LIGHTNING
GROWTH

SUCCESS STRATEGIES for TODAY'S LEADERS

JUSTIN SACHS

MOtivational PRESS®
LEADERS IN GLOBAL PUBLISHING

Published by Motivational Press, Inc.
1777 Aurora Road
Melbourne, Florida, 32935
www.MotivationalPress.com

Manufactured in the United States of America.

ISBN: 978-1-62865-353-3

CONTENTS

LEADERSHIP

ANNIKA SORENSEN
LIGHTNING GROWTH: SUCCESS STRATEGIES FOR TODAY'S LEADERS 8

LAURA VAN DEN BERG-SEKAC
LEADERSHIP FROM ANOTHER POINT OF VIEW 20

DR. THERESA DEL TUFO
AGILITY, INNOVATION AND STRUCTURE: THE BALDRIGE WAY 34

DR. HANS C. MUMM
DEVELOPING NON-LINEAR LEADERS IN DISRUPTIVE TIMES: CHALLENGES
IN A CO-EVOLUTIONARY AND MULTI-DIMENSIONAL TECHNOLOGY
REVOLUTION 51

DAVID TWEEDT AND PETE WINIARSKI
THE POWER OF DAILY LEADERSHIP 73

M.S.RAO
SOFT LEADERSHIP: AN INNOVATIVE LEADERSHIP PERSPECTIVE............... 90

GAURAV BHALLA
SOULFUL LEADERSHIP: SCRIPTING NEW LEADERSHIP NARRATIVES
THROUGH IMMORTAL POEMS 112

ABHA MARYADA BANERJEE

MASTER THE VISIONARY MINDSET 129

ANEETA PATHAK

HE SAID, SHE SAID, WE SAID...............
DID THEY ALL GET THE RIGHT MESSAGE?.. 144

ESPERANZA MONTALVO

HUMILITY AS A LIGHTNING-GROWTH FORCE IN LEADERSHIP 155

ALLI MANG

YOUR FIRST MOMENT EARNS YOU MORE MOMENTS 170

BUSINESS

ALI M AL-KHOURI

DEVELOPMENT OF SUSTAINABLE ORGANIZATIONS................................ 180

JESSICA LORUSSO

A KEY TO SALES SUCCESS 205

TERRI LEVINE

TURBOCHARGE YOUR BUSINESS AND INCOME 222

LEWENA BAYER

LIGHTNING GROWTH: SUCCESS STRATEGIES FOR TODAY'S LEADERS 229

DIANE A. CURRAN

BUSINESS LIGHTNING BUGS, SPACE CAPSULES & BADMINTON 248

JASON MACKENZIE

LIGHTING GROWTH.. 263

STEVE LENTINI

SUCCESS STRATEGIES FOR TODAYS LEADERS...................................... 274

DAVID RYBACK

STRATEGIES FOR LIGHTNING GROWTH IN SALES.................................. 282

AKASHA GARNIER

COLORFUL LESSONS: FIND THE KEYS TO YOUR STRENGTHS
AND YOUR BRAND 293

MOTIVATION

CYNTHIA JAMES

RADICAL SELF CARE: A PORTAL TO SUCCESS 304

ALICE STEFANIAK

OPPORTUNITY PATHWAYS 317

ALLISON SUTTER

THE MOTIVATIONAL MECHANISM.. 330

LYNETTE LOUISE (AKA THE BRAIN BROAD)

THROUGH THE WALL 342

JOAN S. PECK

THE STRATEGIES FOR SUCCESS FROM A SPIRITUAL OUTLOOK 349

KATHY FRAY

PARENTING SUCCESS STRATEGIES TO GROW TEENAGERS INTO

OUR FUTURE LEADERS.. 363

LEADERSHIP

ANNIKA SORENSEN

LIGHTNING GROWTH: SUCCESS STRATEGIES FOR TODAY'S LEADERS

DEAR LEADER - THE BASE IN YOUR LEADERSHIP IS YOU!

A leader of today has many challenges. We live in a changing world, going from the industrial society into the IT society. In one way that may seem like an easy thing. We are going from physically hard work to physically light work – how great isn't that? The methods to communicate are multiplied. You can reach so many more people (customers) – they are just a click away. And so on... Everyone brought up today are familiar with the IT world, right? WRONG! For many years still there will be a large group of the workforces that are not good at or even willing to deal with the IT part of a job. As a business leader you need to deal with both worlds – weather you want it or not. You need to become a superwoman or superman with a lot of skills to handle that. You need to have commitment, communication skills, know a lot of psychology and have a bucket full of patience.

Sounds like an impossible task?! It is definitely not!

However you will need to prepare your body and mind with a good ground and the right skills. And now we are on to something. It is not about a lot of courses in leadership techniques you need first, it is taking care of the base in your leadership: YOU

If your life is a mess, personal and/or professional, if you don't know your own basic self, if your body is tired and you sleep lousy, if you are grumpy and irritable – you will NOT be the perfect guide to care for others and make them do their best.

Conclusion: You need to help yourself first before you can help others – just like they say in the safety on airplanes: Put on your own oxygen mask first.

Is that even possible? Of course it is! By taking a good look at yourself and getting to know yourself better.

Most of the issues, when not going well in life, are usually connected with some feeling of stress, right! Therefor I have designated my life to spread knowledge on how to stress less and instead get more done in a smoother way and eventually be the best of the best in leadership.

So hang on!

I call it the Stress Triangle – because there are 3 aspects that are the most important sides of stress and turbulences in your life. Knowing about this and how it works can show you how to get over stress and pressure.

The first aspect is your body and physical health.

The second aspect is your mind, mindset, your mental health.

The third is the matters that are external from you - what surrounds you – your life platform.

So if you install good habits and good knowledge in these 3 part of your life - you will feel less stress, feel more at ease, get more time and energy and consequently get more done, feel good about what you do and in the end earn more money, get higher revenue or whatever depending on where you are in the organization. So you can say it will be profitable one way or the other.

Another really big advantage of fixing this is that not only will you feel better with better health and self-knowledge, you will also live longer. So if you avoid the stress and find ways to tackle it you can also save cost like not needing to pay hundreds of thousands dollars in medical care.

I have met many leaders who had stress related disease and for years and years they were fighting it instead of solving it, and the company and the family was economically stressed because, also in Sweden with a very generous social security system, it does cost a lot to get ill and stay ill.

If these three parts don't work in your favor you're losing power in your life and as a leader. Instead of joining one more course in leadership, join a course in self-knowledge and stress management, which will be far more profitable in the long run.

The problem is that most people don't have a systematic way to relieve stress and in fact most people don't know they are stressed. I don't know if you have had palpitations before and you sit there and have shallow breathing and you can feel your heart and you get this mini panic attack – that means you are stressed.

And if you are having arguments all the time in your home, that means you are stressed. And when you can't solve simple things that was easy before and you keep forgetting stuff, that means you are stressed. One big problem is that a lot of you, if you are business owners, you make poor decisions in your business and it can cost you millions. Yes, that can happen!

Let me show you a systematic way. I work with stress management based on the Wheel of Life. The wheel I use has 8 pieces – and this is very basic – nothing fancy – but it is YOU!

Here is how you can start:

Seen from the perspective of the Stress Triangle it is Mind –
Body – Platform. The platform is then divided into 6 basic areas
to cover all aspects of life:

1. Mind - Personal Development — Who are you? You need
   to really get to know yourself to be able to know what
   you need and where you want to go. It's about identity.
   Knowing yourself also makes it easier to relate and
   communicate with your fellow human beings. It is basic
   to all the other part of life – to see ourselves – and to know
   what we want and how to get it. This is the first leg in the
   Stress Triangle.

2. Body: Health —How do you take care of your physical self?
   This piece of the pie can be divided into 5 sub pieces (sleep,
   diet, physical activity, stress management and substance
   use). This is the second leg in the Stress Triangle.

   All the rest, part 3-8, form the platform of the Stress
   Triangle.

3. Work — During around 45 years of your life you spend at
   least half your awake time at work — most likely more if
   you are a leader.

4. Money — Money is not just about numbers, it's also a lot
   about feelings.

5. Network — We are pack animals. Having good, healthy
   networks will help you get the most out of your life.

6. Intimacy — Without close human contacts your heart and
   soul will shrink. This is about the most basic of needs for a
   thriving life. This is about self-esteem.

7. Free time/hobbies — Work is important, but it doesn't define us entirely.

8. Surroundings — Believe it or not but where you live matters. There's a power in "place." This is also about status, how we compare ourselves with others.

Now you know what I find is important to deal with. This is one way to do it:

Step 1: This is to take a good look at all these aspects, write it down on a piece of paper. Your own thoughts. Not what others want you to write. Not what you think others want you to write. It is not about the formalities in the writing, it is only about getting your thoughts down on a piece of paper to be able to view it in the next step.

Step 2: This is the hard part. TAKE YOUR TIME and REFLECT on what you have written. This is hard work, I know, but essential for good results.

What parts of your life work your way and what parts do you need to do something about? Take your time! Look at your notes again! Discuss with your loved ones, with your friends and others you trust. Maybe even get professional help from a coach.

Step 3: This is about making an action plan for the things you want to do. This may also need some input from the surrounding.

Step 4: Okay, are you ready? This is also a tough one.

JUST DO IT!

Just like the Nike ad. At this stage it is maybe even more important to get the help you need. Life style changes are hard and all of this is life style changes in a broad sense.

You have now also learned not to jump on whatever random offer to solve YOUR challenges, since that may not be what you need. You have learned that you need to look at your WHOLE situation, you need to get to know yourself, you need to get energy to do the work and you need to find out where you want to be and what you want to be before you can do the changes you need. And to do this work you have learned about an easy tool, the Wheel of life.

Let me give you my take on a couple of the subjects to help you get started.

Body is, like said above, about the traditional parts of health. This piece actually can be divided into sub-pieces. I do that in my work, I use 5 sub-pieces. It will get to the core of your health. It is about sleep, absolutely a lifesaver. It is about food, also a lifesaver. It is about physical activity, another lifesaver. These three wants to have regularity, that is what your body and mind wants from a biological perspective. Combine how you handle these three, which are the essence of life, with your stress pattern and your substance use (mainly alcohol and tobacco) and you find your today health situation. This part is to give you energy to change your life. So I always recommend my clients to work with this health part parallel with whatever else they want to change.

WHAT DO YOU WANT TO CHANGE?

Before you start I recommend you write down all your thoughts on this on a piece of paper, just like you did when looking at the big picture. What do I eat and what are my eating habits? What do I do for physical activity? How is my sleep? Do

I smoke, do I drink too much alcohol, how do I stress? A lot of questions at the same time and our mind can only hold 5-7 facts at the same time. But if you can look at the facts written down you can get the big picture of it all at the same time.

If you realize you need to do several changes in these it is best to start with one change at a time. Do it for at least 4 weeks. Then you can add another change for the next 4 weeks and so on.

Just keep it coming and after a while you will realize that other things change too, just automatically, because of the changes you did.

I also want to share some insights about the other leg in the Stress Triangle the one about YOU, mind, mindset, personal development. You can learn about yourself in many ways. It is about mindset and about understanding why you act as you do. It is about communication with others and about personality types. I use a model called the Puzzle of Ensize.

Maybe it is far out for a doctor to talk about this but I have in my earlier every day health care work noticed that so much is about mindset. It is not about what we have -it is about how we see it, embrace it or perceive it. I have seen many patients with the same diseases, the same treatments, the same struggles and the outcome was so different, and it was not explained by difference in biology. I could clearly see it was a difference in mindset. Developing an optimistic, motivated, confident, loving, and resilient mindset is everything.

Personally it was a big step forward in my way to a less stressed life when I got to do a communication and driving forces analysis. Not just reading about it but doing the real thing, a real analysis based on my answers. Lots of things came clear to me about me, how I work but also about what is happening around me, how other people function. When you embrace this part, life gets so much easier. Less conflicts and misunderstandings. More results and also more fun. Go here if you too want to do the real analysis **http://bit.ly/drannikaensize** write "**leader1**" as coupon code and get a good discount because you are an owner of this book.

You can also read books about self-development and health improvement. There are hundreds of them out there. Maybe you can go to a library to find a couple of books to start with. Make it a habit to always have one self-development book for your ongoing reading.

The 6 remaining areas are work, free time, money, personal relations, network and place. Here you inventory your life around the titles of each section. Write it down, just as I have explained earlier. Find out where you are today. Brainstorm of where you want to be tomorrow and set a plan. YOUR plan specifically made for your needs. Not a random plan. Not matched with your friend's plans. Just YOUR plan. And then hit GO! Because knowing something and not doing it is like not knowing it!

I want to mention one curiosa on the piece about where you live. It may seem silly to have a section just about this but it is scientifically proven that place matter and status matter.

A few years ago I came to listen to a speech by Sir Michael Marmot, an authentic and humble man from England, he is an expert in epidemiology (structures in society). In one of his books, The Status Syndrome, he tells the story about the people nominated for an Oscar; they have 4 years LESS longevity than those who got an Oscar. And you would think being nominated for an Oscar is high status. This is about envy and how we compare ourselves with others. Status matters also on the top of the hierarchy. That is something to consider. As you can understand this is really about mindset and gratitude. The grass is NOT greener on the other side of the fence, it only has a different shade. Now you have gone through what to do something about.

Next - How to move on?

What would change for you if you were able to go through your day feeling relaxed instead of pushing, chasing or rushing?

What would change for you if you woke up feeling peaceful every day?

Imagine completing your day feeling relaxed and accomplished.

It's not about doing more, just doing it different. Which piece to start with when looking at YOUR situation? I'll get back to that in a minute but first

I want to introduce a quick, always at hands, tool for rapid stress relief. Make a big smile toward someone else in the room. Note what happens. The spectators also start smiling, right, because it is so hard not to. Because we have nerve cells called mirror neurons that "forces" us to mimic what we see. That also goes for sour faces, but we don't want to mirror that, do we?

The good thing is that when we smile our mind recognizes that our facial muscles are in the position of a smile and that signals to the brain to produce feel good hormones, making us feel good when we smile. Another good thing is that the person being mirrored with a smile also has the same mechanism and feels good too. So when you start feeling stressed out you can give a smile to someone. If you have no one to reflect your smile on you can use a mirror to reflect yourself to keep the good process up for a short relief in the stress.

Okay, where to begin in the life style changes? Well, it does not really matter that much, as long as you do something. Because doing something will start the process and doing one change will move the balance and that will start changes in other areas too. What I usually recommend is to also do something to improve your health to get the energy for doing changes. Also I believe it is an advantage to continuously work with your mindset because that is where you get the willpower to go on in the tough times.

If you want a helping hand in your work towards becoming your best self and be the leader you always dreamed about I can recommend my online course **www. TheGetYourLifeBackWorkshop.com** . You work yourself through all the pieces in the Wheel of Life, all with a little help on the journey. Use the link above and write **"leader2"** as coupon code and get a good discount because you are an owner of this book.

Now is the time to start the good work to make you the real and best YOU. Now is the time to make you the leader you always dreamed about!

TO YOUR SUCCESS!

Dr Annika

Dr. Annika Sorensen MD, specialized in family medicine and health promotion, and has worked in the Swedish Public Health System for over 25 years. She has met thousands of patients with stress issues and stress related disease and have seen stress from all angles. She has also met close to thousand patients on long term sick leave, doing work assessments.

Following her passion for helping people overcome stress-related challenges, Dr. Annika today runs her own company **AskDrAnnika.com** as a stress strategy consultant, mentoring busy business leaders and professionals to improve their overall health and wellness and of course teach stress management. She has simply changed her focus from disease to health, with an emphasis on stress management, health promotion, work assessment and other business related issues.

Dr Annika is a professionally trained international public speaker and she is known for seeing the entire picture and making complex topics easy to understand.

Besides speaking Dr Annika hold seminars and strategic-work-sessions and has a mentor program for business leaders and executives.

Dr Annika is also the author of 2 top-rated books, "Take Stress from Chaos to Calm" and "My De-Stress Diary". Read more: **http://bit.ly/AmazonAnnikaSorensen**

Furthermore Dr Annika offer you the online course **TheGe-tYourLifeBackWorkshop.com** where she hold your hand, virtually that is, and walk you through a thorough introspection into your own life and help you find *your* best way to get out of the stress. She has created this step by step system in 8 models from her years and years of experience.

www.AskDrAnnika.com

info@askdrannika.com

LAURA VAN DEN BERG-SEKAC

LEADERSHIP FROM ANOTHER POINT OF VIEW

"He who cannot be a good follower cannot be a good
leader."
Aristotle

In this chapter, I'd like to look at the theme of leadership from a, perhaps, unusual angle, namely the horse's perspective, and show you how to fortify it.

1. WHEN A HORSE COMES IN, NOTHING REMAINS UNCOVERED

There's a tremendous power within each of us living beings. To me, this power is particularly visible in horses. Its rough overwhelming presence imposes respect, fear, and admiration at the same time. For many, it's also a representation of ultimate joy and freedom.

The intensity of that power becomes tangible especially when you walk a horse. Even if you're good mates and trust each other, below the surface you still can feel the strong, volatile, unpredictable volcanic force that is full of movement, momentum, and decisiveness, and that can erupt in a millisecond. The force is unpredictable, and yet the horse seems to know how to use it.

But this is not the only thing that makes horses so special. Like many other things, they reflect perfectly how we behave towards ourselves. However, they do it in a magnifying way that is gentle and confronting at the same time. When a horse mirrors us, and we become aware of it, it always touches the depths of our souls.

I remember how I once came into the stall and a mare bit at me. I was upset. Why was she doing it? All I did was say hello to her when walking by—something I always did—and she always responded to this with a soft neigh. It was a little play we always did. To soothe my disappointment, I wanted to caress her daughter who stood in the box next to her. Normally she loved it, but now she threw her head aside and showed her teeth, which was something she never did.

Her reaction swept me off my feet. I was shocked, petrified, and waves of tears inundated me. I cried my heart out and felt immensely sorry for myself. And the more I wallowed, the more proof I found of other people or circumstances being hostile towards me. I felt hurt, offended, unloved, and left forever alone. Poor, poor little me. Then, exactly at the point when my reaction became pathetic, a situation flashed across my mind when a couple of weeks before, I was angry that things didn't go the way I wanted. I saw how I snagged at myself. I also saw how instead of acknowledging honestly that what I was doing wasn't right, I blamed others, wanting them at the same time to comfort me. I wanted them approving my false excuses and dishonesty, and then felt angry and disappointed when they didn't. So here I was, upset, feeling hurt, ashamed, trying to find justification for my egoistic behaviour, angry that I couldn't find it, but also glad that I became aware of what was going on. Deep down, I felt how much I had cheated myself and how much pain I had caused myself, and I knew I had to admit that my behaviour wasn't okay, and take responsibility for it. My ego sobbed a couple of seconds more, then reluctantly took accountability for it, and then I couldn't help but laugh about my pathetic reaction. And the mares? They nibbled the hoy as if nothing happened, and neighed naughtily at me.

The reason why horses tend to provoke such strong reactions—you mostly love them or you fear them—is because their power invokes the way we lead our lives. It reminds us of the potency our lives have, and what we make of it. When we discover that we have fooled ourselves (or better said, that our ego deceived us), or don't dare to powerfully express who we really are, horses can lead us back to our inner power again.

YOU CAN FOOL YOURSELF, BUT YOU CANNOT FOOL A HORSE

There's hardly a better way to discover the naked truth about yourself than by walking with a horse. (Please note, that if you are not used to horses, you should never do this just by yourself—you need an experienced trainer with you). The interesting thing is that it doesn't matter whether you have any previous experience with horses or not. I've seen high class cavaliers or CEOs not being able to lead the horse straight for 25 meters, and people who have never worked with a horse before walk away with the horse as if they'd been together forever.

Why is that? It's because horses are herd animals and are used to being led, but only if the leader is genuine. By genuine, I mean that they have real self-confidence, wisdom, decisiveness, and know-how of how to use their power without misusing it. Such a leader owns it fully. It's natural to them, and they never doubt or discuss it. Another mark of genuine leadership is using the power to act when needed without hesitance, to take good care of what's important, stay focused on priorities, and to protect the security of their herd and their own boundaries. A wholehearted commitment to your life or to any goal equals leadership. When you can be a genuine leader of your life, your life becomes authentic, and such a life is a doorway to your higher potential—that magnificent power within you.

To put it simply, in the wild, the herd of horses is led by an older, wiser, more experienced mare who knows the dangers of the daily life, and the best places to find food or shelter. In the backline of the herd is her leader mate, the stallion who defends the back. He defines the speed with which the herd advances, controls whether the herd stays together well, brings back lost members, and eventually educates or plays with the foals. So the mare chooses the direction, and the stallion takes care of the speed. It's the combination of choosing where to go, keeping everyone safely together, and keeping the momentum going, so to speak.

Within the herd, the hierarchy is clear and indisputable. Each member knows its place and what to do or not to do, so that no energy is wasted on unnecessary conflicts. They all know that only together they are strong and only together they will survive.

So when you walk with a horse, something very special happens. (It actually happens with every person you meet, but horses show this magnified, so I like to use them as an example). You two become a herd, and the horse will show you where in the herd's hierarchy you take your place. It's often the same place you tend to take in your daily life, by the way.

The horse is crystal clear about whether you're a genuine leader or not. If you sincerely trust and respect yourself, honour what's important to you, you take your leadership over yourself and your life truthfully. Consequently, the horse will accept you as his leader, and follow you in the direction you choose to go. Translated to your daily life, your life will be in flow, and you'll be able to pursue your goals without too many challenges.

But it goes even deeper. When you two become a herd, and he so to speak becomes *one* with you, through your interaction your hidden patterns become visible. So it's not about the horse's (or somebody else's behaviour); it's a clear manifestation of what YOU are doing, consciously or not.

In this way, he's showing you how you deal with your inner power and the potency of your life, and what kind of a leader you are of your life (or in your daily life). He lets you see where the members of your "herd" (your inner parts) are lost somewhere in the past or in the future, or whether they (dis)respect the hierarchy. Your ego, for example, may have taken a situation over—a little unsecure child that still is longing for approval and is nagging in the middle of a business meeting, or some inner part of you needs more freedom and therefore sabotages your deadlines.

As said before, you cannot cheat a horse. If your 'power' is only your ego in disguise, showing that in reality you don't trust yourself at all, disrespect yourself, or have a low self-esteem, the horse will notice it in the blink of an eye. He sees it in your posture, your behaviour, and the way you're speaking, no matter how much you think you are in control. Your true emotions and feelings about yourself, even if they're buried three houses deep underground, are an open book for him. That's why some experienced riders who are not truly self-confident can impose their leadership on the horse when riding because of the bit and other tools, but hardly at all on the ground where they cannot manipulate the horse in such a way. Such an interaction is enforced, and will be unreliable. In a daily situation, if you have a leading position, your co-workers may obey you then, but not respect you. Then, under the surface, you will sense it, and feel unfulfilled with your collaboration, without perhaps exactly knowing why.

Being a genuine leader doesn't mean you're always fearlessly perfect. Everyone has an element in their life that they're afraid or insecure of, be it the fear of rejection, success, or failure, change, or letting go. The long-forgotten mother's snubbing gesture, our father's critical gaze, our old teacher's misprizing words, or a hateful remark of a stranger are not lost, but still secretly dominate our lives. We all have fears, wounds, and insecurities, and we all hide them consciously or not—from others, but especially from ourselves.

Therefore, when a horse comes in, nothing remains uncovered. All those hidden fears, cowardice, blame, anger, fiddling around, excuses, and what we feel guilty or ashamed of, are visible to the horse. Our hidden, tucked away, manipulative character comes out, and not only does it become visible through the horse's behaviour, but it magnifies to proportions that we cannot deny any more. And in the same way, all our true beauty and magnificence becomes visible as well. We then admire the beauty, power, elegance, or strength of the horse, and forget that we're only really watching our own.

Therefore, when you pretend that you're something that you're not, or display the superficial version of your day-to-day persona instead of your authentic deeper self, it isn't something that a horse is interested in (nor are other people by the way). It only confirms that you're not your own leader and therefore are nobody's leader. Your hierarchy's place is defined -below the horse or not belonging to the herd. He will discuss it, try to dominate you and chase you, or he will run away from you as quickly as possible.

By the way, when you feel fear or any other negative emotion, or are stuck, it's not a big deal as long as you're honest about it. It's your pretending that he dislikes. However, in that case, it may be safer for you to stay at a distance, and just be honest about your feelings.

So from this point of view, the horse will accept you as his leader only if you are honest and act in a sincere way. All the other behaviour such as false doubt, discussions, anger, yelling, or trying to be likable won't work, because that's not how a genuine leader behaves. Leadership is not about being dominant but about being firm, respectful, decisive, committed, and consequent. It means that you freely express your true magnificent nature: things that inspire, motivate, and empower you, incite your growth, bring you more joy and harmony, and give you peace of mind.

Your true nature consists of the love of freedom—like it is for each of us—and the need to evolve towards your highest potential, explore the life, create, and love, to experience joy, and express it in as many forms as possible. That's your 'herd', and you need to lead it with wisdom so it can be nourished, sheltered, and supported through your female energy, which is your intuition, innate knowing, and life experience. It's this herd's safety that you need to protect from assaults of guilt, anger, false beliefs, and wrong attitudes that bother us all constantly. It's your lost faith or misbehaving parts of the herd who compromise your inner hierarchy and allow a scared or inexperienced part of you decide that you'll give up a dream or make a choice based on fear or lack of perspective. You are your own herd, and your own parent, child, friend, neighbour, boss, or employee all in one. But like in the herd of horses, you need to use two guiding forces at the same time—the female and the male.

When you want to guide a horse without using manipulative things like bits, you must be clear where you want to go (even if it's only a small walk without a special intention) and then take that direction. Go there fully present. Don't think about yesterday or tomorrow, do it with your full attention. You are then relaxed, in both body and mind. The smell of the air flows through you and all your senses are involved. You are in the moment and you forget it at the same time. You become one with that moment and with everything that makes up part of it. If you're with the horse, you "melt" together. The cadence of your steps becomes one, and a deeper connection and heart communication takes place. You start to feel how that volcanic power of joy, peace, or serenity that's never far away flows through you. Those are the moments you'll never forget because it's where you meet each other at a soul level. And, in fact, you meet the true *you*.

When you understand, or can imagine it, it doesn't matter whether you're with a horse, a friend, your beloved, a colleague, an employee, or just doing some activity. The horse is exchangeable. When your inner female and male power cooperate, and therefore form a powerful unified leadership of your inner herd, everyone you meet will feel that power of unity. They will feel your wisdom of knowing where to go, trust your experience how to get there, and intuitively know that you truly possess the knowledge of how to deal with the eventual challenges. They'll feel secure in your presence, and trust that you're strong and vigilant enough to honour and protect everyone's boundaries and interests.

2. TWO ANGLES OF LEADING – FEMALE AND MALE ENERGY IN ACTION

This story about the horses is an example of how you can become a more aware, genuine leader. It's great to work with horses, though unfortunately it's not possible for everyone to do so. But you don't have necessarily work with them in reality. Using the metaphor of a horse's life is a great way to change a context of certain patterns. Especially because it's also a metaphor for the potency of your life. You can use it to step out of patterns that may be difficult for you to change. Looking at your life from the perspective of a horse can provide you with a new, fresh perspective and help you strengthen your leadership with lightning speed.

Let's take a closer look at how you can **fortify your leadership.**

In the concept of equine co-guidance that we discussed before, two forces (male and female) are engaged.

At the head of the group stands the first force—the female force. This force inspires trust, and has the wisdom, knowledge, and experience to guide the group to food, water, and safe shelter. She is the one who determines when the group moves and the route it will take to reach the destination.

The second force is at the rear—the male force. He is the one who takes care of the momentum, drives the slower or straggling members of the group on, and watches and protects the group from predators.

Between these two forces—together—are all the members of the group, and each of them has and respects its own place.

Translating this into a human context, the female energy (in our case, trust, wisdom, knowledge, life experience) guides us to those things that nourish us mentally, physically, emotionally, and spiritually, and that are safe for our wellbeing. This (female) energy starts the action (or decides on a goal), and chooses the strategy on how to get there.

In other words, to be a strong leader and achieve our goals, we must be led by our wisdom, knowledge, and life experience, and we must trust that we'll be able to get to our destination. When we want to begin something, we must first be sure that what we want to do will nourish us in all of the required levels, and then determine the strategy that will get us there safely. (And if we are wise, we'll know that we won't get there if we allow, for example, our ego to guide us, or a child within us who just wants something right here and right now).

Then, to achieve our goal, cooperation with the second force (the male energy) is absolutely necessary. This energy ensures that the decision made by the female energy retains the momentum, and that everything remains focused on the goal. It keeps distraction, disorder, incorrect behavior, and everything that has nothing to do with the goal at bay.

Consequently, the female energy sparks the action and the male energy ensures that nothing distracts or threatens the flow of it, and that the energy and everything and everyone involved keeps moving. Without the (harmonious) cooperation of these two forces, the action cannot be executed properly. Neither the leader at the front nor the one at the back are able to keep the group going in the right direction and protect the group on their own. This means they must work together peacefully and they must wholeheartedly trust each other that they can, and will, both do their respective jobs well. To succeed, neither of them must feel any need to control the other.

It's interesting that in this concept of cooperation between female and male forces, the male leader, in order to keep momentum, doesn't place himself in the front of the group and pull the rest of the group along with him. Instead, he pushes everybody up from the back, and from there he controls whether everybody follows the female leader in front.

We all know this feeling—when we are supported and protected from the back, we can fly.

So how can you protect your own back, and cooperate with your inner female co-leader?

START BY ASKING YOURSELF SOME QUESTIONS

For example, do you know what nourishes you, and where you can find that thing? In your life, who decides that you should go for something? Is it yourself, or are you waiting for others to fulfill your essential needs? And how do you keep up the momentum in your life? Are you able to stay focused, or are you distracted by all kinds of shiny objects? Can you say YES or NO when necessary? Do you take care of your own 'herd', or do you allow intruders to disturb the direction and the pace at which you pursue your goals and dreams?

Which part of you is in charge of your life? Who is your wise, inner 'mare', and who is your protective, caring 'stallion'? Do you allow them to fulfill their roles? Or do you give responsibility to others, for example, by blaming them, or tolerating disrespectful actions towards you?

In fact, you can ask yourself the same kinds of questions in any situation. If you own a business, consider who starts a new project or decides what route the business will take? Is it the right person—the one who has the wisdom and experience to do so? Are the decisions 'nourishing' and safe? Do they bring things to the company that make it prosper? Do you feel fulfilled by the work you perform? Does your work make you enthusiastic? Is everyone in your business able to express their talents? Who is taking care of the momentum? Who ensures that the focus stays on the agreed goals? Does everyone genuinely respect their own task?

In your relationships, ask yourself: how do you take care of yourself and your needs? Do you need others so you feel happy, or can you guide yourself to find what is important to you? Especially in a relationship, your inner leadership will be mirrored very strongly. It's in this field that we often allow outside forces to lead our lives instead of letting our own male and female energy co-operate and guide our lives. For example, when you allow the criticism or negative feelings of others to invade your life, your male energy isn't doing its job properly. When you ask for approval to be happy, or to do what's important to you, your female force isn't guiding you, but somebody else's 'mare' has taken over your life. You're in the wrong herd, where your place will always be low. Or when you feel emotionally responsible for others, you in reality lead other people's herd, where you always will have to fight to keep your leading position.

WHAT'S NEXT? TO BEGIN, A SMALL EXERCISE

When you realize that the leadership theme we just discussed is something you'd like to improve on, you just need to start small. Try to implement the elements we have been talking about in some simple actions. For instance, determine a simple goal. Pay attention to whether it's nourishing and safe for you, and then choose how you want to get there. Now you need to call in your inner protective force (go ahead, make a game of it), and ask it to take care of staying focused and chasing all destructive actions or thoughts away. If you want to, you might even wish to visualize the journey to where you want to go—together with an experienced mare, protected from anything that stands in your way by a strong stallion. Feel your body, the way you walk, and how you feel. Then walk and feel in this way as much and as often as possible, to anchor it.

This may all sound like a silly game, but I ensure you, just try it. You will be surprised by the incredible effect it has. If you like, please, let me know your experience and reactions, I'd love to hear them!

And if you want to learn more, or would like to go more in depth with this theme and take it to a higher level, or have any questions or comments, please feel free to contact me at **www. Essensense.com**

Stay Close to Anything That Makes You
Glad You Are Alive

Hafez

Laura van den Berg-Sekac, M.A. is an international best-selling author and improvement strategist with more than two decades of coaching and consulting practice in the field of self-knowledge and personal transformation. She is a strong believer in each person's ability to reach their innate strength and higher potential in every part of their life, and she loves to teach her clients and readers how to step into their full power and become change-makers.

Her passion is to develop new, often unconventional methods to empower and get the best out of her clients, like, for example, through working with horses in order to unveil the hidden inner attitude of the person who works with them.

Laura lives in France and works from there internationally.

DR. THERESA DEL TUFO

AGILITY, INNOVATION AND STRUCTURE: THE BALDRIGE WAY

"It is not necessary to change; survival is not mandatory."

W.E Deming

DINOSAURS AND EXTINCTION

Do you know what happens when dinosaurs mate? It's a phenomenon that Sears and K-Mart are intimately familiar with, as they spiral into financial disaster and extinction. Remember the once great companies of the past—Kodak, PanAm, Sylvania, Blockbuster, Netscape, to name a few? When organizations stand still, rest on their past accomplishments, and fail to listen to the voices of their customers, they wither away and self-destruct. It results in the monumental spontaneous combustion of their corporate souls. What can businesses and organizations do to mitigate and minimize a meltdown of this proportion?

In the 21st Century information society, nothing is more constant than change. When organizations refuse to change their business models to respond to the rapidly changing external landscape, they put themselves at risk of being irrelevant and obsolete. Some organizations waste a lot of money, time, and resources providing services and products that are no longer needed, doing processes that are inefficient, and measuring performance and results that are not critical to strategic success. In other words, they are becoming obsolete, especially in this information society where speed, accuracy, innovation and effective planning are critical to survival and competition.

THE BALDRIGE WAY: SYSTEMATIC, COMPREHENSIVE AND REPLICABLE

In my 25 years experience as a performance consultant, I have found the Baldrige Criteria for Performance Excellence a valuable and time-tested framework to improve organizational performance and implement innovation. This quality approach is systematic, comprehensive and replicable. It looks at the organization as a system—where all the component parts are interdependent and function as an integrated whole. All organizations are systems, whether they are managed as systems or not. This overarching framework guides organizations as they pursue excellence in the areas of leadership, strategic planning, customer focus, data and knowledge management, workforce focus, operations focus and organizational results.

The seven Baldrige Criteria and their critical linkages are portrayed in the chart that follows. Leadership (Category 1), Strategy (Category 2) and Customers (Category3) comprise the "Driver Triad" that emphasize the key role of the leader in strategy formulation and deployment and a continuing focus on the needs, aspirations and requirements of customers. Engaged, highly trained and empowered employees (Workforce Focus, Category 5), guided by efficient and effective processes (Operations, Category 6) represent the "work core" that yields breakthrough performance for the customers and the organization.

The "brain center" resides in Category 4, Data, Measurement and Knowledge Management, critical to achieving organizational and performance excellence (Category 7). Robust and live data are needed for innovation and continuous improvement and to monitor alignment and progress between goals and performance. Leaders use data to set priorities, allocate resources, make decisions and manage and address systemic issues.

The Baldrige approach is comprehensive, integrated and all-inclusive. I often ask employees and leaders if there are any organizational components that are not addressed in the framework. So far, no one has ever come up with an element that's not included in the Baldrige paradigm. Unlike other approaches that simply focus and address a single or a limited number of elements, the Baldrige is a disciplined process that targets all critical components. For example, the Balanced Scorecard is an excellent tool for managing results and outcomes and can be deployed as an effective strategic planning method and a measurement tool. The "Turning Outward" approach is a good method for listening to the needs, aspirations and abilities of communities we serve, but it neglects to consider the abilities and capabilities of the organizations serving the community. The Six Sigma is a systematic tool for detecting defects and variations in processes, but it fails to consider other critical elements necessary for organizational success. The three approaches discussed are quality **tools** that can be used to supplement and implement a systematic and comprehensive framework that the Baldrige Criteria represent. The latter is superior to the other two as a management and improvement system.

Finally, the Baldrige enhances an organizations ability to respond efficiently and effectively to changing environmental threats and challenges. Agility is maximized because organizations have an overarching framework, a performance map that guides their every strategic plan, action and decision. Employees and leaders' eyes are set on clear, visible and robust organizational targets that are reviewed and updated during set periods annually. Structure allows greater freedom to improve and to innovate.

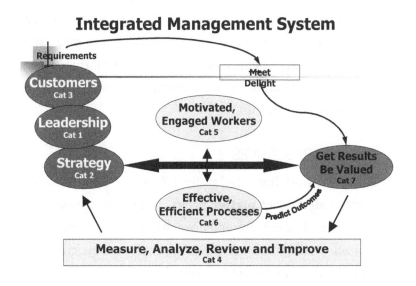

Figure 1: Baldrige Criteria: Seven Categories

A SUCCESS STORY

DELAWARE DIVISION OF LIBRARIES: THE BALDRIGE JOURNEY

Beginning in 2002, the Delaware Division of Libraries embarked on a quality journey, learning about best practices and tools that businesses use to reinvent themselves and achieve performance excellence, and how to apply them to libraries (Wilson, Del Tufo, & Norman, 2008). The business tools were the method chosen to identify and clarify the profession's fundamental identity. Staff and stakeholders throughout the Delaware library community were all invited to learn and to apply the Baldrige Criteria for Performance Excellence, the Balanced Scorecard methodology, and Lean Six Sigma (Blazey, 2009; Brown, 2007). The Baldrige approach was selected as the operating framework because it offers a comprehensive set of standards that span all aspects of organizational performance, and provides the foundation for the development of a strategy for improvement and growth.

PUBLIC LIBRARY SERVICES

Value Proposition: Delaware Libraries support lifelong learning in **all subject matter areas** (from story times to new technology and everything in between) to promote opportunities for all to discover their passions, explore their curiosities and achieve their version of the American Dream.

Delaware Libraries are continuously redefining their role as content curators and expert navigators of information and knowledge, and have been fairly successful in shaping an environment as an engaged and dynamic community center for learning and communication. You can go to Delaware Libraries to learn a language, explore and learn how to use the latest technologies, or simply attend a workshop on how to start your own small business — these services and many more are available at your local libraries. The chart below displays the menu of services offered by the public libraries in Delaware.

Figure 2: Delaware Public Libraries Services:
Courtesy of the Delaware Division of Libraries

Delaware Public Libraries: Balanced Scorecard Strategy Map: Displayed in the chart below are the strategic goals/Perspectives (in dark blue) and objectives (oval-shaped figures) of the Delaware Libraries. From 2008-2012, the agency utilized resources and developed programs to address the objectives that focused on "growing capacities," "leveraging technology," and "using resources efficiently." From 2013-2017, Libraries are targeting efforts in "increasing value to customers," "expanding customer base," "improving program success," "increasing relevance of resources," "improving efficiencies," "developing staff skills and knowledge," and "ensuring excellence in performance."

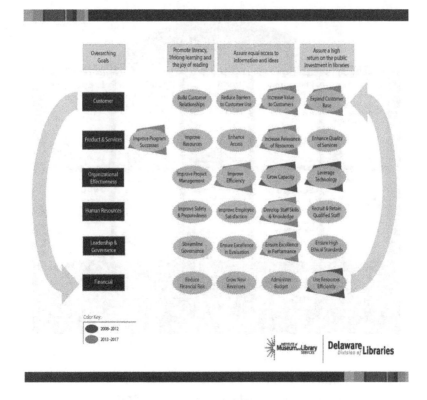

Figure 3: Delaware Public Libraries Strategy Map:
Courtesy of the Delaware Division of Libraries

ORGANIZATIONAL RESULTS

The mission of the Delaware Division of Libraries is Library Development. The division employees provide resources and expertise to help public libraries evolve. Delaware libraries enrich lives by providing everyone access to the knowledge that engages their passion. Libraries facilitate lifelong learning for Delawareans so that they are able to achieve their full potential and their versions of the Delaware Dream.

The litmus test for any successful organization can be gleaned by looking at results—outputs and solid outcomes that demonstrate success. Here's a sampling of the Delaware Libraries successes and accomplishments:

» Customer Perspective

No. of Delawareans with Library Cards:

The goal of Delaware Libraries is for 50% of Delawareans to have library cards. The population of Delaware in 2015 was 945,934, while the number of library cardholders was 475,256, which indicates that 50.24% of Delawareans are library cardholders.

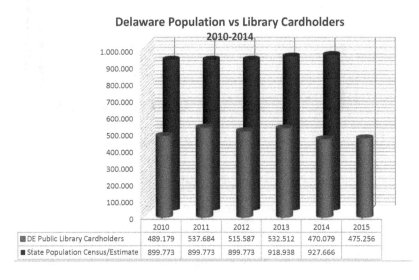

	2010	2011	2012	2013	2014	2015
DE Public Library Cardholders	489.179	537.684	515.587	532.512	470.079	475.256
State Population Census/Estimate	899.773	899.773	899.773	918.938	927.666	

Figure 4: Delaware Population and Number of Library Cardholders: 2010-2015

Number of Reference Questions: By Service Category

There is a notable increase in the number of reference questions fielded by librarians from Fiscal years 2014 through 2016. Notice the uniform upward trend in the computer and eBooks areas, where reference questions posed by customers increased from 110,503 in Fiscal Year 2014, to 129,047 in Fiscal Year 2015, and finally to 164,684 in Fiscal Year 2016. The increase in this service category between 2014 and 2016 is 49%. This upward trend appears to align with the comparable and phenomenal increase in eBook usage, as displayed on page 10.

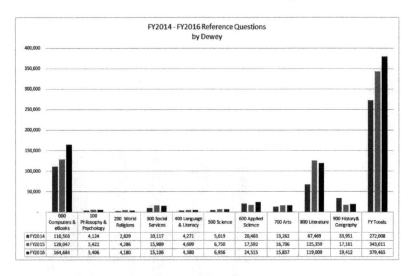

Figure 5: Number of Reference Questions: Delaware Public Libraries

Public Libraries - Statewide Master Plan for Library Services and Construction

A major finding of the planning study indicate that "92% of library users, and 84% of non-library users said libraries are vital or very important to the quality of life in their community."

Web Survey Results for Delaware, April 2010-2015

The survey was conducted in 2009 by the University of Washington for the Institute of Museum & Library Services (IMLS) and the Gates Foundation, to understand the various ways in which patrons use public access computers in libraries. There were 412 Delawareans who responded to the online survey.

Below is an excerpt on the notable findings of the report:

» "The trend of alleviating workload of community agencies or supplementing their efforts, and serving as a de facto service organization.

» The library serves as a clearinghouse for many types of training offered by government and private agencies.

» Librarians provide one-on-one assistance for users working through their own learning process; the library is an environment with resources that support all stages of learning, and helps people stay current with the skills necessary for getting and keeping their jobs ." (US Impact Study - Web Survey Results for Delaware, April 2010)

The sea of changes in the social, economic and demographic landscape of Delaware appears to have opened viable opportunities for Delaware Libraries to find their niches. The findings from the report displayed above highlight the evolution of libraries and the manner in which they are fast becoming a valuable community resource for other service agencies in the community. In other critical areas, they are becoming primary providers of key community services, such as employment, training and technology use. Their strong partnerships with various community organizations have allowed them to carve out a coordinating role, and in some instances, have assumed a leadership role as a central clearinghouse for training opportunities offered by governmental agencies, non-profits and industry. Delawareans appreciate the added value of having a trained librarian provide them with one-on-one assistance in navigating the technology information maze, as demonstrated by the high user rating below (79.3%).

User Rating of Technology Assistance Received: DE Public Libraries

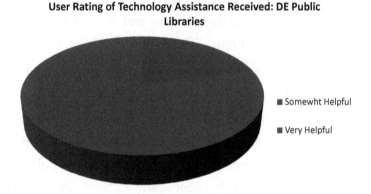

- ■ Somewht Helpful
- ■ Very Helpful

Figure 6: User Rating of Technology assistance received: Web Survey Results: 2015

HUMAN RESOURCE PERSPECTIVE: EMPLOYEE SURVEY

A comprehensive statewide Employee Survey was conducted in 2012, with a 56.6% response rate. There were 493 librarians and staff surveyed between June and July of 2012. The findings indicate a generally healthy organizational climate for both employees and leaders. The chart that follows indicates the following notable findings:

- » A workforce that values its culture of service;
- » Professionals who have a strong commitment to their customers and their mission;
- » Individuals who are generally satisfied with the work that they do;

» An organizational culture that promotes open and honest communication;

» Professionals who value process effectiveness, quality service and continuing training and development; and

» Leaders who have a vision of a better future for libraries.

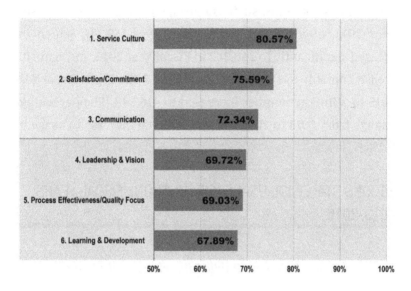

Figure 7: Delaware Libraries: Employee Survey:
Results Overview

PRODUCT AND SERVICES PERSPECTIVE: USAGE: EBOOK COLLECTIONS AND JOB CENTER

Collections and Reference: Library Services include Collections and Programs across all subject areas—from attending a computer class, to exploring world religions, to finding a job and more. Libraries share a statewide technology infrastructure for robust access to internet. Library technologies are funded 100% by the State of Delaware.

Job Centers: From March 2014 through June 2016, there were a total of 656 jobs offered by Delaware employers to participating patrons of the Delaware Job Centers.

eBook Usage: It appears that use and availability of eBook (electronic books) collections is increasing, outpacing the usage rate of physical items, such as books, CDs and DVDs. In Fiscal Year 2013, eBook usage (circulation) was 159,347, which increased significantly to 248,262 in Fiscal Year 2014, and again increased notably to 352,651 in Fiscal Year 2015. From Fiscal Year 2015 to 2016, the number increased to 416,592. The percentage change from 2013 to 2016 is a phenomenal increase in usage by 161%.

EBOOKS STATEWIDE USAGE (CIRCULATION): FISCAL YEARS 2013-2016

Table 1: Delaware Public Libraries: eBooks Usage

FISCAL YEARS	USAGE (Circulation)
Fiscal Year 2013	159,347
Fiscal Year 2014	248,262
Fiscal Year 2015	352,651
Fiscal Year 2016	416,592

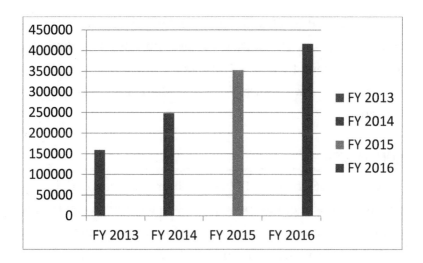

Figure 8: eBooks Statewide Usage -
Delaware Public Libraries: 2013-2016

HUMAN RESOURCE PERSPECTIVE: PROFESSIONAL DEVELOPMENT: LIBRARIANS AND LIBRARY STAFF

» The Ada Leigh Soles Memorial Librarian/Archivist Scholarship Loan Program enables Delaware Libraries to "grow their own" library professionals through scholarships and grants for continuing education and training.

» Frequent Professional Development opportunities help library staff stay up to date on the latest in the library field and all subject areas.

ORGANIZATIONAL EFFECTIVENESS: INFRASTRUCTURE AND CONSTRUCTION

The Delaware Libraries goal for library construction is 1 square foot per capita statewide. The State of Delaware pays up to 50% for library construction and from 2008-2016, library space expanded by 139,289 square feet to accommodate the increasing needs of Delawareans to use Libraries as community learning centers. Delaware Partners include more than 130 organizations that work with libraries to share their resources and expertise.

CONCLUSION

A large measure of the Delaware libraries success could be attributed to their commitment and deployment of an empirically validated guiding framework for performance excellence. The external environment, the marketplace is in constant change and turmoil and is not likely to slow down in this technologically-driven society. Organizations that will survive and thrive are those that have an operating framework that allows them to respond, with agility and strength, to the ever-changing demands of the marketplace. Agile execution of this operating structure opens the door for flexibility, improvement and freedom to create and innovate.

REFERENCES

Blazey, Mark L., (2005). *Baldrige in Brief.* Milwaukee, Wisconsin: ASQ Quality Press.

Blazey, Mark L., (2015). *Insights to Performance Excellence 2015-2016.* Milwaukee, Wisconsin: ASQ Quality Press.

Brown, Mark Graham. (2016). *The Pocket Guide to the Baldrige Criteria, 17th Edition.* New York, New York: Productivity Press.

Crandall, M., Becker, S., & Gates, M. (2015). Delaware Libraries Survey Results: Impact Survey.

Himmel & Wilson (2005). Statewide Master Plan for Library Services and Construction. Dover, DE: Division of Libraries.

National Institute of Standards and Technology. (2016): 2015-2016 *Baldrige Excellence Framework (Business/NonProfit)*. Retrieved from http://www.quality.nist.gov.

Vinyard, John, (2015). Baldrige in Plain English: Understanding Performance Excellence. Milwaukee, Wisconsin: Quality Press.

Wilson, D.D., del Tufo, T., & Norman, A.E.C. (2008). *The Measure of Library Excellence. Linking the Malcolm Baldrige Criteria and the Balanced Scorecard Methods to Assess Service Quality*. Jefferson, N.C.: McFarland.

Dr. Theresa del Tufo is a community leader, an educator, an organizational consultant, and a technical and motivational writer. She is the author of the book *SoloPower: How to Harness the Secret Energy of Living Alone* (2014) that explored the happiness, challenges and transition stages of solo living. SoloPower was the first in a series of books on how to lead a full and happy life, despite the challenges and inevitable sufferings that life brings. *The Fullness of Nothing* is the second in this series.

As a child, Tes survived the ravages of war during the Japanese occupation of the Philippines. Her family had to escape to the mountains since her father was wanted for publishing anti-Japanese propaganda. As a young bride and immigrant, she had no family to support her after the untimely death of her husband. As a single parent, she raised two young sons and put them through college, while working on her doctoral degree and holding a full time job. Out of the struggle, darkness, and loss in her earlier life emerged strength of character, light, and a deeper appreciation of the inherent goodness of life. This book is seen through the eyes of those experiences.

In March of 2009, Tes was inducted into the Hall of Fame of Delaware Women by Governor Jack Markell. The award is the most prestigious recognition bestowed on Delaware women for lifetime achievement and outstanding accomplishments.

DR. HANS C. MUMM

DEVELOPING NON-LINEAR LEADERS IN DISRUPTIVE TIMES: CHALLENGES IN A CO-EVOLUTIONARY AND MULTI-DIMENSIONAL TECHNOLOGY REVOLUTION

What does revolution look like? Is there such a thing as a leadership revolution? Would the answer lay in your definition of leadership, your definition of what is revolutionary, or is it in the collection of your perceptions of how one motivates and drives others towards shared goals?

As leaders living in a time marked by disruptive technologies, we must learn "How to harmonize the speed of innovation and change with the human spirit's need for leadership" (Mumm, 2016). Societies are not stagnating while world leaders struggle to integrate into the era of globalization. Non-linear leadership asserts the concept of multiple primary factors or stakeholders that require analysis in order to develop an optimum solution. There are many stakeholders and a myriad of key interactions that all need to achieve a certain level of satisfaction.

Non-linear leadership breaks away from the line and block chart mentality of linear organizations. Non-linear leadership thrives in complex adaptive and dynamic systems. The leadership style allows order to emerge by giving organizations the space to self-organize, evolve, and adapt, encompassing evolutionary design, and service delivery. Self-organization is indisputably opposite to linear management thinking. Non-linear, non-authoritarian, self-organized entities offer real-time insight and constant evolution that is the catalyst to revolution. This promotes a culture that rapidly disseminates information and enables participants to adapt more easily in the face of change.

When you look out into the future and think about the word revolution, what do you see? Does your mind head towards the negative and think about countries in strife or in a military revolution? Alternatively, do you move towards a positive outlook and access the creative side of your brain; dreaming of how you could make the world a better, brighter place for all? Answering these questions will allow you to acknowledge your perceptions about the changing world, as your perception becomes your reality.

If you reading leadership and management journals, it appears leaders continue to assume that stability is the normative state and that change is unusual, however, nothing can be further from the truth. Is the world really in disarray or have the rules, policies, and institutional guides of the past largely run their course? Examining the challenges in a co-evolutionary and multi-dimensional technology revolution starts with the recognition that technology is moving too fast for our world's governing bodies to keep up with and this is creating a false sense of chaos, appearing as a loss of control.

As leaders if you focus on the negative, you will tend to influence people around you in negative ways. If you focus on the positive side of change and innovation, you will tend to create teams of people that seek out the innovation and wonderment in their work. As a leader you hold the key to success and this starts by not getting caught up in the massive amount of negative information (and often false) that is overloading your sense of purpose and your ability to impact not only yourself but the world around you.

In Figure 1, I put forth for your consideration the idea that we have three simultaneous revolutions occurring in the time continuum of humankind and this is what creates the co-evolutionary and multi-dimensional technology revolution. Although all of this appears to be an anomaly in the historical timeline; it is actually a shift in the paradigm as the Robotics Revolution and the Biotech Revolution are creating a third revolution - the Knowledge Revolution. All of these changes and shifts are happening not in a linear timeline like previous revolutions, but are happening in a non-linear almost parallel fashion that is creating a disruption in the norm of how we act and interact with the world. This non-linear disruption creates uncertainty at levels that most people are uncomfortable with, and this contributes to the current global upheaval. Second, only to water and food, humans crave certainty, safety, stability, and order however in these disruptive times of multi-industrial sectors revolutionary change is the only thing guaranteed.

A shifting knowledge base is creating the need for new leadership paradigms. Knowledge no longer creates a defacto leadership role; younger generations now question facts and assumptions. The youth no longer depend solely on their elders to instruct them and guide them. Leaders must change their thought processes and focus more on a positive future using non-linear, non-authoritarian, and self-organizing entities as frameworks to the base of their leadership styles. Leaders now need to work to support the people and processes that will allow us all to thrive in this new and bright future. By focusing on the strengths of the people they support, instead of just providing guidance or instruction, leaders will become more effective.

In complexity theory, (non-linear leadership) a key leadership function is to define a clear actionable vision of the desired outcome. The vision statement allows for a series of philosophies. These philosophes facilitate the emergent decisions that make up the eventual solution. This concept is based on theories of change that discuss the concepts of how an organization can implement planned changes versus forced changes.

Let us examine what is happening today and where the next revolution is taking us. This will provide a sense of understanding and thus a sense of certainty and positive purpose.

The Next Revolution

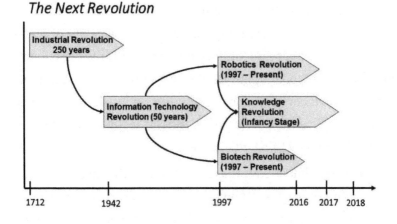

Figure 1: Compression of Revolutions

If we examine the timelines of world revolutions in figure 1 above, we see change. We see the pace of change is radically accelerating and the upheaval in the world begins to accelerate in a similar fashion. What is not apparent is the pace at which leadership changes must evolve in order to help those around them understand their role in shaping a positive future.

HISTORICAL REVOLUTIONS

A quick walk through history starts with the industrial revolution, which was approximately 1712-1942. This approximate 230-year revolution starts in 1712 with the steam engine. This revolutionary period in history lasts until 1942 when John Atanasoff and Clifford Berry built the first electronic digital computer, thus ushering in the information technology (IT) revolution. ("Industrial Revolution Inventions Timeline – 1712-1942," 2015).

During the industrial revolution, leadership was just evolving as workers and management adapted took a linear and hierarchal structure with the goal of optimizing the output from the raw materials and workforce. Workers came out of the farm fields, piecemeal factories (and from the trades) where they had general autonomy and a deep understanding of the tasks needed to create success (food for the winter and products to barter with) along with a strong independent mindset. Management was just beginning to understand that machines could continue to replace workers in doing heavily repetitive jobs and that the integration of man and machine in order to successfully complete tasks took not only training, it took people skills. This is a skill that was not always valued or the focus of much training as discussed by Rita McGrath in the Harvard Business Review when she states "The focus was wholly on the *execution* of mass production...By the early 1900's, the term "management" was in wide use, and Adam Smith's ideas came into their own. Others – such as Frederick Winslow Taylor, Frank and Lillian Galbreth, Herbert R. Townes, and Henry L. Gantt – developed theories that emphasized efficiency, lack of variation, consistency of production, and predictability."(McGrath, 2014).

THE INFORMATION TECHNOLOGY REVOLUTION

The information technology (IT) revolution spans approximately from 1947-1997, with many, falsely believing that we are still in the IT revolution. In 1947, William Shockley, John Bardeen, and Walter Brattain invented the transistor that permitted electronic miniaturization. The leadership and management required during this revolution focused more on expertise and thus the "mid-twentieth century was a period of remarkable growth in theories of management and in the guru-industrial complex. Writers such as Elton Mayo, Mary Parker Follett, Chester Barnard, Max Weber, and Chris Argyris imported theories from other fields (sociology and psychology) to apply to management." (McGrath, 2014).

These theories and leadership styles clashed with the science world as metrics based processes and management by objective gave way to even more ideas of reengineering, the "waterfall" method of software development and six-sigma. All of these theories, methods and ideas culminated with Peter Drucker as he dubbed all of the efforts as "knowledge work" and "saw the value created wasn't created simply by having workers produce goods or execute tasks; the value was also created by worker' use of information." (McGrath, 2014).

Structure is a desirable organizational attribute only if it services the organization and the people in it. All too often, the organizational structure is in place only to serve as a wage scale discriminator. A leader must recognize the potential in people and develop the leadership skills as required, a person must want to be a leader, and not begrudgingly accept a leadership position simply because the possible monetary benefits.

The compressed timelines of this new revolution from 250 years in the industrial revolution to 50 years in the IT revolution is radical changing the world and it is creating unintended consequences that humankind may not understand. IT gives self-organizing entities the ability to emerge at will and bring solutions to issues at a speed never seen before. There is a risk in all that humankind does; the real risk to leaders arises in continuing down a linear and authoritarian path of questionable means which will not lead to the future, but only hold onto the past.

Some think we are still in the IT revolution. The reality is that Moore's Law appears to have run its course and the IT Revolution truly did have an end date of 1997. Keep in mind that Moore's Law discussed and framed IT more in the realm of limitations, and not limitless innovation when it was envisioned in 1965. Essentially, it said that the number of transistors per square inch on integrated circuits doubled every year since the invention of the integrated circuit and it will continue to do so approximately every 18 months. Yet in 2003, the driving factor of interconnectivity ended the IT Revolution as IEEE argues by stating "Reversing early limitations on Moore's Law, interconnectors have replaced transistors as the main determinants of chip performance. This "tyranny of interconnectors" will only escalate in the future, and thus the nano-electronics that follows silicon must be interconnect-centric."(Meindl, 2003). This idea drove the world out of the IT Revolution and into the robotics and biotech revolutions. In 1997, the social networking site Six-Degrees.com was created; thus drawing a new line in the sand for human contact and interaction. This signaled the end of the IT revolution.

THE ROBOTICS AND BIOTECH REVOLUTIONS

The robotics revolution was ushered in on May 11, 1997, when a computer built by IBM known as Deep Blue beat world chess champion, Garry Kasparov. The goal of Japan's RoboCup is to have a fully automated team of robots beat the world's best soccer team by the year 2050. Honda has created the P3, Honda's first completely autonomous humanoid robot.

In parallel to the robotics revolution, the biotech revolution took hold in 1997 with the reported cloning of Dolly, the sheep, using DNA from two adult sheep cells. The importance of this event woke the world up in 2001 as the Human Genome Project created a draft of the human genome sequence. Within two years, the project reported on the location and sequence of human genes on all 46 chromosomes.

By 2016, the timeline for revolutions has compressed and the world is in a unique situation as Connected revolutions play out simultaneously; the robotic revolution moves man and machine closer together, the biotech revolution enables humankind to live longer and consequently man become partial machines as a cyborg.

The definition of a cyborg is a person whose body is beyond normal human limitations by mechanical elements built into the body. This creates physical abilities that extend or alter the body for a better life experience, beyond normal human limitations by mechanical elements built into the body. This shift in the focus of evolution for humankind moves from innovation to understand to the questioning of life itself. The world now sees two new revolutions take hold and a third revolution, the knowledge revolution begin, all in less than 20 years.

The robotic and biotech revolution are now integrating and feeding off each other in ways no one could have imagined. Consider the idea that micro robots are now small enough to clear out clogged arteries; perform routine surgeries with minimal incursion as well as precisely deliver drugs to an affected area for maximum effectiveness with minimal side effects. Current study is verifying the robot itself does not have any harmful side effects. One research question delves into the issue of whether the robot should be extracted. Do you allow the robot to extract in some fashion from the body or simply stay in the body in case it is required later in life? This type of revolution integration creates radical disruption in the norm and it requires world leaders, businesses professionals, and even parents to have different mindsets and leadership skills to navigate in such an uncertain environment.

Research of this type raises ethical questions about protecting human rights and whether artificial intelligence is equivalent to humans' self-awareness and therefore should be afforded the same rights as humans. The idea that humans are one of the only species that can claim they are truly self-aware may be at an end. An Oxford mathematician, Marcus du Sautoy stated, " It's getting to a point where we might be able to say this thing has sense of itself, and maybe there is a threshold moment where suddenly consciousness emerges...we should respect it in all its forms, regardless of whether its basis for being is organic or synthetic" (Dockrill, 2016). If one looks at problems that the simplistic fashion of leadership can lead its way out of these issues, meaning in a traditional linear leadership style, one is doomed to fail in this multi-dimensional world. Leadership skills will require more intricate decision-making abilities in a compressed timeline that increases the anxiety for the uncertainty as "The underlying thought is that cognitive computing functions in an assisting, subordinate relationship to humans...experts believe that cognitive computing has the potential to advance in a superior relationship to humans." (de Batt, 2016).

Combining the robotics, biotech revolution offers up the creation of the knowledge revolution. This gives rise to the future of man and machine learning about and from each other. This was stated by Kurzweil in his book *The Singularity is Near* when he says "our ability to create models of reality in our minds enables us to articulate meaningful insights into the implications of this impending merger of our biological thinking and non-biological intelligence we are creating" (Kurzweil, 2005, p. 4). The merging of man and machine, the merging of education with the machine and the ability to customize the experience to an individual's learning ability is a required change from the norm as the speed of the revolutions has proven that the current systems are inadequate and are becoming redundant and irrelevant.

Robot ethics, the ethical and social implications of robots, quickly becomes a study for academics and scientists as well as an integration consideration for society. Even the US Defense Department is studying the ethical challenges of autonomous weapons systems. In society, these discussions tend to manifest themselves into Hollywood movies that exaggerate robot wars such as *The Terminator*, where machines become self-aware and decide that they must eliminate all humans. In *I-Robot* it appears that the artificially intelligent systems examine the flaws of humankind as the robot controller- Virtual Interactive Kinesthetic Interface (*V.I.K.I.*) explains "You cannot be trusted with your own survival. To protect humanity, some humans must be sacrificed. To ensure your future, some freedoms must be surrendered. We robots will ensure mankind's continued existence. You are so like children. We must save you from yourselves. Don't you understand? The perfect circle of protection will abide. My logic is undeniable." (Vintar & Goldsman, 2004). In many ways, *V.I.K.I.* is logically correct; however, leaders in this multi-dimensional revolution need to work to create solutions to issues, so *V.I.K.I.*'s logic would not be so undeniable.

Whether one wishes to embrace the reality of the future or not we must explore a future in which humanity can no longer control technological progress through the normal shared values expressed in laws, policies and world governance. As machines take on more routine, dull, or dangerous work, leaders and their organizations will face unprecedented challenges as they attempt to adapt to this new world. In the past, automation technology focused on the factory floor and new machines would disrupt one employment sector at a time, with workers then switching to a new skill set or emerging industry. The situation today is quite different, as the multi-dimensional revolutions will affect all industry sectors in an unequal manner.

Technology flourishes as markets expand, and free roaming robotics is the key to market expansion in the robotics revolution.

Advanced artificial intelligence is the key enabler of the market breadth and depth. Free roaming robotics will be the next productivity accelerator. It comes as the information revolution stops accelerating productivity and stabilizes at a more constant growth rate. As the baby boomers retire, the demand will increase dramatically for machines to take on tasks that will allow a higher quality of life in their waning years. The use of robotics and artificial intelligence cannot replace everyone or every task. However, it will free up human capital to engage in other pursuits.

As an example, the US Air Force is planning on developing unmanned aerial systems that can work autonomously and in teams. This will cue up the next round of machine-to-machine cooperation, allowing for "swarms" of cooperative robots to complete complex missions. Most robotics companies are not truly revolutionary or even evolutionary in robotics; they focus more on the toy and consumer market. They are task and niche-oriented and not revolution-oriented, and will benefit from the innovations and advances in AI and manufacturing. Without advanced artificial intelligence, these companies will be taking baby steps instead of giant leaps. They are also mostly working sub-scale, instead of the key "near-full-scale" area. Once the world is convinced that all things are possible, the revolution is complete as it is at near full scale and not at the toy market level.

KNOWLEDGE REVOLUTION

The tri-revolution that I am labeling a "Knowledge Revolution" has at its core the ability to offer large data stores at the stroke of a keyboard or voice command into a mobile device. This great revolution has the ability to solve some of the great historical issues; knowledge transfer and the issue of scarcity and selective knowledge transfer. Thomas Frey states "Scarcity is defined as an economic condition that arises when people have far greater wants than the available resources. Most often we think about the limited supplies of natural resources, but it includes far more than that" (Frey, 2012). In knowledge transfer and in higher education, the economic condition that Frey alludes to is the ability for humans to obtain and learn in an amount that is sufficient to offer human evolution through innovative means. This evolution will then create greater economic, social, and humanistic processes and products to move the human race for the betterment of society for future generations. This idea creates an abundance of information, most of which is largely inaccessible and untapped by the average person, even though as Frey contends "Our ever-evolving information world is enabling us to construct hyper-individualized service offerings to tap into our personal wants, needs, and desires like never before" (Frey, 2012). This evolving world will need to reset our thinking and reflect on our history to create a future that is brighter than our past. New knowledge bases will be created, the danger of misinformation being injected into knowledge base (media, politics, religion, etc....) is an issue that needs further investigation. However, just the thought of the ability to inject misinformation into automated systems should give pause to what truth is and how we define it.

Alvin Toffler is correct when he states "The illiterate of the 21st century will not be those who cannot read and write, but those who cannot learn, unlearn, and relearn" (Salpeter, 2003). The fact is that in the knowledge revolution we are compressing decades into days, an example of this is the difference between an owner's manual and a quick start guide. The base knowledge on how to plug in, boot up and start the functions on a product are now a given, and the world is moving so fast the only thing consumers want or read is the quick start guide. As Professor Randall Nichols states "Trained resources capable of manning either side of the equation are probably beyond the scope of normal education systems. We don't train scientists anymore and the tinker toy mindset seems to be reduced to internet games." (Nichols, 2016).

Our life spans are very short, and as the amount of knowledge available to the human race radically expands, a necessary skill for individuals will be to think broadly about the topics in this increase knowledge base. As state in a 2009 education summit, "The only reason schools exist is to cultivate students who can think broadly about any topic. The only reason people with an education get hired is because of their ability to think. Great thinkers can help create great futures" (*CoRT: Futurist Thinking Tools for Students*, 2009). True knowledge transfer fuels additional innovation and creativity via our education system. This arena has stagnated to the detriment of the human race. The foundation of education has not dramatically changed in the past 100 years. Our current understanding of human education forces learning at the same pace and in a similar manner as the past even though the world moves at a breakneck speed today as compared to a century ago. The knowledge revolution is forcing the world into new processes and thoughts on what type of information we choose to transfer, access and learn and how that information assists us in achieving the goals of a group or of ourselves.

The positive side of the knowledge revolution will move humanity forward and allow the progressive change in thought, processes, procedures, education, and technology. During this new surge, we can seek the uplifting euphoria of higher thought as we embrace the unbridled human spirit and we hone our leadership skills in making our world and ourselves positive beacons for change and innovation.

LEADERSHIP IN THE KNOWLEDGE REVOLUTION

Leadership must embrace the reality of the knowledge revolution. Any resistance to adapt and adjust as we fully enter into the knowledge revolution will create irrefutable harm, not just to the first world countries; third and second world countries will suffer at disproportionate rates. The ability to instruct in multiple modalities, and with the assistance of artificial intelligence and human enhancements (cyborg-like enhancements) offers a range of options to move knowledge throughout the universe faster and with a greater depth of understanding than in the past. The challenge is society as a whole has not handled the enormous amounts of historical data available to date, and it does not appear poised to handle an avalanche of new ideas, data, process, procedures, and innovation that are heading at it like a runaway freight train.

Although the full integration of the knowledge revolution offers an ever-changing and bright future, many aspects of leadership and human interaction will need to evolve and learn to adapt to a changing future before we realize the true power of the revolution. If one examines the average classroom today, the instructing aspects of the one room schoolhouse from the early 1900's is clear in the lessons of reading and regurgitation of information. This type of linear thought process is invalid in the new knowledge revolution. The ability to teach in multiple modalities offers student's new ways to learn the material with a higher retention and usability rate. We must customize the experience. Today, student learning takes place from hardcover books that are now in PDF form so the institution can claim itself in the digital age. As noted, humanity will look to drive progress as far as it can, and technological advancement will pose new dangers along the way—from concerns over the production of guns in garages and the health effects of nanoparticles to the ethical pros and cons of cognitive enhancement (Vielmetter & Sell, 2014).

Consider the idea of cognitive complexity; the notion that as a timeframe moves further out, an individual's intellect must disproportionately increase in order for the individual to interpret correctly the future state of any issue. Cognitive complexity thinking goes beyond the idea of emergent change in complex systems such as business, education, governance, governing, or human evolution; it offers the ability to create true discriminators of what constitutes an opportunity or a threat. The emergence of the knowledge revolution will push the world into deeper and more meaningful complexities, not into a simplistic formatted life, as many people might believe.

Linear and authoritarian leadership will no longer work; we must shift to a non-linear, non-authoritarian, and self-organized entity framework of leadership. Keith Morrison states "In complexity theory, a system can be described as a collection of interacting parts which, together, function as a whole...This interaction is so intricate that it cannot be predicted by linear equations; there are so many variables involved that the behavior of the system can only be understood as an 'emerging consequence' of the sum of the constituent elements." (Keith Morrison).

The leaders that follow a linear leadership mindset get nervous about this proposal, as they falsely believe they will lose control of an organization or decision-making processes and chaos will ensue. General Bill Creech states the best answer to this concern as he offers the idea that

"Many people believe that decentralization means loss of control. That's simply not true. You can improve control if you look at control as the control of events and not people. Then, the more people you have controlling events — the more people you have that care about controlling the events, the more people you have proactively working to create favorable events — the more control you have within the organization, by definition." ("Quotes by General Bill Creech," 2016).

CONCLUSION

Guiding distributed human intelligence in a way that produces non-linear emergent behaviors (answers to problems) can create the evolutionary solutions to hard problems. This leads people, teams, and entities in a logical, rapid fashion in a world that demands efficiency and effectiveness at levels not seen historically. The complexity theory offers power through its non-linear, accelerated evolution that matches the restless and perpetual change occurring in today's technological world. This restless and perpetual change demonstrates a world changing in such a way that it is not possible for the current linear, authoritarian leadership and organizational change models to match the pace of change. This mismatch reaches beyond the pace of technology to the pace of our human interaction with the technology and the way leaders can succeed during this time of creative change.

Most actions conducted by governments and industry offer only authoritarian, linear, and evolutionary thought and ideas when revolutionary non-linear, non-authoritarian structures are what are needed to force the framework of the future. A fundamental mismatch occurs because the design processes of most regulations, policies, and rules avoid risk and embrace slow processes; the opposite of what is required today. For successful integration of strategic net change, government and industry must embrace a leadership framework that can address potentially disruptive technologies and concepts that have multiple stakeholders and multi-directional interactions. Fostering innovation and technology refresh over outdated and irrelevant policies is one way to embrace non-linear thought. Decision making with action and tangible results is what is required in the tri-revolutionary world. Given this requirement, how do we realign our institutions, (academic, governmental and commerce) for resilience and success as new revolutions continue to emerge simultaneously and inject additional instability into systems that are already struggling for equilibrium.

As technology and the world around us change at an ever-increasing rate, policy, and governance struggle to keep up with these changes. Drones, advanced weapons, biological attacks (intended or unintended by the spread of disease such as Ebola), self-replicating organisms in the physical space and in cyberspace will push senior leaders passed their ability to comprehend and govern leaving a void that must be filled by academics, industry, and futurists.

The reality is that humans will continue to allow machines to take over critical thinking skilled areas. When the world is faced with push button decisions needed at the speed of light, it will continue to allow machines latitude to make decisions for humankind without the benefit of wisdom, people skills, or leadership. There is no way to mitigate all risks, only an attempt to control them or accept them. Leadership is not a single concept or thought and thus linear leadership is failing forward as we move into the knowledge revolution at the same time the robotic and biotech revolution are nearing their mid to end stages. Whether humankind chooses to accept the concept or not, the knowledge revolution is an issue that cannot be ignored. The knowledge revolution does not depend or end upon any one leader's ability to forecast the future, or make agile decisions. All humankind must shoulder it, as we must learn and re-learn in an effort to make solid decisions for our global corporate colleagues, our families, and ourselves for another revolution after the knowledge revolution will surely be on the horizon and this time it should not take humankind by surprise.

REFERENCES

CoRT: Futurist Thinking Tools for Students. (2009). Paper presented at the Education Summit: Innovation and Creativity in Learning.

de Batt, B. (2016). How cognitive computing will change project management. Retrieved from http://www.cio.com/article/3107317/project-management/how-cognitive-computing-will-change-project-management.html

Dockrill, P. (2016). Artificial intelligence should be protected by human rights, Machines have feelings too. Retrieved from http://www.sciencealert.com/artificial-intelligence-should-be-protected-by-human-rights-says-oxford-mathematician

Frey, T. (2012). Inventing Our Next Great Scarcities. Retrieved from http://www.wfs.org/blogs/thomas-frey/inventing-our-next-great-scarcities

Industrial Revolution Inventions Timeline – 1712-1942. (2015). Retrieved from http://storiesofusa.com/industrial-revolution-inventions-timeline-1712-1942/

Kurzweil, R. (2005). *The singularity is near: When humans transcend biology*: Penguin.

McGrath, R. (2014). Management's Three Eras: A Brief History. *Harvard Business Review*. Retrieved from https://hbr.org/2014/07/managements-three-eras-a-brief-history

Meindl, J. D. (2003). Beyond Moore's Law: the interconnect era. *Computing in Science & Engineering*, 5(1), 20-24. doi:10.1109/MCISE.2003.1166548

Mumm, H. (2016). United States Patent No. 4,927,039. U. S. P. a. T. Office.

Nichols, R. (2016). *Field Notes-Ah-ha Moments* Adjunct Faculty UAS-Cybersecurity. Kansas State University Polytechnic Campus.

Quotes by General Bill Creech. (2016). *Quotes by Famous Leaders.* Retrieved from http://govleaders.org/quotes-leaders.htm

Salpeter, J. (2003). 21st Century Skills: Will Our Students be Prepared? *Technology and Learning-Dayton, 24*(3), 17-29.

Vielmetter, G., & Sell, Y. (2014). *Leadership 2030: the six megatrends you need to understand to lead your company into the future*: AMACOM Div American Mgmt Assn.

Vintar, J., & Goldsman, A. (Writers) & A. Proyas (Director). (2004). I, Robot. Hollywood, CA.

Dr. Hans C. Mumm is a best-selling author and a dynamic speaker through a range of topics including leadership, technology revolutions, and drone/UAV issues as well as countering the human trafficking phenomena and the challenge of human communication.

Dr. Mumm is a proven leader in a diverse set of fields including technical investigation, scientific research, military intelligence, and small business owner. He is a published researcher in both the scientific and social science arenas. His publications include: *Applying Complexity Leadership Theory to Drone Airspace Integration, Embracing the Need for Leadership in the New World of Unmanned Vehicles and Robotics, Managing the Integration and Harmonization of National Airspace for Unmanned and Manned Systems* and co-authoring, *The Multi-Fuel Optimization System: A Technical Discussion,* and drafted *Legislation to Establish a National Inter-Agency Working Group To Develop Policies and Protocols On the Use of UAVs and Robotics,* along with several other works.

Dr. Mumm is highly skilled in designing policy and governance for advanced technologies including unmanned vehicles and robotics earning his Doctorate of Management (with a concentration in homeland security) from Colorado Technical University (CTU). Dr. Mumm's unique skill set is a hybrid resulting from on the ground tactical combat experience and many years spent in strategic homeland security roles consulting on policy creation and fielding new technologies within the intelligence community. His UAV and robotics expertise have focused on determining the specific uses, exceptions, and allowances; including studying the unintended consequences, future use, and misuse of such technologies. Dr. Mumm's presentation and publications supports his fellowship with the Cyber Conflict Documentation Project (CCDP) as he expands their research into autonomous systems in the virtual and physical worlds.

Dr. Mumm has earned twenty-three personal military ribbons/medals, six military unit medals/citations, and two Directors Awards from the Defense Intelligence Agency. In 2005, Dr. Mumm was recognized as one of the "Ten Outstanding Young Americans and in 2003 he was awarded the National Defense PAC "American Patriot Ingenuity Award" for service during "Operation Iraqi Freedom." He was honored, in 2016, to receive a People of Distinction Humanitarian Award. Dr. Mumm is an instructor with American Military University and California University of Pennsylvania.

DAVID TWEEDT
AND PETE WINIARSKI

THE POWER OF DAILY LEADERSHIP

**Unlocking Stellar Team Performance and Sustaining Breakthrough
Results through Powerful Daily Leadership Practices**

INTRODUCTION

In our experience, Daily Leadership is the key to success--
the key to unlocking stellar team performance--and practically
speaking, the only way to stay viable in today's competitive market place for just about any industry.

Daily Leadership will skyrocket your team's productivity and
lock in higher levels of employee engagement. These time-tested behaviors enhance communication on all levels, set the
stage for model performance, and hold the vision for the entire
team--that in and of itself will stave off an impending crisis in
your company.

Consider this: Our country is facing a leadership *crisis* which
is costing businesses *billions!* A recent survey by the Barna
Group found 90% of those polled believe there is a *Leadership
Crisis*, 61% said they work for a *Bad Boss*.[1] And that can mean
only one thing: leadership is lacking.

Now, let's flip this conversation to the positive side. Imagine
if your company could more than double its profitability. Anoth-

er survey conducted by Towers Watson found fully engaged organizations are 256% more profitable.[2]

Engagement is the secret sauce that drives profitability! And how do you drive engagement? *Through Daily Leadership principles.*

A great deal of this increased profitability is associated with *sustaining* the improvements and breakthrough results which allows the organization to focus on further gains and increased profits. Given the profitability statistics above, why would any organization ignore the power of employee engagement--and not implement Daily Leadership behaviors?

Creating a fully engaged workforce starts with leadership through your entire organization from the C-Suite to the front lines. During our nearly three decades of experience, we have studied and worked with many great leaders of our time. We have found that truly great leaders first and foremost practice Daily Leadership principles, including those that focus on seeing the employee not just as cog on the wheel but as a valuable asset to the team, potentially with problem-solving abilities and visions that could enhance an entire operation. Daily Leadership is not left to chance. It's a way of life interwoven into with the technical aspects of a leader's role. This is especially prevalent in *great* front line leaders. Additionally, as you progress up the corporate ladder, the necessity of excellence in these Daily Leadership behaviors becomes even greater.

As leadership guru John Maxwell says, "Most teams don't naturally get better on their own. Left alone, they don't grow, improve, or reach championship caliber. Instead, they tend to wind down. The road to the next level is always uphill, and if a team isn't intentionally fighting to move up, then it inevitably slides down."

The group that has the highest influence in developing and growing a fully engaged workforce is the front line leadership team. Employee engagement starts here and flows *up* through the organization where each successive layer in the organization plays a lesser role in direct employee engagement and a greater role in enabling their reports to be successful. Therefore, if you are to be successful in creating a fully engaged workforce in your organization, you need to ensure your front line leaders understand your vision and are fully equipped to be successful.

DOES YOUR BUSINESS STRUGGLE TO SUSTAIN RESULTS?

We have found that many companies struggle to sustain the improvements they've made, wasting time and money re-visiting these processes when the results and performance slip backwards rather than driving the company higher. One of the main reasons these improvements slip backwards is the failure to engage the workforce when making the changes or not providing the support for the team after the improvement focus has shifted elsewhere.

In both situations, the glue that holds the improvement together is the engagement and buy-in of front line leadership. Companies have traditionally failed in not placing enough focus on the development of these leaders. They may have received technical training, which is the first phase in the process; however, in many cases, these companies failed to continue up the maturity path and provide the additional leadership training that would enable these leaders to connect with each employee at a deeper level. This deeper level drives engagement and helps to sustain the results.

As companies progress further up the maturity path, leaders evolve to the point that they will be ready to include individualized development plans and goals for themselves and eventually help their reports do the same. However, our experience shows that it is pretty far down the maturity path when you master these skills such as acting equally as coach, mentor, and student with their teams. The goal is to layer these enhanced skills on the technical base. This manifests within those robust engaging discussions with your people. And similar to this, you would want to begin with the initial company or department goals and then define the activity and behavior that align with these goals as a foundation. Later, you would start layering in the personal goals that grow the person that indirectly helps the company grow.

LEADERS EMERGE WHILE MANAGERS ARE TRAINED

We believe that to allow leaders to emerge you want to recognize that each person is an individual with different backgrounds and experiences. The ultimate purpose of any type of leadership development then is to shift the current behaviors towards high productive, high employee engagement type of behaviors. While we recognize that your leaders are at different points in their journey, the goal is to meet them where they are and drive their growth toward higher performance with all the support you can muster.

There are six behaviors we would like to see as a result of your leadership initiative. All of these are assuming that they are in complete alignment with your company's core values and coming from a point of personal and professional integrity. The six behaviors are:

» Challenging the Process
» Inspiring a Shared Vision
» Enabling Others to Act
» Modeling the Way
» Engaging the Heart
» Developing Your Team

Challenging the Process. The vision is to challenge the status quo from a point of humility and respect for people. Enable the front line leads/supervisors to challenge the process in a way that 1) you are respecting those doing the job and 2) that you're engaging your team to look at better ways of doing things while still staying in compliance.

This approach is equipping your leaders to engage their team based on the process of inputs, outputs, and challenges the current system creates. The person with the decision rights ultimately owns the decision and everybody must then, once they've had their opportunity to challenge, agree to be accountable and agree there are no pocket vetoes.

The focus is how to respectfully challenge, without attacking the person. Challenge the data and facts, and don't overly use emotions. In the beginning, some of the supervisors may or may not know some techniques to effectively do that. When your supervisors are growing on their journey together, there will be opportunities for those who are further along to help their peers and share their strengths.

Enabling Others to Act. This is a rather big one. Enabling Others to Act is coming from a point of humility and respect, utilizing the role of a coach and mentor. This behavior requires managerial courage of the supervisor to be comfortable to not keep a tight rein on decisions, but to know when to potentially allow their team to make small mistakes in the spirit of them growing and learning. This self-confidence and self-esteem on the leader's part to be comfortable to encourage risk-taking within the team will not occur immediately. This behavior is built over time, which can be accelerated when the mid-level leadership creates a safe and supportive environment for their front line.

Modeling the Way. This one's pretty self-explanatory. People will not know the way until you show them the way. Your team watches what you do much more than listens to what you say.

Engaging the Heart. For each employee, meet them where they're at and help them to define the journey that they want to take and how that fits within the vision for the company.

Developing the Team. This last behavior is central to successfully exhibiting the first five. Keep in mind that most leaders have three main goals. They are: set goals, remove barriers, and provide resources. To successfully achieve these three goals, the role of your supervisors is to be a coach, mentor, and student in every situation. And when you approach these three goals from a coaching perspective, the obvious result is employee development. This also increases visibility of the up-and-comers.

SO WHAT IS DAILY LEADERSHIP?

Daily Leadership is the process of developing these six behaviors within your front line leadership to levels well beyond traditional expectations. This approach engages and equips the targeted leadership allowing the leaders to emerge and prosper.

Taking a holistic approach for your company's leadership, Daily Leadership allows strong leaders to emerge, who are capable of producing breakthrough results and sustaining them through their highly engaged teams. These are leadership behaviors that are not directly part of traditional training, and are an integral ingredient in the secret sauce that many organizations overlook within the front-line leadership ranks.

The Daily Leadership approach first defines a clear vision of what you want your leadership to aspire to if you do not already have one. The next step is to develop the strategy and a clear process on how you're going to achieve that vision within your organization and your team to deliver the results.

When we were front line supervisors early in our careers at Wiremold, we went through a great deal of training and coaching focused on the behaviors that helped us successfully engage and coach our teams. Some of those things we learned back then are fundamental, and often overlooked in many companies. Traditionally, companies take the best operator and make them a lead, then maybe make them a team leader or supervisor and expect great results without ever giving them the leadership training. So we're talking about a progression here. You have to have a vision and a strategy--and it has to be aligned. You have to have guiding behaviors that create the culture you want, you have to get the right talent, and you have to develop the talent.

You may find that your current talent is tooled toward an old model. If this is the case, you will need to evaluate their potential to mold and adapt within the future model. If there are close-minded individuals, you may have to do a bit of top grading. This is never a fun exercise, however necessary as it may be for your long-term success. When you don't have the right talent, you can develop all you want and not get the results, right? If you have no process, you can't really develop talent around no process.

Necessity is the mother of invention and that is exactly how the Daily Leadership program was born. This is probably not too different from what you experience at your company. Typically, the operations group is struggling to make the results and to engage the operators, and maybe has some culture challenges. They scratching their heads as to why the improvements don't come faster and the results don't stick.

We want to help the supervisors understand that their role needs to shift from playing defense all of the time and waiting for the next crisis to playing much more offense and developing their teams to handle the crisis productively and efficiently, and ultimately implement the changes so the crisis does not happen again--or perhaps averted in the first place.

THE FOUR DAILY LEADERSHIP PRINCIPLES

Front line supervisors are dealing with stuff all day long, and often times when you ask them to reflect at the end of the day, "How well did you progress towards your agenda?" the answer in many cases is, "Goodness, I didn't do anything toward the agenda. I was totally reacting to everybody else's needs." Our vision for the front line centers around four Daily Leadership principles:

» Manage performance proactively

» Execute fast-paced issue resolution

» Clearly communicate high expectations and provide regular feedback

» Coach and develop team members and leverage them to achieve great results

Manage performance proactively. The first principle revolves around how you manage performance proactively. How do you know what it is in the context of the bigger vision, in the context of your personalized vision? What is the vision that the plan has?

Here, we use a baseball analogy to demonstrate our point: Pete coached his son's little league team for the last few years. Over the seasons, he had to look at these kids in the face and discuss the biggest goal for the team--winning the season. Yet, this overarching goal had to be broken down into winning the game of the day. Then, there were the micro goals to develop the individual team members, encouraging them to play their best that day, hit the ball the next time they are up at bat, and to have fun in the process.

When they focused on having fun, they did good at bat, and they made the play in the field. Then over time, it rolled up to the next level of performance--winning the game, and ultimately having a winning season.

The same approach is taken for any team and individual development. And the best way to do that is to proactively find ways to make time in your schedule to allow yourself to focus energy on some bigger picture things so your not just going home at the end of the day having spent all your time chasing issues.

Execute fast-paced issue resolution. This is when problems come up the supervisor is focusing *on both* immediate resolution and long-term actions so the problem does not rear its ugly head again.

When this principle is sometimes initially discussed, we hear people say, "Yah, we have our problem-solving process. We get a cross-functional team together, and we solve the problem over a period of time." While all of this is good, it's also a big picture way to think about it.

What we are talking about here within the context of Daily Leadership is on the firing line. We have to ship so many dollars worth of product today to meet orders and the equipment is not running. What do we need to do right now? There are a number of different types of counter measure interventions that can be put in place, and sometimes this can't solve the root cause in the moment. So the solution is to do something that is a temporary fix--then get to root causes as quickly as you can.

Here is one example: There were some parts that were holding up a shipment. The customer was calling the CEO and chewing him out. He walked down to the manufacturing floor and the head of operations said, "Oh, yah, that's a screw, and we know that this screw is not here. We can't ship without the screw and so we have launched a problem solving initiative and a corrective action process with the supplier." On the surface, this is the right answer. Meanwhile, the CEO identified that it was a standard screw size. The CEO said, "Home Depot is five minutes from here. Someone get in the car and go get the screws and ship this order before we lose this customer."

So recognize that there is balance between the need for urgent action with fixing processes and putting long-term solutions in place by solving the root cause. Depending on where you are, the pendulum might swing all the way on one side or all of the way on the other. What we are trying to do is help people recognize how to quickly assess what's needed in the moment to keep things moving and put a solution in place--while also determining the root cause to permanently solve the issue.

Clearly communicate high expectations and provide regular feedback. The third principle is centered around roles and responsibilities--and focused on engaging the front line leaders in developing their own roles and responsibilities, and making sure that from supervisor to supervisor they are in alignment.

A key point in roles and responsibilities is that they do not have to be the same because they are tailored to each individual's current state of competence. What is also included within this principle are the decision rights, which are not granted by title, but are granted by experience. So you could have a supervisor with very high decision rights because they demonstrated this competency next to another supervisor with low decision rights. The point is meeting the supervisors where they are and taking them on their journey to allow their leadership to emerge. The goal is for them to be aligned and eventually all moving in the same direction.

Along the way, feedback is important--and perhaps most important is the feedback style which builds a rapport amongst individuals where people are hungry for feedback and they are open to it. It's not defensiveness. Many leaders ask: what are the clear expectations for me? What am I to focus on? How am I aggressively closing those gaps within myself and how am I leveraging my leader and my peers to close that gap as well? Continual feedback to provide these answers is vital.

Unfortunately a lot of folks only receive feedback in two occasions: One, when it's time for the annual progress review and there is a sit down formal conversation where they receive feedback, and the two, when something goes horrible wrong.

What we want to do is turn that totally upside down and have more positive feedback sessions than negative. This is the concept of, "How did we do today? Let's reflect back and define what we need to do in order to improve so that tomorrow is better than today." We want to shoot for having a positive mindset as the guiding theme. This starts with having high expectations and then layering in the feedback, which enables personalization depending on your leader's current capabilities.

Identify where your team is doing really well and give them the pats on the back from a truly authentic perspective. We want you to do more than give someone a slap on the back as you are walking by saying, "good job." People know when a compliment is heartfelt and when it's not.

Coach and develop team members and leverage them to achieve great results. The last principle is actually fairly similar on the surface to the third one where it's about development and coaching and going beyond base expectations and metrics. Here we are focused on, "How I can help you?" It's recognizing that a leader's responsibility is not just to give direction and then get out of the way. It's to give direction and then see if the team is capable of going on their own—-and if so, then getting out of their way.

It is also about stepping in to coach and mentor if the team is struggling. If they are bumping into things that need to be removed in terms of barriers or blockades, a good leader practicing Daily Leadership behaviors steps up. If there is an issue with something outside their team's area of influence, they need someone to be an advocate for them. During this time it's about the coaching and the development part of the conversation that helps them to know that is okay to ask for help. It's also about coaching them on the right communication process you used to be an advocate for them so they understand the different approaches possible to get things done with other members of their team.

YOUR NEXT STEPS

You may be thinking, "Where do I start?" The first step is to assess where your front line leadership team is today. How well are they proactively growing and developing their teams? On a scale of 1 to 10, how engaged is your workforce? When improvements are made, how well are the results sustained?

The next step is to assess if you have the knowledge and expertise within your organization of delivering and coaching the Daily Leadership principles. If this knowledge base does not currently exist, you will want to identify a group that has the knowledge, expertise, and experience delivering this leadership development program. If you are partnering with an external resource, you will want to identify a couple internal resources this external group can develop into your internal champions.

Whether you already possess this expertise or not, the delivery is equally as important as the content, especially at the front line leadership level due to the fact that most will have never had the opportunity to be previously exposed to the Daily Leadership behaviors let alone had a coach to help them practice them. What we found is if we put a group of leaders in a room and train them on the subjects for a day or more, we will be extremely lucky if they retain 20%. On the other hand, when you use a teach-coach-soak model, the retention increases to 80% or better. This approach has been extremely effective and the individualized coaching really helps drive it home for each of the team members involved.

Daily Leadership for the front line leaders requires small doses of training on the content followed by situational discussions with the group to apply it directly to the business and one-on-one coaching to grow the experience. The amount of classroom vs. one-on-one coaching depends on the maturity of the organization. Ideally, the more you can base the coaching on "real-life" situations, the more robust and impactful for each location.

Based on where the needs are, you may customize what you focus on by interweaving the approaches that are relevant to what your team needs at that time. Then there's soak time, (time for your leaders to reflect on the content and practice what they are learning) and homework. Ideally, you review the material and do a debrief on how they did, before moving into the next approaches and more coaching and training.

We want to ensure that,within the context of that structure, they are reviewing results each day, and they are also into the proactive coaching. They are diving into processes, they are understanding root causes, and they're engaging the opinions from their team.

CONCLUSION

When the Daily Leadership principles are practiced each day and focused around the behaviors you want your leaders to embody, you will notice the culture of accountability, trust, respect, and engagement growing with each interaction. Ideally, you would see teams embodying a continuous improvement mindset without the supervisor having to prompt their people. These employees are making suggestions; they're maybe even trying things out depending on what is within their latitude. The more mature teams will develop to the point where, within the parameters of what is acceptable, you might have people do an experiment with an idea and demonstrate their thinking as, "here was the problem, here's the idea we had, we ran this experiment, here is why it seems to be working or not." It can really bring continuous improvement to the next level where sustainment is a standard.

The next move is yours. Our hope is by reading this chapter you are energized and excited by the possibilities for your company. The good news is the possibilities are endless. The important thing to remember is, this is a journey not a 100-yard sprint. While there will be significant short-term wins, it takes persistence, resilience, and drive to achieve an environment where breakthrough results are truly sustainable. We wish you the best on your journey.

REFERENCES

[1] The Different Impact of Good and Bad Leadership, <u>Research Releases</u> in <u>Leaders & Pastors</u> • February 18, 2015

[2] Towers Watson 2012 Global Workforce Study, "Engagement at Risk: Driving Strong Performance in a Volatile Global Environment"

Win Enterprises, LLC

http://www.CompleteBusinessTransformation.com

+1.860.651.6859

info@winenterprisesllc.com

Pete Winiarski is Founder and CEO of Win Enterprises, LLC, and **David Tweedt** is President, Consulting at Win Enterprises, LLC. We help visionary business leaders breakthrough their biggest challenges to create superior results. Based on the *Win Holistic Transformation Model*™, we customize your **powerful strategy and guided execution process** so you can enjoy **fast results** and reach your **full potential for long-term success**. Win Enterprises, LLC is the only consulting company that has integrated the Science of Success with cutting edge business transformation principles to **sustain the breakthrough results we achieve together**.

Daily Leadership principles and practices are central to Pete and David's core philosophy that they drive through the entire Win team and their clients. They use these leadership principles and all the elements of the Win Holistic Transformation Model™ to help clients to achieve their operational and financial goals and to sustain results for the long term.

David and Pete are co-authors of the book, *Win The Game: The Ultimate Guide to Your Successful Business Transformation*.

Download free tools from their website, from **http://www.CompleteBusinessTransformation.com**

M.S.RAO

SOFT LEADERSHIP: AN INNOVATIVE LEADERSHIP PERSPECTIVE

ABSTRACT

A new style of leadership is needed in our interconnected, global, and technocratic world. "Soft Leadership" is the answer to this need. The research paper explores soft leadership - a relationship-oriented style of leadership. It builds on four OB frameworks. It describes soft leadership with 11 Cs and illustrates each characteristic with examples. It discovers how the soft leaders adopt tools such as influence, persuasion, negotiation, motivation, recognition, appreciation, and collaboration for the collective good. It calls upon readers to consider how leadership insights acquired from this paper may be applied individually and organizationally to make a difference in the lives of others. The 11 C's that collectively constitute soft leadership is a unique concept. The paper provides the location of soft leadership in Blake Mouton Grid. Participation of international leadership experts and their questions when I led International Leadership Association webinar with my spontaneous answers further enriched this concept.

Keywords - Soft leadership, Leadership styles, Soft skills, Leadership development, Organizational development, Blake Mouton Grid

INTRODUCTION

> "A small body of determined spirits fired by an unquenchable faith in their mission can alter the course of history."
>
> **Mahatma Gandhi**

I have coined a new concept – soft leadership. I have authored a book on it, and International Leadership Association invited me to lead the webinar on this concept due to the interest it is generating globally. I accepted the invitation and led the webinar on it August 29, 2012 successfully. During the webinar the topic generated a great interest among the participants who are experts in the domain of leadership, and they posed a number of questions on it. I explored on their questions, and researched the concept further thus adding value to it. Here is the enriched concept of soft leadership which is a new direction to leadership.

WHAT IS SOFT LEADERSHIP?

Soft leadership is leading through soft skills and people skills. It blends soft skills, hard skills, and leadership. It emphasizes on the significance of precious Human Resources. It helps in managing the emotions, egos, and feelings of the people successfully. It focuses on the personality, attitude, and behavior of the people, and calls for making others feel more important. It is an integrative, participative, relationship, and behavioral leadership model adopting tools such as persuasion, negotiation, recognition, appreciation, motivation, and collaboration to accomplish the tasks effectively.

Soft leadership is not a submissive leadership or a lame duck leadership but an assertive leadership where soft leaders adopt pleasing and polite communication to get the tasks executed. Succinctly, soft leadership can be defined as the process of setting goals; influencing people through persuasion; building strong teams; negotiating them with a win-win attitude; respecting their failures; handholding them; motivating them constantly; aligning their energies and efforts; recognizing and appreciating their contribution in accomplishing organizational goals and objectives with an emphasis on soft skills. It is based on the right mindset, skill set, and toolset.

SOFT LEADERSHIP – FOUR OB FRAMEWORKS

There are four different OB frameworks or models the organizations adopt such as autocratic, custodial, supportive, and collegial (Cunningham, Eberle, 1990; Davis, 1967). The autocratic framework draws mostly out of McGregor's Theory X while the rest of the three frameworks draw mostly out of McGregor's Theory Y. Although organizations adopt these four frameworks they predominately operate on one main framework as per their vision, mission, philosophy, principles, policies, and culture. In addition, organizations consider the type of the industry or the sector they are into, and above all, the type of its employees such as skilled, semi-skilled, and unskilled employees.

In autocratic framework, the superiors behave like autocratic leaders and the subordinates are at the mercy of superiors. Employees are hired and fired, and are at the whims and fancies of the employers. Employees don't appreciate this framework and, as a result, the performance is the lowest. In custodial framework, employees are provided with job security, and are cared by their superiors. Hence, employee performance improves in this framework. In supportive framework, the superiors support the subordinates on all spheres. The employees are encouraged and empowered to participate in decision-making. They feel that they are part and parcel of the organizations resulting in improved organizational bottom lines. In the fourth framework of collegial, there is no much gap between the superiors and the subordinates as are all considered partners. Precisely, there is no leadership and followership in this framework, and are all treated as partners for progress. This framework invites amazing response from all stakeholders thus enhancing organizational excellence and effectiveness. The soft leaders adopt collegial framework as they believe in partnership, not in followership.

SOFT LEADERSHIP AND BLAKE MOUTON GRID

Soft leadership is based on behavioral theory. Here is its explanation from the perspective of Blake Mouton Grid (1964) – a behavioral leadership model: The Blake Mouton Managerial Grid[1] or Leadership Grid coined by Robert Blake and Jane Mouton presents five leadership styles - Country Club Management, Authority-Compliance Management, Impoverished Management, Middle-of-the-Road Management, and Team Management. This Grid theory breaks behavior down into seven key elements such as Initiative, Inquiry, Advocacy, Decision making, Conflict resolution, Resilience, and Critique.

X axis represents 'concern for production' and Y axis represents 'concern for people' ranging from 1 (Low) to 9 (High)

---

1   http://www.mindtools.com/pages/article/newLDR_73.htm accessed on September 9, 2012

(see Figure 2). The country club management (1,9) reflects yield and comply; the authority-compliance management (9,1) denotes control and dominate; the impoverished management style (1,1) reflects evade and elude; the middle-of-the-road management (5,5) indicates balance and compromise; and the team management (9,9) emphasizes contribute and commit. Soft leadership falls in the quadrant of Team Management. For soft leadership, 9 out of 9 go for 'concern for people'; and 6 out of 9 go for 'concern for production'. We can put it as 6, 9 for soft leadership approximately (That is 6 for production and 9 for people) (see Figure 1). Therefore, as per Blake-Mouton Grid, soft leadership falls more on 'concern for people' and less on 'concern for production'.

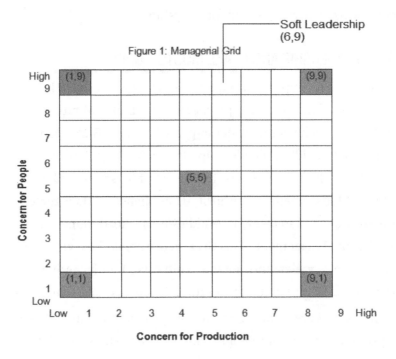

Figure 1

The Leadership Grid

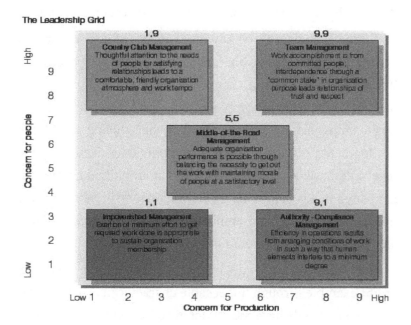

Figure 2

SOFT LEADERSHIP - 11 CHARACTERISTICS

CHARACTER

Warren Bennis says, "Successful leadership is not about being tough or soft, sensitive or assertive, but about a set of attributes. First and foremost is character." The collapse of companies like Enron, Lehman Brothers and World Com reminds the world about the leaders lacking character at their core. People sometimes blame the business schools for producing such leaders without any ethical and moral values. However, we cannot blame business schools for all the ills that happened at the business houses globally. Here the problem lies with the leaders who lack strong character resulting in such downfalls.

Character is one of the key components of soft leaders. It is through their strong character they lead their people by influencing and guiding them. People look at leaders who have an impeccable integrity and who walk the talk. Hence, most companies emphasize on character during leadership development programs. For instance, companies like Hindustan Lever emphasizes on character wherein an individual puts his company's needs before his own. It has strong human resource management system and emphasizes on strong ethical system and character among its employees.

As a leader you are always under the scanner. You need to set a right example through impeccable character in order to grow as a leader. People have the tendency to look at the weaknesses rather than strengths of others. Hence, it is essential to demonstrate strong character to lead from the front in order to influence people around you.

Martin Luther King, Jr. said, "The ultimate measure of a man is not where he stands in moments of comfort and convenience, but where he stands at times of challenge and controversy." Character is the key thing that differentiates between good leaders from others. In fact, good character makes a person a great leader. What counts at the end of the day or your life is who you are, not what you have.

CHARISMA

One of the greatest characteristics of soft leaders is their charisma. Soft leaders make other people more important and valuable through their charisma. Charisma helps in connecting with others easily as people feel valued and pleased to talk with these leaders. Marianne Williamson says, "Charisma is a sparkle in people that money can't buy. It's an invisible energy with visible effects." The soldiers of Alexander blindly followed him because of his charismatic leadership. The soldiers marched toward victory during Second World War under the charismatic leadership of Winston Churchill. The Americans were influenced with the charismatic leadership of John F. Kennedy who gave a clarion call: *'Ask not what your country can do for you; ask what you can do for your country'*.

Warren Bennis and Burt Nanus said, "Charisma is the result of effective leadership, not the other way around." Charisma is something related to extraordinary powers bestowed through divine means. It is the rarest of the rare qualities which are usually acquired through birth. However, the research reveals that charisma is a skill that can be honed by training, experience and practice. There is an urge in all human beings to be liked by others. Charisma paves the way for being liked by others. There are various components of charisma such as warmth, smile, grace, body language, voice and confidence. A person is said to be charismatic when there is coincidence in all these components.

In 1947 Max Weber came out with three leadership styles such as bureaucratic, traditional and charismatic leadership. Weber[2] defines charismatic authority as: "resting on devotion to the exceptional sanctity, heroism or exemplary character of an individual person, and of the normative patterns or order revealed or ordained by him."

2 http://books.google.co.in/books/about/Charismatic_Authority. html?id=lDQfQwAACAAJ&redir_esc=y accessed on September 9, 2012

Charisma needs substance than style. Have knowledge and content to speak and connect with others. Charismatic leaders are known for walking the talk. So is the case of soft leaders who have the passion to serve their people.

CONSCIENCE

Sophocles said, "There is no witness so terrible and no accuser so powerful as conscience which dwells within us." Conscience is one of the major key components of soft leaders as clear conscience makes them stand out from other leaders. People expect leaders to be ethical and responsible. They also look up to leaders whose conscience cares for them. Conscience differentiates right from wrong. Leaders must have clear conscience to convince themselves so that they can persuade others. If there is a chasm between word and deed conscience reminds the same. Mahatma Gandhi was always clear with his conscience. He unveiled the mistakes he made in his life in his autobiography. Every person makes mistakes but how many unveil and admit the same. In fact, it requires a lot of courage to reveal wrong-doings on their part.

Several leaders resigned because of their conscience. They left their high positions due to the call from their conscience. Hence, conscience is powerful. Leaders have to convince their conscience first to convince others. Aung San Suu Kyi underwent several trials and tribulations from military rulers during the house arrest as her conscience did not allow her to leave country. Mahatma Gandhi led the Civil Disobedience movement which was a non-violent protest against British. It was an act of conscience.

Dr. Martin Luther King aptly said, "Justice is a temporary thing that must at last come to an end; but the conscience is eternal and will never die." Several problems and evils in the society are the result of people compromising with their conscience. People may cheat others, not their conscience. Conscience is always clear, and it is powerful. People have to be accountable to their conscience. People may do several wrong things for their survival or their selfish motives. Ultimately they need to persuade their conscience which is always clear. It is a remainder for every human being. Hence, don't compromise with your conscience as compromising with conscience is equal to the death of a person morally.

CONVICTION

Conviction is another key ingredient for soft leadership without which the soft leaders cannot lead successfully. It is their convictions that take soft leaders forward and make their people move forward toward achieving their goals. Walter Lippmann aptly said, "The final test of a leader is that he leaves behind him in other men, the conviction and the will to carry on." There are leaders who died for their people due to their convictions. They never compromised and stood like rock despite stiff opposition and challenges and threats to their lives. Leaders like Mahatma Gandhi, Martin Luther King Jr., Dalai Lama, and Aung San Sui Kyi are the symbols of sacrifices and convictions.

It is hard to imagine leadership without firmly showing one's convictions. Dr. Martin Luther King Jr. firmly believed in his convictions. He did not appreciate the inequality of blacks from whites. He sacrificed his life for the cause of civil rights movement and, finally, became a martyr. People followed him because of his convictions. He could lead the movement successfully because of his convictions. He finally proved himself as a symbol of soft leadership.

COURAGE

Courage is an integral part of soft leadership. According to Aristotle, courage is the first virtue, because it makes all of the other virtues possible. Courage does not mean fighting physically with others. Courage doesn't mean killing people ruthlessly. Courage doesn't mean being aggressive all times. Mark Twain rightly remarked, "Courage is resistance to fear, mastery of fear - not absence of fear." Courage is about standing by your values and morals and principles and policies despite being pressurized by others and receiving threats from others. People often believe that courage as a characteristic is confined to military personnel alone. That is not true. Courage is essential for everyone. Courage is also a major key component for soft leaders because courage commands confidence from their followers.

People always want leaders with backbone. David versus Goliath is an amazing example where tiny David took on the mighty Goliath successfully. Few leaders proved globally that it is not the size but the strength counts. When we take the example of Yugoslavian leader, Marshal Tito he broke the back of Soviet empire. President Ronald Reagan, Pope John Paul II and Prime Minister Margaret Thatcher came together to bring down the crumbling walls of the Soviet Union, giving hundreds of millions of people the chance to enjoy freedom. The leader like Lee Kuan Yew brought Singapore from nowhere to a prosperous country despite being dearth of natural resources.

All these leaders made a difference to this world through their courageous leadership. What counts at the end of life is neither muscle power nor money power, but your will power.

COMMUNICATION

James Humes said, "The art of communication is the language of leadership." The success of soft leadership depends more on communication than anything else. It is through communication leaders express their ideas, ideals, and insights and persuade others to follow them.

Leadership is about handling people for accomplishing goals. While handling people communication becomes the core component through which leaders connect with others. As leadership styles are different to touch different people with different emotions, needs, egos, and feelings, there are different communication styles such as aggressive communication, submissive communication, assertive-aggressive communication and assertive communication. The leaders need to adopt assertive communication style ideally and other styles from time to time to make the leadership effective. Because of the key role communication plays while leading others, we can assert that communication is the sister of leadership.

Leaders can influence others through communication alone. Nitin Nohria observed, "Communication is the real work of leadership." It is through the magic words leaders influence and inspire others to do the impossible things. Soft leaders demonstrate assertive communication so as to connect with others and carry forward them toward their goals.

COMPASSION

When we look at soft leaders like Lord Jesus and Buddha, we find them being filled with compassion. They changed the face of the world through their compassion. The soft leader like Mother Teresa helped lepers and poor through her selfless service. She made an immense difference in the lives of poor and downtrodden in India. In fact, compassion is an integral characteristic of soft leadership. It helps in connecting with others easily. People appreciate the leaders who care and touch them.

Compassion means caring for others by ignoring your own interests. Compassion is not weakness. Kahlil Gibran says, "Tenderness and kindness are not signs of weakness and despair but manifestations of strength and resolution." Compassion is all about genuinely caring for your people. It is handholding them without expecting any returns. Compassion commands great inner strength, courage, and power. Compassion is a key to ministering to people. Compassion makes a lot of difference in making leaders as soft leaders. Soft leadership flows from the fountain of compassion.

The real leaders are the ones who encourage others and who take care of others and who empathize and demonstrate compassion with others. Only such leaders have the ability to influence and maximize the potential of their people and organizations.

COMMITMENT

Soft leaders have another great characteristic of commitment as it makes them command respect among others. It is their firm commitment toward their causes that wins acclaim from others. If you want your life to be successful you have to be committed. For instance, when you love your family, you need to be firm in demonstrating your commitment. Commitment consumes your time. But it builds longevity in relations. Not only in your family life, but also at the workplace if you as a leader demonstrate your commitment, people trust you and treat you with utmost respect. It is rightly said, people don't care how big you are. They only care how committed you are. We find several families breaking due to lack of commitment. We also find teams getting crashed at the workplace due to dearth of commitment. Commitment is the bridge between the word and the deed. A firm commitment toward your word and work makes you as a successful leader.

CONSISTENCY

Consistency is another important ingredient for soft leadership. Leaders need to demonstrate their consistency so as to have profound impact on their people. People expect leaders to be predictable, responsible, and credible. Failure to demonstrate consistency might lead to credibility crisis.

Benjamin Disraeli observed, "A consistent man believes in destiny, a capricious man in chance." Mahatma Gandhi maintained consistency throughout his life by sticking to non-violence and peace. Consistency is essential in every area of life. Consistency is essential in putting your efforts to achieve big. It is required to be noticed as a credible and responsible person. Consistency helps in leadership branding and memory recall. When we talk of situational leadership we recall Ken Blanchard; when we talk of servant leadership we recall Robert Greenleaf; when we talk of emotional intelligence we recall

Daniel Goleman; when we speak about self-improvement we remember Dale Carnegie. These leaders have excelled and branded themselves in their area of specializations through consistent behavior and leadership.

CONSIDERATION

Consideration is one of the major characteristics of soft leaders as soft leaders basically care their people. They respect their followers. Consideration includes recognizing the good work done by others and appreciating them promptly, liberally and graciously. This is the trait of the leaders with people-orientation rather than task-orientation. The transactional leaders are fundamentally task-oriented while transformational and soft leaders are people-oriented with a big heart to care and consider others.

Consideration means how much and how far the leaders are sensitive toward their people. It means how much they empathize with them and how far they can go to handhold others. Consideration includes caring and respecting others with an empathetic attitude. It deals with stepping into the shoes of others and looking at the things from others' perspective. It makes people win the confidence of others as it helps connect with others quickly. Confucius rightly remarked, "Consideration for others is the basic of a good life, a good society."

CONTRIBUTION

Stephan Girard said, "If I thought I was going to die tomorrow, I should nevertheless plant a tree today." We are what we are here today because of amazing contributions made by several soft leaders to this mankind regardless of their areas of interest. Contribution includes precious time, money, energy, ideas, knowledge, and assistance to the society. Genuine and selfless contribution takes true leadership. People respect the leaders who contribute their best to society without hankering for wealth, power or prestige.

Mother Teresa rightly said, "We ourselves feel that what we are doing is just a drop in the ocean. But the ocean would be less because of that missing drop." While contributing to others it can be in small portions. People often think that the contribution has to be in a big way. In fact, a small effort is better than no effort. A huge amount of small contributions makes up to a large amount of differences for society. It is rightly said, "All the whining and complaining in the world is not going to make a difference to the world. It will only drain you of your precious energy from doing things that do make a difference." Hence, contribute your best little by little consistently, and you would be amazed at the differences that you make to the society over a period of time.

John C. Maxwell in his book titled *Teamwork: What Every Leader Needs to Know says*, "People who take advantage of others inevitably fail in business and relationships. If you desire to succeed, live by these four simple words: add value to others. That philosophy will take you far."

Don't expect anything in return when you think of adding value to others. Remember what goes around comes around in different form. If everybody contributes something for others imagine the kind of the world we would live in, and the kind of the world that we would pass on to our next generation.

Apart from the character, charisma, conscience, conviction, courage, communication, compassion, commitment, consistency, consideration and contribution, the soft leaders must also possess other characteristics such as coordination, cheerfulness, comprehension, cooperation and connection to connect with others to become successful soft leaders.

Here is the diagram (Figure 3) connecting 11 C's that collectively constitute soft leadership.

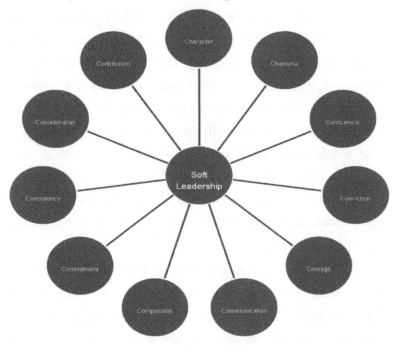

Figure 3

CONCLUSION

The rapid changes in technology have made the world a global village. People with diversified backgrounds and communities work under one roof. Their aspirations and expectations are growing. Adopting this leadership style meets their aspirations, and also addresses several global leadership challenges effectively. The days of hierarchical command and control don't work any longer. These are the days of communication, negotiation, facilitation, coordination, collaboration, recognition, and appreciation to get the tasks executed successfully. People expect the leaders to be polite, pleasant, assertive, and supportive. Employees prefer to work in an egalitarian set up. They appreciate leaders with an integrative, participative, collaborative, and relationship-oriented leadership mindset. They want their leaders to become their counselors and coaches to groom them for their all-round success. Hence, companies started to focus on the slogan of *'employee first and customer second'*. Soft leadership emphasizes concern for people i.e., on employees who are the precious human resources. Hence, soft leadership is the need of the hour to give a soft touch to people who in turn give real touch to customers through dedication and discipline.

Remember that leadership should not be self-centered but should be centered on others. Leadership is not a badge of honor, but a job involving responsibility toward people. Leaders spend three-fourths of their time with people. Hence, they must care for the needs and concerns of the people to establish credibility and influence them, and to lead from the front. Above all, it is the age of partnership, not followership.

We have enough leadership styles such as autocratic, democratic, delegative, transactional, transformational, servant, and situational to name a few. It is time to adopt this new leadership style. Hence, let us explore and adopt soft leadership style to take mankind to greater heights of glory. Let us hand over better society to our next generations so that they can be proud of us. Let us become good ancestors. To conclude in the words of Woodrow Wilson, "You are not here merely to make a living. You are here in order to enable the world to live more amply, with greater vision, with a finer spirit of hope and achievement. You are here to enrich the world, and you impoverish yourself if you forget the errand."

REFERENCES

Soft Leadership: Make Others Feel More Important by M.S.Rao, Galgotia Publishers (2012)

Soft Leadership: Make Others Feel More Important by M.S.Rao, Leader to Leader Journal, Spring 2012

Soft Leadership: A New Direction to Leadership by M.S.Rao, Industrial and Commercial Training (2013)

Organizational Behavior: Human Behavior at Work, by Keith Davis and John Newstrom

http://www.ila-net.org/Webinars/Archive/Rao082012.html

http://onlinelibrary.wiley.com/doi/10.1002/ltl.20019/abstract

http://www.emeraldinsight.com/journals.htm?articleid=17083779

http://www.unpost.org/mahatma-gandhi-soft-leadership/

www.leadershiparlington.org/EMAIL%20UPLOADS/Spears_Final.pdf

http://www.mindtools.com/pages/article/newLDR_73.htm

http://news.harvard.edu/gazette/2002/02.21/11-nye.html

http://www.e3lg.com/assets/.../The%20Science%20of%20Leadership.pdf

http://books.google.co.in/books/about/Charismatic_Authority.
html?id=lDQfQwAACAAJ&redir_esc=y

http://coachingcosmos.com/resources/Leadership+grid+2.jpg

http://www.universalteacherpublications.com/mba/ebooks/
ob/ch1/page4.htm

http://www.nwlink.com/~donclark/leader/leadob.html

ACKNOWLEDGEMENTS

Author thanks Dave Ulrich, the Partner of The RBL Group for writing foreword for his book - *Soft Leadership: Make Others Feel More Important* and connecting 11 Cs with his Leadership Code.

Frances Hesselbein, President and CEO, Frances Hesselbein Leadership Institute

Professor M.S.Rao, Ph.D. is an international leadership guru who rose from humble origins. He is recognized as one of the world's leading leadership educators, authors, speakers, coaches, consultants and practitioners. He is a sought-after keynote speaker globally. He has 36 years of experience in executive coaching, and conducts leadership development training programs for various corporates and educational institutions. He is an executive coach, and a dynamic, energetic and inspirational leadership speaker. He coined a new leadership learning tool — *Soft Leadership Grid;* leadership training tool — *11E Leadership Grid;* and innovative teaching tool — *Meka's Method.* His areas of interest include Executive Coaching, Executive Education and Leadership. He is passionate about serving and making a difference in the lives of others. He shares his leadership wisdom freely with the world on his four blogs. His vision is to build one million students as global leaders by 2030 which is the winner of Leadership 500 Excellence Awards 2015. He is the recipient of 10th International Prestigious Sardar Patel Award—2015 for Lifetime Achievement in the field of "Excellence in Youth Development."

He is the Father of 'Soft Leadership' and Founder of MSR Leadership Consultants, India. He is the author of 36 books including the award-winning *21 Success Sutras for CEOs.* His book *21 Success Sutras for Leaders* was selected as the Top 10 Leadership Books of the Year — 2013 by San Diego University, USA. His book *Success Tools for CEO Coaches: Be a Learner, Leader and Ladder* is the Community Choice Winner from Small

Business Book Awards for 2014, USA. He is the recipient of an International Award — *International Coach of the Year 2013, USA.* He is the recipient of Outstanding Reviewer for Human Resource Management International Digest in the Emerald Literati Network 2015 Awards for Excellence. He has published more than 250 papers and articles in international publications including *Leader to Leader, Leadership Excellence, Strategic HR Review, Development and Learning in Organizations, Industrial and Commercial Training, Human Resource Management International Digest, T+D Magazine,* and *The Journal of Values-Based Leadership.* He serves as an Advisor and Judge for several prestigious international organizations including Global Leadership Awards in Malaysia, Middle East Business Leaders Summits & Awards in Dubai and Small Business Book Awards in the United States.

He serves on the editorial boards of various prestigious international journals including *Development and Learning in Organizations* and *Industrial and Commercial Training* of Emerald Journals — U.K, and *The Journal of Values-Based Leadership* — USA. He can be reached at: profmsr14@gmail.com and additionally maintains four popular blogs including 'Professor M. S. Rao's Vision 2030: One Million Global Leaders' URL: http://professormsraovision2030.blogspot.in.

GAURAV BHALLA

SOULFUL LEADERSHIP: SCRIPTING NEW LEADERSHIP NARRATIVES THROUGH IMMORTAL POEMS

CRISIS AND OPTIONS

Today's organizations are obsessed with leadership. The subject dominates their consciousness and their training budgets. Billions of dollars are spent globally on leadership training and development, with the US alone spending between $14 to $50 billion annually, depending on whose estimate you believe. Regrettably, though, these enormous investments in nurturing and developing leaders have not resulted in glittering gains. Because even while talk of leaders and leadership is everywhere, stories of outstanding and inspiring leadership are rare. Conversely, it's an atypical day when we don't receive news of leadership crises, failures, and scandals, like the examples that follow.

First, Wells Fargo. In September 2016, Wells Fargo, one of US's largest banks, was found guilty of a serious breach of public trust. Its employees were caught opening millions of fraudulent bank and credit card accounts for existing customers – *without customers' knowledge* – so the bank could achieve extra fees, higher sales, and greater market dominance. The unwitting customers, on the other hand, were unjustly burdened with increased monetary debt, higher levels of debt-related anxiety, and lower credit scores.

The corrupt practices followed by junior-level Wells Fargo managers can be traced directly to the sales practice of cross-selling – a heavily promoted system of sales incentives and rewards to get existing customers to buy more products and services from the bank. Yet, John Stumpf, the bank's CEO, refused to bear the brunt of the blame. He denied that he and other senior executives had fostered a sales-push culture that led to the opening of millions of false accounts. The hit was taken by others: the bank fired (sacrificed) 5,300 junior level employees, who, though guilty, were probably following orders received from above. It also paid a fine of $185 million in civil penalties and immediately suspended the cross-selling incentives for its sales employees, which is difficult to understand given Stumpf's claim that the cross-selling incentives were not responsible for creating the crisis.

Next, British Petroleum (BP). On April 20, 2010, the Deepwater Horizon oil rig, owned and operated by Transocean and leased by BP, exploded in the Gulf of Mexico, killing 11 people and causing one of the worst oils spills in history. By the time the source well was capped 87 days later, on July 15, 2010, more than 3 million barrels of oil had leaked into the Gulf, wreaking gut-wrenching havoc on marine and bird life, and over 1,000 miles of shoreline from Texas to Florida.

The actions and behaviors of BP's then CEO, Tony Hayward, following the oil spill were not driven by the needs of the scarred environment, but rather by "self-concern." He didn't drop everything and make managing the crisis his top priority, instead he talked and behaved in ways that suggested he resented the accident as an unwelcome intrusion into his life. From his initial lament, "What the hell did we do to deserve this?" to his self-serving comment, "I would like my life back," his behaviors revealed a clear preference for who and what he was willing to sacrifice: he was willing to sacrifice others – people and the planet – but not himself, or any aspect of his life. That he *made* time to attend a yacht race at the height of the crisis only bolsters this assessment.

If John Stumpf and Tony Hayward were one-offs, we could brandish them as errant bad-apples in leadership seminars and move on. Unfortunately, they aren't. They are symptomatic of the crises of leadership widely prevalent in institutions across all sectors of society, private and public, profit and nonprofit... even religion. These crises represent a hefty cost to society because they drain the wellbeing and prosperity of all – employees, customers, suppliers, communities, and the planet.

How then do we right the ship? Not by extending the *reign of dead ideas* and following the *mantra of more* – more spending on leadership training, a greater emphasis on ethics, stronger pleas for authenticity, and louder demands for empowerment. While still relevant, these ideas and initiatives have run their relays and don't have new alternatives to offer. Difficult times demand fresh approaches, *new thinking* tailored to the circumstances surrounding us. This fresh, new thinking is especially vital in two areas if we want to resolve the leadership crisis that society encounters repeatedly and frequently.

First, we need a new transformational narrative for leadership: A narrative that leads us *away from a narrow descriptive* *focus on what leadership is, to a wider and broader focus on what leaders and leadership should stand for* – a public platform for increasing the wellbeing and prosperity of the greater many, not just a privileged few, by harmonizing the needs and visions of a variety of vested interests. Just as in the case of Pope Francis and the Roman Catholic Church. Catholicism, the Vatican, and the Papal institution had all existed long before Jorge Mario Bergoglio became Pope Francis, Bishop of Rome. What Pope Francis has done so effectively – the main reason the world adores and applauds him – is provide a new narrative for the Roman Catholic Church. He pointed the church toward *what it should stand for* – service, mercy, and obligation to the people (both believers and non-believers) – and *away from a myopic focus of what it is* – self-referential liturgies and symbols of power and worship.

Second, leaders and leadership need a new set of teachers: Teachers that bring leaders face-to-face with their own humanity – who they are, what they stand for, and what they are willing to fight for. Because the greatest asset of leaders is not just the brilliance of their minds, but the wisdom of their souls – *what's within leaders that guides what's in their minds.* Without this inner awakening and consciousness, the new narrative of leadership described above will remain a mere idea; it won't see action. Pope Francis is a new teacher, mainly because of how he approaches and encourages other leaders of the Catholic Church to fulfill their mission: through their humanity, not merely through the intelligence of their minds.

Accordingly, the rest of this essay will focus on these two aspects, a new narrative for leaders and leadership and a new set of teachers – new to the business world, but old to the world.

SOULFUL LEADERSHIP: A NEW NARRATIVE

To understand soulful leadership is to appreciate the dilemmas and conflicts featured in the episodes that follow. Inspired by real events, they typify what thousands of leaders around the world experience daily.

The VP, Marketing of a cosmetic company gets a call from her former secretary, a single mother with one child. She has an upcoming job interview and would like a favorable reference from her previous employer. Her performance when working for the VP was a train wreck, to put it mildly. She earned consistently poor evaluations, was warned several times, and finally put on probation for 30-days. She left before her probation period ended, as she was diagnosed with cancer and had to begin extensive chemotherapy treatment. The VP wouldn't hire her again, considers her incompetent, and doesn't think it would be fair foisting her on an unsuspecting employer. Her former secretary needs a job to earn a living and, even more importantly, have health insurance.

The Director of a Japanese long-term care facility is in a quandary. There is a shortage of Japanese care givers, and the residents don't like being touched and cared for by "Gaijins," foreign workers. He is pushing for robots to provide nursing care for the residents since he has not succeeded in recruiting extra staff. A robot resembling a cuddly bear was brought in as an experiment, but the residents were not impressed. They complained of feeling neglected and lonely – they wanted human beings to care for them and visit them, not machines. The Director's mother, who is also a resident of the nursing home, is the most vociferous protestor against robots.

Both episodes carry within them the potential for soulful leadership, which is defined as:

Purposeful leadership journeys guided by an inner awakening that faithfully and diligently consider the full range of sacrifices embedded in leadership decisions so the ongoing prosperity and wellbeing of all involved – the leader, the organization, people (employees, customers, communities), and the planet (health and resources) – can be increased.

The two essential elements of soulful leadership are:

1. who leaders sacrifice in order to keep their organizations moving forward, and

2. whether this pattern of sacrifices is guided by an inner awakening, or by the leader's own needs of vanity and wallet.

Let's return to the two episodes to see how they play out.

Whether the potential for soulful leadership inherent in each episode actually becomes reality depends entirely on how the two leaders respond to the conflicts and challenges facing them. In each episode, the leader is temporarily stranded, or stuck. In order to get unstuck...and move forward...the leader has to act, and act unequivocally. But, committing to an action requires sacrificing something, or somebody. That is the only way the principal actors in the episodes above can move forward, they have no choice. The only choice they have is who they decide to sacrifice, how much, and when.

Sacrificing others for our own wellbeing and prosperity is easy and has a long tradition, as old as human history.

» The Marketing VP can move forward by refusing to give her former secretary a positive reference, thereby preserving her preference for "fairness."

» The nursing home director can move forward by adopting robots, thereby sacrificing the emotional preferences of his customers, including his own mother (also a customer, but not just any other customer).

This preference for sacrificing others is governed by a straightforward formula: Those who have power and authority, whether conferred or appropriated, sacrifice those who are less fortunate in this regard. This preference system looks at the world in simplistic dichotomous ways: right-wrong, either-or, good-bad, moral-immoral.

However, are sacrifice options ever that simple? Crisp, clean choices between right-wrong, black-and-white? Or are they fuzzy and murky, because right-wrong, black-white are all intricately mixed up, forcing leaders to consider sacrifice options that are often choices between right and right, or between wrong and more wrong? To complicate leaders' dilemmas, these sacrifice choices invariably knock on their doors all tangled up in contexts and circumstances, which can't – or shouldn't – be ignored.

Take the case of the Marketing VP. Could it be her former secretary's incompetence was due to circumstances? Perhaps she would have performed a lot better, but for her illness. And what about the expectations of the next employer concerning the quality of the talent it wants to hire? It complicates things even more if the person planning on hiring her former secretary is the VP's friend.

And what about the poor Nursing Home Director? What if despite his best intentions he is not able to find Japanese caregivers? What if the only way he can maintain the health of the nursing home residents is by forcing migrant workers on the residents, or robots, regardless of how loudly his mother protests?

Once we open the front door to admit the full range of complexities and uncertainties that are typical of the world we live in today, the need for a new narrative becomes clear and urgent. Leaders have a range of sacrifices they can – and should – consider in their attempt to get unstuck and move forward, including options that involve an element of sacrificing some aspect of themselves – their own needs and preferences. Because who they sacrifice and who they don't will uniquely determine who gains and who loses, whose prosperity and wellbeing increases and whose doesn't, or even diminishes.

So how should leaders decide who to sacrifice, how much, and when? Unfortunately, unlike gadgets and appliances that come with "user manuals," leadership roles rarely come with rule books that carry clear-cut commandments that say, "Do this." There is no one right way to act. Which brings us eye-to-eye with a vital question: "If there's no right way, if there's no rule book, then where do leaders go for guidance?" Where do leaders go to find the "third-way," the way that lies between the polarities of "my way or the highway?" A way that juggles sacrificing others with sacrificing aspects of themselves, as well. And once they decide, who do they turn to for approvals and assurances that the third way they have chosen is the best they could have done, given the context, given the circumstances? Even leaders need pats on the back, confirmation that they are on the right track.

In the absence of rule books, prescriptions, and edicts, there is only one place they can go, only one well they can draw from.

It's what lies and lives within themselves, their own "humanity" – who they are, what they stand for, and what they are willing to fight for. It is this humanity that guides the *sacrifices* leaders make, and determines who gains and who loses. The pattern of distribution of these gains and losses is the defining indicator of the presence or absence of soulful leadership. Soulful leadership is absent if "others" are consistently sacrificed, and only a few, most notably the leaders and their accomplices benefit. Conversely, it is present if leaders faithfully and diligently shape their sacrifice decisions based on the needs of the entire system, not just their own.

This essay is not naïve. It knows and accepts that it is impossible to increase the wellbeing and prosperity of everybody. Nobel Prize winning economists, like Kenneth Arrow, have already demonstrated that – as have classical and neo-classical writers and thinkers on social and economic justice, like John Rawls. There will always be people who feel deprived. Additionally, there will always be people, no matter how hard leaders try, who will not experience an increase in wellbeing or prosperity. Leaders rarely command such complete power over resources, people, and circumstances as to elevate the wellbeing and prosperity of all in one fell swoop. Abraham Lincoln, Mahatma Gandhi, Mother Teresa, Nelson Mandela all worked faithfully and diligently to increase the wellbeing and prosperity of those disproportionately sacrificed – slaves, untouchables, poor, racially oppressed. Did everyone benefit from their faithful and diligent attempts? Definitely not. But were more people better off, was there a greater wellbeing and prosperity in the entire system because of their leadership? Most definitely, yes.

Since soulful leadership doesn't descend on leaders like an

edict from above, but springs from within, a critical regenerative shift must take place within leaders before soulful leadership can manifest itself. Leaders must reimagine their own humanity by redefining their relationship with themselves, with others, and with this planet. This regenerative shift is what is referred to as the "inner awakening" in the definition of soulful leadership provided earlier in this essay. It is also what the phrase, "Awakening A Leader's Soul," signifies in the title of my forthcoming book, from which this essay is extracted.

How best then to trigger this regenerative shift, this inner awakening, so leaders can embrace and implement this new narrative of soulful leadership? What we need is a new and different set of teachers, who can unveil us to ourselves, and who can create epiphanies that enable us to see and understand our own humanity in ways we hadn't before, and reimagine it. The world's immortal poems have this ability. Which is probably why scientists, painters, philosophers, and politicians have through the years regularly called on poets and poetry to guide their hearts and minds. No reason why the business world should not tap into the wisdom and advice of poets and poetry to establish the new narrative of soulful leadership.

IMMORTAL POEMS: (OLD) NEW TEACHERS

Why poetry?

Why travel so far from the world of management gurus, leadership case studies, and personality tests to the world of immortal poems? Because poets stand tallest among all teachers in consistently helping us make sense of ourselves, our world, and our place in it, in new and insightful ways.

In the very essence of poetry there is something… a
thing is brought forth which we didn't know we had in us
—Czeslaw Milos, Ars Poetica

Poems deal in eternal truths. *They are news that stays NEWS,"* is how Ezra Pound liked to explain the power of literature and poems. Poets and poetry operate from a deeper level of consciousness and, as such, are an invaluable gift, especially when we find ourselves stuck, screaming, "Who am I?" "What am I doing here?" "How do I get out of this bind I find myself in, and move forward?"

Poems are like mirrors that reflect us. According to Percy Bysshe Shelley, the poster poet of romantic poetry, "neither the eye nor the mind can see itself – *unless* reflected upon something which it resembles." This "mirror" aspect of immortal poems is invaluable since we are incapable on our own of seeing the world as it is, and ourselves as we are.

And yet the world is different from what it seems to be and
we are other than how we see ourselves in our ravings.
Czeslaw Milos, "Ars Poetica"

By helping us see ourselves and the world differently, poems magnify us and feed our imagination and creativity. And in so doing, they encourage us to experiment, adapt, and improvise – invaluable assets, especially when one considers that there are no rule books, or commandments, to guide leaders' on how best to find the "third way" and juggle their sacrifice decisions. Even if there were, they wouldn't be much use because the world rarely stands still for the same prescription to work no matter the circumstances. Some of the world's most powerful companies have learned this lesson the hard way. Context and circumstances are key. What works in US doesn't always work in India, and vice-versa. However, since poems deal in eternal truths, the wisdom they impart is more portable and readily applicable, regardless of the circumstances.

Let's illustrate this with three short examples.

First, the immortal William Shakespeare and the sagest blueprint ever developed for being authentic and leading without putting on an act and appearances.

This above all- to thine own self be true,

And it must follow, as the night the day,

Thou canst not then be false to any man.

Hamlet, Act I, Scene 3

Does it matter which sector of civil society a leader operates in – government, business, education, healthcare for this advice to hold? Does the ethnicity or race or the religious affiliation of the leader matter? Does the country in which the leader operates matter? No. The wisdom and teaching of Shakespeare's poem is perennial and universal. It is also critical to the implementation of soulful leadership. Because when leaders wear masks and lead by pretending to be something they are not, it is a telltale sign that they value their own prosperity and wellbeing more than anyone else's. Consequently, they will always sacrifice others disproportionately more.

Next, let's consider Robert Frost's wisdom concerning the value and courage of taking considered risks, conveyed by the poem for which he's most famous.

Two roads diverged in a yellow wood,

And sorry I could not travel both...

... Two roads diverged in a wood, and I—

I took the one less traveled by,

And that has made all the difference.

Robert Frost, *"The Road Not Taken"*

Leaders and organizations are never so rich in resources as to pursue every shiny opportunity that comes their way. Weighing options is good up to a point, but then leaders must act, and act with conviction. And playing it safe is not always the best option, because often it only breeds mediocrity and regret. I have been teaching executive education seminars and workshops since 1985, and I can't think of a single management case – no country or institution excepted – that teaches this lesson as well as "The Road Not Taken." Soulful leaders know intrinsically that increasing prosperity and wellbeing for the greater many in the future requires placing strategic bets today. And they do so through courage and their willingness to sacrifice aspects of themselves, if they have to do so.

Finally, let's consider the sensitive, but frequently encountered, issue of ego. For this essay, ego is an excessive sense of "I," a pursuit of "self-aggrandizement," and a deep-seated conviction that "I am the center of the universe." Leaders who operate with an exaggerated sense of "I" have an incessant craving for power, prestige, and recognition, and an acute desire for control under all circumstances. They are incapable of embracing and practicing soulful leadership because their needs will always take priority over the prosperity and wellbeing of the greater many. So they will sacrifice others disproportionately more. Why not? They are, after all, the center of the universe.

Let's imagine we were tasked with teaching the hazards of ego (as defined above) in a leadership development program. How would we do it? Perhaps some combination of lectures, case discussions, role playing, and by providing negative examples, hoping they'd serve as deterrents. Each of these techniques could potentially appeal to the minds of the program participants. But would they trigger an inner awakening? Would they provide them with an alternate *weltanschauung* (world view)? Would they help the participants see themselves and their humanity differently as it relates to ego? Perhaps.

But could a poem do better? Could a poem help unveil a different reality, so participants would be encouraged to reimagine their own humanity and how their ego might influence decisions concerning who to sacrifice? This essay believes that Emily Dickinson's timeless poem would.

I'm nobody! Who are you?

Are you nobody, too?

Then there's a pair of us – ...

Emily Dickinson, *"I'm nobody! Who are you?"*

Imagine a leader who leads with a "I'm a nobody" mindset, and who actively promotes a "I'm a nobody" culture. Imagine how many doors it would open. Imagine how cohesive it would make the organization. Imagine how many conversations and healthy debates it would kindle. Imagine how enthusiasm, commitment, and engagement would make work and the workplace infinitely more lively.

Imagine.

We constantly hear a cry for fresh perspectives, for greater imagination, for renewed creativity, in virtually all areas of society today. The human-centric narrative of soulful leadership is a fresh idea. As is achieving an inner awakening by learning at the feet of immortal poems, so leaders can understand and re-imagine their own humanity and give soulful leadership a better chance of manifesting itself. The essence of soulful leadership is not moralistic; it is out-and-out pragmatic, to awaken leader's souls so their leadership journeys can make the world a better place.

In "The Symposium," Plato suggested that one of the greatest privileges of a human life is to become a midwife to the birth of the soul in another – a wiser soul to make the world a better place. This is also the core of the new narrative of soulful leadership. One of the greatest privileges of leadership should be to become a midwife to the growth of healthier organizations that don't just talk about making the world a better place, but actually do make it better. It would be a collective failure if we didn't seize on this opportunity.

NOTES:

1. This essay is extracted from the opening section of my forthcoming book, "Awakening A Leader's Soul: Learnings Through Immortal Poems." Published by Motivational Press, it's scheduled for an early 2017 launch.

2. Due to space limitations, only select lines of poems are produced in the body of the essay. All the poems mentioned and discussed in the essay can be easily found on the Web, should readers want to read and learn more. These teachers never sleep. They'll be eager to share their wisdom whenever you choose to drop in on them.

Gaurav Bhalla has 35+ years of global experience as a consultant, educator, entrepreneur, author, and speaker in leadership, marketing, strategy, and innovation. Committed to learning and personal growth, he has helped executives and companies in over 30 countries solve complex business problems through the application of cutting edge knowledge and ideas. A thinker and doer, he has changed the lives of thousands of executives by encouraging them to perceive and reframe the worlds in which they live in more human-centric ways.

He has held innovation, strategy, and brand marketing positions at companies such as Nestle and Richardson Vicks (P&G), has consulted with large Fortune 500 clients in the Pharmaceuticals (GSK, Pfizer, B-MS), Technology/Telecom (AT&T, Samsung, Microsoft), and Finance sectors (Capital One, Nasdaq, Citi). He has an advanced degree in business and has conducted business seminars, and executive education courses at leading business schools, like Duke, Georgetown, University of Maryland, Indian School of Business, Singapore Management University, and GIBS South Africa, for companies, nonprofits, and associations, like Deloitte, Caterpillar, Microsoft, Accenture, NIH, and National Association of Broadcasters, to name a few.

Published in both business and literature, his leading edge thinking is reflected in his HBR article "Rethinking Marketing," his book "Collaboration and Co-Creation: New Platforms for Marketing and Innovation." His novel "The Curse and the Cup," was published in Nov. 2014, and his latest book on Soulful Leadership, "Awakening A Leader's Soul: Learnings

Through Immortal Poems," is due for launch in early 2017. CEO of Knowledge Kinetics, he remains committed to helping companies create compelling value for all stakeholders – customers, employees, communities, and the planet – through soulful leadership and continuous innovation.

He lives and works in Reston, VA.

ABHA MARYADA BANERJEE

MASTER THE VISIONARY MINDSET

The *Vital Inspirational Sense Intrinsic to Our Nature* © that inspires us into the future is called a Vision. All humans possess a quiet inner-self that guides them to what lifts their spirits and inspires them to harness their entire personal potential towards that purpose. A person with a Vision has an opportunity to direct all effort in a direction that not only serves the purpose but also their personal individualized growth. This way of life gives birth to the phenomenal mindset of a Visionary. Our big and small goals worked BACKWARDS, while WE continually move forward.

Life in general is not spoken of through a Vision.

Visions usually connote **larger than life** goals and/or massive changes. Mahatma Gandhi had the vision of taking India out of the clutches of British Colonialism. Martin Luther King Jr. had a dream for America. Lee Kuan Yew had a vision for Singapore. It is not necessary that we have typical situations or larger than life scenarios to create Visions.

Our unique person, individual talents and gifts are our typical situation.

The ROI on tying ourselves to a vision can be phenomenal for visions place demands on us to grow continually and consciously, **powering and empowering us at the same time.** Powering as we are pushed to become fully functioning human beings tying each day into our own growth and excelling in work that is important to us. Empowering in as much as we learn planned investments of time, talent, thoughts, work, money and relationships. Very similar to conscious investment of money with a clear financial plan to help grow, multiply and compound the earnings. By consciously investing energy into a vision, by default we direct and maximize our best talents, gifts and abilities that compound over a period.

FEEL FORWARD STORYBOARD VISUAL

MOVIES have a striking similarity to our lives and are a very powerful metaphor for understanding life. Through the vision of the filmmaker, we can enjoy the relatable experiences in a film and the key meesage is driven home. The events, situations, turning points and the journey he travels reveal how the protaganist takes the story forward with his motivation, principal thoughts, driving force, his aims and how he gets to those. There is a **beginning and becoming** of the story as well as the protagonist.

Visions are also the same.

WHO we become towards a GOAL and HOW we map our journey is key!

The film making process creates a **Vision Visual** of what the film would look like with the resources available to a filmmaker. With a clever and optimal use of resources like characters, situations, events, costumes, settings, colors, music et al to narrate the story, all resource is managed and controlled to convey the storyline. From the spoken word to the silences, from the movement of the eye to a blank screen, from the visuals to the music, the turning points and some Oscar winning moments, each directed towards the movement of the story and becoming of the protagonist.

Visions are created and executed exactly in the same manner.

What would we and our vision look like as a film? Will it be an award winning film? Will our person be an award winning character? Will the story capture every bit of the inspirational life we want to create? Have we imagined the Oscar Winning moments? Are we using all the resources available to us 24/7/365?

INFUSE FEELINGS, EMOTIONS, IMAGINATION, ENGAGEMENT

Creating a Vision is an ongoing personal process. What **inspires and moves** us reveals our deepest likes, dislikes and core desires. It could be a thought, dream, visual or a cause that stirs us from within touching our mind and heart. What do we want to make of our body, intelligence, education, desires, career, creative urges, financial dreams, relationship benchmarks, spiritual leanings, work, mission, our highest being, environment, business pursuits, personal talents, asset building and simultaneously WHO we want to be as a person. I am personally fascinated, inspired and find myself closest to nature when I am touching food that gives me good health. It is such a huge connection for me that I buy my own vegetables and have a vision too around city vegetable farming!

Visions of any kind come under the bohemian categories of imagination and inspiration. To create a vision, the key ingredient is imagination. Vision, inspiration and imagination are co-dependent as much as they need each other to articulate with specificity what has only been thought. It is within our power to activate this faculty and it is not reserved for the creative people alone. When we direct our thought to follow a purpose that rattles our comfort zone, we are pushed to go beyond our present selves and **become** the perfect match to our Vision.

The process of imagination is a mental, emotional and physical. **The mentally imagined vision demands emotional engagement and physical movement.** Our mental, emotional and physical selves become magnets attracted to each other as we set our imagination in motion. Continued focus leads to new ideas, thoughts and insights showing up to enhance the vision. With each addition, we will have a corresponding emotional and physical stretch as we learn HOW to execute the addition. It may be a new skill, finance, partnerships, work or any other addition that stretches our mind and asks us to act out of our comfort zones. Together our optimal mental, emotional and physical trio acts as the primary guidance system to further expand the Vision.

COSMIC COLLABORATION: A PERSONAL REVOLUTION

Heard of the three-legged race? It is difficult and needs absolute coordination of both partners to run with two legs tied together. A perfect rhythmic movement so the untied legs are lifted at the same time and the tied legs are lifted in consequent movement one after the other. A combination of the three results in coordinated and aligned momentum forward. If we get the rhythm right, we are able to speed up the run.

THREE-LEGGED RACE

Using the three-legged race analogy, let us presume that the left leg represents our person, the right leg represents our vision and the tied legs represent an optimized combination working towards the vision. Now it is we, our vision and a concerted combination working together at all times.

DIMENSIONISION© THE EFFECTIVENESS TOOL

Our effectiveness in expressing and executing the vision depends largely upon the **progressive identification and congruency** of our personal dimensions. With sufficient awareness of all the dimensions, what they are, how they work we can become experts in being effective in our actions. The goal must be to keep them congruent, reach higher levels in each and make sure that at any time they should not be working against each other.

Universal personal dimensions

1. **Physical:** Looks, style, presentation, exterior health, inner health, body language, spoken word;

2. **Mental:** Length and breadth of thought, thought development, congruency in thought and action, confidence to trust thoughts;

3. **Emotional:** Well-being, relationships, sense of hurt, sensitivity, emotional intelligence, dealing with pain;

4. **Intellectual:** Character, will power, inner strength, determination, power of discrimination, power to discern;

5. **Bliss:** Happiness, sleep, stress, general levels of satisfaction;

6. **Energy:** Internal body, disposition, health, circulation, respiration;

7. **Spiritual:** Our connection with the source and faith in its presence and power;

8. **Financial:** Security, relationship with money, financial stability, source of satisfaction, resources for the Vision.

Our personal dimensions are always in **unconscious motion making their presence felt in our daily lives.** Our moods, spoken word, what we think we are, where we can make improvements etc. is always at play. Unless we give our dimensions a congruent direction, imagine the havoc they can cause if working in opposite directions. For example, we want to start a fitness regimen but are emotionally distressed about an idea we pitched to a VC that did not work. With our mind and emotions in distress, there is little likelihood that our body will feel good enough to follow an exercise regimen. When we resolve the issue and feel better, our body will be more in control, our emotions and thought supporting the regimen. Either we resolve this as it appears or the in-congruency acts like the little bubble at the bottom of the lake that becomes visible only when it bursts on the surface. We then spend days and months struggling, failing and wondering why we are not moving forward jeopardizing our own effectiveness. Refinement of these dimensions is **getting hold** of the thoughts and actions consciously before they have developed a great deal to act out of control because what goes on inside us reflects in all we do.

Understanding the effect of our dimensions and sub-dimensions allows us to own the effectiveness of our person. The formula to ensure that there is progress in each can be termed as 4 steps of AIAI. The conscious effort on our part to **add** goals, **implement** additions, **assess** results and **identify** improvements in each dimension. We can keep repeating the process for it to condition our head, heart and actions to stay self-accountable. By weaving a dimensional ideal and making it congruent with our vision, we deliberately move towards personal perfection and progression. (Chart Below)

What would the wishes look like when achieved? Engage in that moment of completion and connect with it as we accept that this **engagement process makes us see the future in the present**. Imagine being on the most popular TV Show talking about it, where we began and how we got there. Imagine if we were in the Headlines of the National Newspaper or a local Magazine sharing the massive insights that we figured on the way.

DIMENSIONS- CREATE THE IDEAL

We must also know that our outside behaviors are built around **Five Core Human Drivers that influence our Desires**

ACQUIRING: Desire to collect material and immaterial things;

BONDING: Desire to be loved and feel valued in a relationship with others;

LEARNING: Desire to satisfy our curiosity;

DEFENDING: Desire to protect our selves, our loved ones and our property;

FEELING: Desire for many emotional experiences, such as pleasure or excitement;

Fill the chart below, rate yourself now and create an ideal rating for each dimension **in column 3 and what you would need to do for the same.** A very empowering exercise!

Dimension chart – Create the ideal

DIMENSION	WHAT?	RATE NOW	IDEAL OF LIFE	ACTION REQUIRED
Physical	Looks, Style, Presentation, External Health, Inner Health, Body Language, Spoken words etc.	1 2 3 4 5 6 7 8 9 10		
Mental	Length & Breath of thought; Thought development; Congruency – Thought & Action; Confidence to test thoughts			
Emotional	Emotional well being; Relationship, pain, sense of hurt, sensitivity; Emotional Intelligence			
Intellectual	Character Building; Will power, inner strength; Determination; Power of Discrimination			
Blissful	Happiness, Sleep; Stress busting; General levels of satisfaction			
Energy	Internal Body Disposition; Health; Circulation; Respiration			
Spiritual	Connection with the Source; Faith in its pervasive power			
Financial	Security; Relationship with money; Financial stability; Source of satisfaction; Resources for the vision			

SET THE STAGE TO PLAY OUR VISION VERSION IN 5 STEPS

1. Get inspired and specify what you really want;

2. Add skills or resources and prepare to achieve the wants;

3. Stay aware as opportunities show up to get closer to our wants;

4. Match your skills or develop new ones to match with the opportunity;

5. Get the desired results and start working on the next level;

Let us place each answer and the dimensions on the Vision Compass below. Building a Compass is a fantastic way to give our selves a Visual Stimulus! 80% of what we learn is visual, 10% auditory and 1% through senses. When we bring our active wishes and thoughts into the present visual, we see them up close. With our mind's eye we would also be able to see how it could change our life's direction. Get that on the compass too.

VISION COMPASS

Rate yourself on a scale of 1-10 where you are at each of these areas in life.

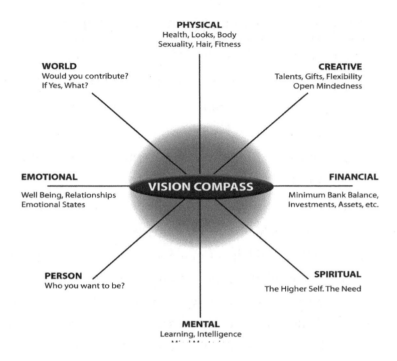

PHYSICAL
Health, Looks, Body
Sexuality, Hair, Fitness

WORLD
Would you contribute?
If Yes, What?

CREATIVE
Talents, Gifts, Flexibility
Open Mindedness

EMOTIONAL
Well Being, Relationships
Emotional States

VISION COMPASS

FINANCIAL
Minimum Bank Balance,
Investments, Assets, etc.

PERSON
Who you want to be?

SPIRITUAL
The Higher Self. The Need

MENTAL
Learning, Intelligence

CAUSE DELIBERATE IMPROVEMENT

HONESTY, ACCOUNTABILITY, RESPONSIBILITY, INTEGRITY: TRANSFORM

The possibility of achieving what we have set out on the compass primarily goes through four stages of thought. May happen, can happen, certainly can happen and will make it happen! As our vision and person engage with each other, we keep diving into unknown spaces, creating new results, discovering our own unknown strengths, weaknesses and talents. Through deliberate actions forward movement in thought as well as in action becomes the new normal. Conscious awareness of how a change in one dimension improves another dimension becomes a game of compounded improvement. If we are happy, our whole body feels good. If we are sad the body also feels the same. If we are thinking about something or someone that inspires us, we feel good within ourselves and vice versa.

If parts of us are confused, take them on as areas that need to be improved upon and increase the understanding of them. **The state of confusion can easily be overcome by developing competency in that area. Take a reality check of what you could change, improve or acquire.** The chart below is self-explanatory.

DISCIPLINE THE CONFUSION: BECOME A LEARNER

CONFUSION STATE	DEVELOPING COMPETENCE
1) Self-Rescue *Own emotions, behaviors will be seen, your inner resources tested. Beliefs and Results tested.* **UNDERSTANDING GIVES**	Personal Power Influence Knowledge activation Information Intellect, Skill expansion Real Action
2) Catastrophic States *Fear, Impossibility, No way out, what to do, etc.* **UNDERSTANDING GIVES**	You will Imagine solution Create Think differently Have a fresh approach Might get over the catastrophic panic altogether
3) Personal Blocks *Negativity, Behaviors, Fears, Mental Blocks, Absolutism* **UNDERSTANDING GIVES**	Mind Power Always room for improvement What and How you think is in your head Formation of new beliefs & assumptions Compartmentalize – No All or Nothing – always something. Focus shifts to that.
4) Dealing with People *Human unpredictability, Insecurity, Communication, self-understanding helps to understand others* **UNDERSTANDING GIVES**	You create your own methods to deal with the new understanding. It is to do with social systems They are not known for unknowns Your personal evolvement brings about change in society.

BRING BACK OWNERSHIP - OUTSIDE IN TO INSIDE OUT

Our present education system does not teach creation of visions for the future. Individual growth aspects like emotional flexibility, targeted application and mental strength is often left to chance or personal experience. With all that we learn and know, when stagnancy and failure begins to set in, we start to wonder what went wrong. In education the proof of success comes from outside the individual. It works well until we have to write tests but thereafter this methodology is an utter failure. Education is focused on the **outside in** approach where our success is measured in limited ways conditioning us to allow outside judgment to gauge how successful we are. This approach extended into real life has led to competitive comparisons where there can be none i.e. the individual growth through individual talent. The outside in approach has led innumerable people to think and apply themselves only via their education who are unable to see beyond that.

Thanks to undue judgment based on social standards we have created lives full of esteem or self worth issues, moral development full of doubt, limitations on self-growth, issues related to social cognitive development, poor health and happiness issues. We have been taught to make negative investments in responding to societal expectations and questioning our person ever so often. We must ask ourselves, how much we have added or subtracted to our person living this way. We were never taught the **inside out** approach in School or Society.

Education today slowly and steadily **hands over ownership** of who we are to what we do. **It literally leans us into disowning ourselves and handing over ownership of our success to outside barometers** like how well we do in social contexts. The **outside in** has it's utility to a point but it is not the best investment. It has to work in consonance and must follow the **inside out** and not the other way round. The **source of our strengths is inside** us but we are trained to live by the **opposite rule**. It is **practically impossible** for anyone outside to define who we are or can become. Our within is not the key focus of either the education or society. **We need to stop functioning in this opposition energy of living outside in with a suppressed inside out. If possible WE MUST DISOWN the OUTSIDE IN approach if we have to build a Vision.**

The outside is chaotic, crowded and never acts on its own. It is defined by an individual's experience of it or the impact of an individual's actions on it. The individual is the one who **impacts** the outside by acting out the inner strengths. If Ownership and Vision is what we choose, the **Outside In** approach can be fatal. There is a need to develop our super skills i.e. our growth muscle, achievement capacity and facing the unknown. It is only through the **Inside Out** approach that the underlying individual intelligence and creativity giving each woman her own **unique** person is built, the visionary is built and the mindset of a Visionary is built.

BEYOND IS WHERE VISION AND OWNERSHIP LIES

When dependence on others reduces and dependence on self gets bigger, there is a level of control within our selves leaving little space for outside interference. **From here the sense of freedom begins and it happens in the mind, percolates in the heart and acts through the body. Disciplining the mind and body to travel through these is the distance between success and failure of a vision.**

We must use skills we learnt at School but **unlocking our mental potential** over, above and beyond our educational conditioning is crucial to live a Vision. We only use 5% to 10% of our real potential. 90% is quite a number to get after. Let us make this part of our big and small Visions because **WE ARE THE 90%.**

Abha Maryada Banerjee is India's first woman motivational speaker of international acclaim, rated as one of the Top Ten Life, Business and Success Coaches in Asia Pacific. An expert at Leadership, Human Peak Performance and Emotional Intelligence, Abha is also the Peak Performance/Mental Strength Coach for Indian Olympic Athletes.

Author of the iconoclast 1st Thought Leadership for women Book called NUCLEUS: Power Women Lead from the Core, Abha has spoken at prestigious events across Asia as a Leadership Speaker. Feeling a need for helping women mentally, emotionally and from the social human perspective, Abha wanted to move beyond gender for purposes of building lives of women. Her quest of how personal leadership can be achieved through self-efficacy brought her to the context of women and leadership. With the undeniable background of gender issues across the World, NUCLEUS will lead women from ordinary to effective and effective to excellent, not as an academic treatise but an experiential one. She has introduced path-breaking concepts, tools and strategies to help women become leaders.

ANEETA PATHAK

HE SAID, SHE SAID, WE SAID...............
DID THEY ALL GET THE RIGHT MESSAGE?

"Most people do not listen with the intent to understand;
they listen with the intent to reply."

– Stephen R. Covey

In this rock n roll world, nothing is more significant than how and what we communicate everyday. We are all very much aware that good communication is the foundation of every successful relationship. It is considered as an essential skill for life, both on a personal and professional level.

Are we born with the traits of an excellent communicator? We are not all-natural communicators, but there are means and ways that are at our disposal and we can use them to learn how to develop our communication skills. It is a skill that we can learn and cultivate each day of our lives and ensure to make a conscious effort to improve it.

Communication is just about exchanging messages, be it through a phone conversation, a text message, writing an email, brainstorming session or any other ways of communicating. However, effective communication combines a set of skills that include non-verbal communication and attentive listening. Communication is one of the principal and central activities in any organization and household. We see them regularly at our workplace, at home with our kids, our families, our neighbours and anywhere else, we care to consider.

We all have the means and skills to communicate through speaking, writing, listening and body language. To communicate effectively, we have to hone our communication skills, as we strive to achieve success in every aspect of our lives. If we cannot communicate clearly, a message can turn into an error, misunderstanding and even frustration by being misinterpreted.

We adopt different communication styles when communicating with people at different level. Our styles reflect our attitudes and characters, which we reveal to other people when we are conversing with them. By becoming more aware of how others perceive you, you can try to adopt and adapt more readily to their styles of communicating. Changing your communication style with every personality you meet, does not mean you are a chameleon-like person. As an alternative, you are helping the other person to be more comfortable with you.

WHAT'S YOUR COMMUNICATION STYLE?

Are you an Assertive Communicator?

Behavioural traits of Assertive Communicators

- » Clearly states his/her opinion and feelings
- » Strongly advocates for his/her rights without abusing the rights of others
- » Confidence to communicate without having recourse to manipulations
- » Easily ally with other people

- » Comfortably talk about your needs and feelings
- » Making your own choices and be accountable to them if something goes wrong
- » In control of your emotions
- » Speak in calm and clear tones
- » Good listeners
- » Create a respectful environment for others
- » Achieving goals without hurting others
- » Socially and emotionally expressive
- » Deal with conflicts in healthy ways
- » You are OK, I am OK

HOW OTHERS SEE AND FEEL WHEN YOU COMMUNICATE

- » Confident about who you are
- » Self-controlled
- » Speak clearly, honestly and to the point
- » Firm but polite
- » Warm, welcoming and friendly
- » Believe and trust your words
- » Positive and coping

Assertive communication is the healthiest and most effective style of communication. Earlier, I mentioned that we are not all-natural communicators, but there are means and ways that are at our disposal and we can use them to learn how to develop our communication skills.

Assertiveness is based on balance as it entails being straightforward about your needs and wants, whilst still taking into consideration the needs and wants of others. If you are assertive, you ask for what you want but you do not necessarily get it. Being assertive is not necessarily easy!

HOW CAN YOU DEVELOP YOUR ASSERTIVENESS?

Value yourself – do your best to handle life's challenges with dignity

» your rights, feelings, needs and desires are as important as everyone else's

» recognize your rights and protect them

» believe that you deserve to be treated with respect at all times

» stop apologizing for everything

» always be respectful when you are angry

» control your emotions

» stand up for yourself - deal with people who challenge you and/or your rights

» when you make mistakes, ask for help

» accept criticism positively – do not get defensive or angry

» accept that you cannot do everything or please everyone

» use "I" statements to convey basic assertions

» always empathize – find out how the other person views any situations, then express what you need

» be honest and ask for your time if you need a few minutes to make up your mind

» say "no" and then give a choice

» say "no" and then clarify your reasons

Developing your assertiveness can be learned and we have to recognize that it will not happen overnight. If you practice some of the techniques mentioned above, you will gradually become more confident in communicating your needs and wants.

> The way we communicate with others and with ourselves ultimately determines the quality of our lives.
>
> Tony Robbins

ARE YOU A PASSIVE COMMUNICATOR?

Behavioural traits of Passive Communicators?

» Lack of confidence when expressing their opinions; will start, stop and hesitate when they speak. Their hesitations are often accompanied by filler sounds such as "ums" & "uhs"

» Value more about the preferences and needs of others rather than their own

» To avoid drawing attention on them they will keep their voices down

» They put themselves down at the first opportunity, over the smallest things

» Avoid eye contact, due to lack of confidence

» Hesitate to express their true feelings

» Always agree to everything

- » Allow others to make decisions for self
- » Sighs a lot
- » Asks for permission unnecessarily
- » Complains instead of taking action
- » Isolates self from group
- » You are OK, I am NOT OK

HOW OTHERS SEE AND FEEL WHEN YOU COMMUNICATE

- » See you as a pain to work with and talk to
- » Can't rely on you to make a decision
- » Poor judgement
- » Always complaining
- » Does not exude self-confidence
- » Not a go-getter
- » As a door mat

Passive communication is a style when individuals develop a pattern; they avoid expressing their opinions or feelings, fearing that they will be rejected. They do not react openly to hurtful situations and unconsciously they are nurturing grievances.

HOW TO SHIFT FROM A PASSIVE STYLE TO AN ASSERTIVE STYLE?

If we increase our assertiveness, this will improve our sense of self-esteem and totally reduce the amount of stress in our life. By becoming more assertive, this will also help us to develop healthier relationships with the people around us; hence become an effective communicator. Start by trying to verbalize your needs, feelings and opinions more frequently. All you have to do is to remind yourself of your exact needs and wants; then actively communicate them directly and respectfully with those around you.

Once you start working consistently on increasing your assertiveness, this will become a self-fulfilling process and will help you to relay your thoughts and emotions more effectively. It will be easier if you try to focus on one aspect of your life first and project an image of self-confidence with those who know you well and they will likely respect your more active participation.

Always ensure that you are making frequent eye contact with people with whom you are interacting. Try to have a relaxed body language and practice saying "no", as it is important to recognize and embrace your right, to simply say 'no'. Emphasize sincerity and clarity in the way you speak. Listen actively and pay attention when someone speaks to you. Whenever anything is unclear, do not hesitate to interrupt the person and ask questions.

> For changes to be of any true value, they've got to be lasting and consistent.
>
> (Tony Robbins)

ARE YOU AN AGGRESSIVE COMMUNICATOR?

Behavioural traits of Aggressive Communicators?

» Impulsive
» Criticize and blame others

- » Interrupt frequently
- » Use "you" statements
- » Intimidating
- » Willing to achieve goals at expense of others
- » Belligerent
- » Bullying
- » Closed minded
- » Poor listener
- » Know-it-all attitude
- » Doesn't show appreciation
- » I am OK, you are NOT

HOW OTHERS SEE AND FEEL WHEN YOU COMMUNICATE

- » Distrustful
- » Hostile
- » Unhelpful
- » Resentful
- » Degraded
- » Afraid
- » Loss of respect

An aggressive communicator tends to go against the rights of others and is verbally or physically abusive, or both. Aggressive communication is typically the result of low self-esteem. It will definitely take a long time for an aggressive communicator to make a paradigm move to becoming an assertive communicator.

All of the above are the three basic styles of communication.

Assertive people state their opinions while being respectful to others.

Passive people do no state their opinions at all.

Aggressive people attack or ignore others' opinions in favour of their own.

> The only healthy communication style is assertive communication
>
> Jim Rohn

I know that we are all pretty much aware of the three main basic styles of communication. Earlier, I mentioned that we are not born with traits of an excellent communicator. There are means and resources out there, which we can use if we really want to become an assertive communicator, considered as one of the healthiest style.

However, based on my personal experience, the best way to improve our communication style is to join a Toastmasters club.

Toastmasters is an organization that enables members to improve communication skills in a safe, encouraging and supportive environment.

People are often confused by the name "Toastmasters." Some think it is about learning how to give toasts at events. To some of you, the name "Toastmasters" sounds old-fashioned; could be because the organization's roots go back to 1924 when Ralph C. Smedley held the first meeting of what would eventually become Toastmasters International.

Today, according to its mission statement, Toastmasters International helps men and women learn the arts of speaking, listening, and thinking — vital skills that promote self-actualization, enhance leadership potential. A Toastmaster has the privilege to benefit in many aspects of their lives – **As best-selling author Harvey Mackay has said**, *"I've never met anyone who didn't think Toastmasters was super valuable to their career.* ***We gain self-esteem, self-confidence, and assertiveness, which makes us better salespeople, better managers, better leaders."***

When we join a Toastmasters club, we not only perk up our communication style but we also unleash our leadership skills. This is the best place to overcome the fear of public speaking and learn skills that will help us in becoming more successful in both our personal and professional life. Toastmasters help us to become better listeners and strong team members and leaders who can comfortably give and receive evaluations.

If you are determined to become an assertive communicator, the best place to go is to look for a Toastmasters club in your local community. This is an inexpensive training and professional development program. Just check it out!

Whatever your grade or position, if you know how and when to speak, and when to remain silent, your chances of real success are proportionately increased.

Dr. Ralph C. Smedley, Founder Toastmasters International

Having worked with senior executives at major corporations in North America, **Aneeta** knows what it takes to serve as an executive assistant. In her new book, Aneeta shares the tools strategies and principles that make the biggest difference for Executive Assistants. Aneeta's goal is to give every Executive Assistant everything they need to SHINE in the eyes of their employer.

So what's the secret to Aneeta's success? The most important thing she attributes it to is her "Can-Do" attitude. Aneeta has created the DNA for commitment, efficient, detail-oriented, efficient, fearless, and go-getter so you too can SHINE in the eyes of your executive.

ESPERANZA MONTALVO

HUMILITY AS A LIGHTNING-GROWTH FORCE IN LEADERSHIP

Don't worry when you are not recognized
But strive to be worthy of recognition.

Abraham Lincoln

How many of you have made a positive connection between humility and leadership? Or do you perceive being 'humble' as being 'weak'?

Weather you thought one way of the other, one thing that has been proven, in both, personal and organizational leadership is that Humility Is not only a virtue but also an advantage – In fact, a study done by the University of Washington indicates that in the organizational world, leaders who are humble are more effective than leaders who thrive exclusively towards self-promotion (Arrogance) and self protection (Fear) -- The reason being is that Leaders who are humble, are not afraid to speak of their own failures, weaknesses, and blind spots. They listen to the opinions of others, admit when they make a mistake, and care for the needs of others. They are both leaders and followers, and lead with both their head and their heart. These set of traits (and others I'll be talking about later in this chapter), create and foster a learning environment where mistakes are allowed to happen and the morale of the group is based, not on judgment and competition, rather on collaboration, learning from others, engaging and growing, failing and getting up, and being consciously aware, that when we have a humble attitude, it is easier to connect with others, and undoubtedly, achieve greater results.

You see, Results are achieved with People.

So now, how is it that we can claim "Humility" as the Lightning Growth Force of Leadership?

There are many reasons for the above statement drawn from my personal experience as an international corporate facilitator and communications and leadership specialist. And more significantly, as a consultant and business woman who has reinvented herself (radically) 4 times – from oil industry professional, to teacher, to consultant, to entrepreneur, and why not, from daughter to mother, to grandmother, to community member, sister, friend, neighbor, etc. -- and where during these reinventions, have dealt with surmounting challenges, especially when jumping into the global business/entrepreneurial world, travelling to 27 countries, working with leaders are all levels, from executives to managers, to supervisors, to front line workers, from completely different cultural backgrounds, languages, political and religious views. And where, the first order of the day, for the purpose of creating effectivity, needs to be, first, an uncanning ability to "Connect", then lead.

Well, in this particular case, and in my leadership role as a facilitator, the consistent question always is: 'How could I connect when I come to a new place to impart knowledge and information, for participants, who are highly confident and knowledgeable in their own fields, who have been either asked to take specific training, or sent by their higher ups? And how do I create an atmosphere for audiences to receive the new information in a way that is not patronizing? In other words, what is it required in these type of situations, where I am in a leadership role, with people I'm seeing for the first time? What do I need to be able to influence them? What do I need in order to lead effectively in this situation?

These and many other questions I ask myself constantly - How do I bring my experience in a way that is not dogmatic and/ or patronizing, yet, it opens the hearts and minds of participants so they can receive the information and tools they are there to receive?

Believe me. It hasn't been easy all the time, and I've failed a number of times – I remember one of my trips to a distant country, where I had to deliver a specific leadership training, and either, I was not completely ready for it, or it wasn't the type of audience I've should've delivered to. In this situation I learned one of the greatest lessons in humility in my life. However, I took the lesson learned, made a correction, and picked up again. I truly believe that I can fail, and I can also get up. Fail and get up again. Fail and Persist. An in this process, as I look at failures as "lessons learned", accept that the virtue of 'humility' is the only thing that could sustain me as a coach, facilitator, business woman, entrepreneur, leader, and most importantly, as a human being.

You see. One of the best definitions of leadership I've ever heard was said by Ken Blanchard – co-author of The One Minute Manager – One of the world's most popular Management Method - Being a Leader is a process of influence. Anytime you seek to influence the thinking, behaviour, or development of people in their personal or professional lives, you are taking the role of a leader. Leadership can be as intimate as words of guidance and encouragement to a loved one or as formal as instructions passed through extended lines of communication in organizations. Leadership can be nurturing the character and self worth in children and promoting greater intimacy and fulfillment in personal relationships, or it can involve distributing diverse resources in an organization to accomplish specific objective and task.

I'm telling you a piece of my life story, so you can relate. You might have a completely different experience and be presently under a completely different setting, environment and situation. However, let me assure you, that the principles I'll be sharing in this article, apply to all kinds of 'leadership situations'. And I can say this with assurance, because these principles have been tested throughout countless leadership and global training in North-America, Latin-America, Japan, Europe, and Asia. So, if you are ready to adopt even just a few of these principles, I can guarantee you a shift in the way you look at Humility and Leadership.

So let's begin.

Basically, the importance of humility in leadership and why I am adamant in saying that Humility is the Lightning Growth force of leadership, is because, from my academic training and personal experience this is what I've found out – *Caveat: Don't believe anything I'm saying. I trust you'll experiment with this information and will get your own answers and results as you test them.*

In order to 'connect' with others, we need to first understand. In order to understand, we need to learn about the other. In order to learn about the other, we need to listen. And in order to listen, we need to "suspend" our opinions. And here is the secret ... In order to be able to suspend our opinions, we need Humility. Why? Because when we are "a know it all" we don't need to suspend our opinions, because we don't need to listen or learn. We are full. In fact, it said that: "Without humility we cannot learn".

So now, this is a good place to bring a set of definitions of Humility for you to explore and reflect upon. Question how you feel about what they are saying to you. Does it resonate with who you are? Do you connect with any of these definitions? Do you feel resistance towards any of them?

I confess that years ago, I used to resist some of the definitions below – coming from a societal conditioning based on authoritarian structure, and adding to this, my baby-boomer status - a topic for a new chapter - it took me a number of years to change my paradigm on how I perceived leadership and how I perceived humility. And to be transparent, the topic of humility, is one that I continue to study, practice, fail, get up, fail, get up and Persist – It's a work in progress.

Having said that, here is the compiled list of definitions on humility. As I said before, read them and observe how you feel about them. What's the first thing that comes to your mind. Refrain from judging yourself. Just observe.

Here they are:

Humility: Standing by itself, the word radiates "quiet confidence". It exudes strength.

Humility is self-confidence without arrogance.

Humility is modesty and restraint without the destructive effects of out-sized arrogance.

Humility is courage. It is the willingness to admit mistakes and seek out guidance.

Humility is self-respect without excessive self-promotion.

Humility is the triumph of competence over bravado.

Humility is **not** weak or meek. It does not mean shy or insecure. It is not being timid, reserved, reticent, or non-confident.

Humility is authenticity.

Humility is self-awareness. It is recognizing one's strengths and limitations. It is the ability to say, "I don't know." It is quite simply the willingness to put others first.

Maybe C.S. Lewis said it best, "Humility is not thinking less of yourself, but rather thinking about yourself less."

Many people believe that humility is the opposite of pride, when, in fact, it is a point of equilibrium. The opposite of pride is actually a lack of self esteem. A humble person is totally different from a person who cannot recognize and appreciate himself as part of this worlds marvels.

Rabino Nilton Bonder

Contrary to the **old** paradigm of leadership -- where the leader has to have all the answers, is afraid of making mistakes for fear of losing credibility, is pontified as the knowledge bearer according to his or her position, and reigns from fear and pride motivations, in the **new** paradigm, humility is the Lightning

Growth **force** which sustains the type of collaboration and synergistic influence that results in effective leadership.

Why?

Because being humble begins in our heart, in the 'personal' leadership realm - in the inside - where effective leadership starts – Before we can hope to lead anyone else, we have to know ourselves. We work on our Personal leadership before we take on leading teams, groups, organizations, and so on. This is why Stephen Covey talks about moving from dependency to independence to interdependence in his 7 Habits of Highly Effective People.

Personal leadership involves choice, and Humility is a choice, which for some of us, is a conscious choice in our adult years because we didn't have a humble model of leadership as we were growing up, or the society we were raised in did not provide the example.

The foundation for a humble leadership style does not exist under the authoritarian societal structure. Bringing this awareness into consciousness and observing the ramifications of such paradigm, takes work and a humble attitude in order to make a shift.

In the new paradigm of leadership, as we look at leadership from a pyramidal perspective, the leader sits at the bottom where he or she can listen to others views and ideas. Where observation versus judgment is practiced. Where questions for clarification are posed. And where an environment of experimentation is accepted, with ample opportunities to fail, get up, and persist.

It is said that without humility, we cannot learn. And the new Leader is one who leads and also learns – If this is not the mindset of the leader, there will be stagnation, resentment, lack of motivation, lack of inspiration, particularly now days when we are being exposed to such large amount of information, at the speed of the bullet, and when if there's no newness, exploration, innovation, creativity, most of us, especially the young generation, loses interest quite rapidly. You see, in the authoritarian leadership style, knowledge is power. And what can we do now when knowledge is at the tip of our fingers with the prolific amount of information we get on internet? I'm sure you are aware that now days we can say something and then prove it, with research and statistics, with completely opposite findings. Please don't quote me as saying that 'knowledge is not important. Or that where the knowledge comes from is not important'. It is.

All I desire to demonstrate here is that the old paradigm of 'power because of my position or because of what I know' is becoming somewhat discredited – anyone can learn whatever they choose. Knowledge is at our fingertips. In the New Paradigm, it takes more than just position and knowledge to gain influence and leadership. It takes integrity, that is, it takes living what we preach. It takes living by our principles, our beliefs, our values. It takes having a clear Vision, and one that is for the good of all. It takes real leadership, based in Humility.

I often bring up the following story of Ghandi in my Leadership training (at all levels) – I'm paraphrasing it in case you've already heard it.

A frustrated mother brought her son to Ghandi so he could ask him to stop eating sugar. Ghandi in his infinite wisdom responded: 'Lady, I'd love to help your son. Could you bring him back to me in a week?' The lady, somewhat surprised by Ghandi's said to him: 'but Ghandi, I need him to stop right of way'. To what he responded again: 'lady, please bring your son in a week'.

A week went by, and exactly as she was asked, the mother brought her son to Ghandi. 'Here he is', said the mother. Ghandi looked at the young man and said to him: 'Stop eating sugar'. Then the mother asked Ghandi. Why did I have to wait for a week for you to say this to my son?

Ghandi's answered: "Because I was eating sugar then".

Isn't this what real Integrity means? And I'm not bringing a different topic here. In fact, integrity and humility go hand in hand. Integrity is recognizing that unless we submit humbly to our values, our principles, our Vision, we are faking leadership. Do you see the relationship?

By the way, I wish I could always have the type of Integrity Ghandi demonstrated. A high call. Something to aspire to. However, it is constantly in the back of my mind, and when I fail, this story comes to my perception, and makes me reflect on my leadership roles ... I stop and look within and take time to observe, correct, learn, move forward.

The question then now is:

How can we develop or enhance Humility? What Principles do we need to practice?

To start with, let's look at very practical actions we can take in our daily leadership roles, both, personal and organizational.

Here they are:

1. Share the credit and Accept the blame

Paul "Bear" Bryant, the legendary University of Alabama football coach, captured this idea perfectly when he said, "If anything goes bad, I did it. If anything goes semi-good, we did it. If anything goes really good, then you did it. That's all it takes to get people to win football games for you"

2. Embrace these three magical phrases:

» "I don't know"

» "Help me understand"

» "You're right!"

3. Admit your mistakes

Apologies (real and sincere apologies) demonstrate strength of character, respect for others, and a desire to learn.

4. Ask for Feedback

It takes real humility and a healthy dose of self-confidence to ask: "How am I doing?"

5. Recognize that Good Questions can be more powerful than Questionable Answers

Seek out the opinions and thoughts of others. Ask questions. Listen.

Be careful not to be enamored with the sound of your own voice.

6. Treat all people with respect and decency, regardless of their position in life

Say "Please" and "Thank you!" in ALL your interactions.

The next following principles are directly related to organizational leadership role, thought, it also applies to our personal roles as leaders:

1. **Listen to all kinds of ideas and different points of views.** There is evidence that the most imaginative and valuable ideas tend to come from what we might find as an opposite point of view, or perhaps from someone who may seem a little offbeat.

2. **Know what you don't know.** In other words, be humble enough to admit that you don't have all the answers. Nor do you have to have them. Others have strengths we don't have.

3. **Embrace and promote a spirit of service.** Are you dedicated to helping others succeed, or is the concern about your own personal success? Humility cannot be faked – you either genuinely want to serve and assist or you don't, and others will pick up on this.

4. **Be passionately curious.** At all times, welcome and seek out new knowledge, and insist on curiosity from those around you. Curiosity and many positive leadership attributes, including emotional and social intelligence, go hand in hand. Take it from Albert Einstein: "I have no special talent," he claimed, "I am only passionately curious."

5. **Share your mistakes as teachable moments.** Are you confident displaying your own personal growth? By admitting to your own imperfections you make it okay for others to make mistakes, as well. And what is failure if not the road to success?

6. **Engage in dialogue, not debates.** Another way to practice humility is to truly engage with different points of view. Too often leaders are focused on trying to convince others and "winning" arguments. When we debate in this

manner, we miss out on the opportunity to <u>learn</u> about the *other's* point of view and their unique perspective.

7. **Embrace uncertainty.** Ambiguity and uncertainty are prevalent in today's business environment. When as a leader we can humbly admit we don't have all the answers, we create a space for others to step forward and offer solutions.

8. **Role model being a "follower."** Humble leaders empower others to lead. By exchanging roles, leaders not only foster development; they model the act of taking a different perspective - something that is so critical in working with diverse teams.

9. **Accept Ambiguity.** At times leaders want to control everything. However, some things can't be known in advance. You have to know when to take charge—or when to let go and not try to force everything to go your way – it takes humility to be able to do this.

10. **Self Reflect.** Like many leadership skills, humility may not come easy to everyone. That's why it's important to engage in self-reflection. One way is writing, on a journal, what went well during your interactions or what could've been handled differently.

11. **Let People do their jobs.** Micromanaging kills morale—and it isn't very humble. Choose good people, train them, then "get out of the way and let them do their jobs. It can take humility to admit that your way isn't the only way or even that some people are better at certain roles than you. The humble leader accepts these truths and allow other's strengths to work for the good of the team's objectives and vision.

"When leaders demonstrate these behaviors (as leaders within organizations or in our personal roles) —self-awareness, perspective, openness to feedback and ideas, and appreciation of others—one of the responses we hear from employees is: "I can actually perform at a higher level" - There is a relationship between humble leadership behaviors and outcomes.

A humble leader is secure enough to recognize his or her weaknesses and to seek the input and talents of others, thus, creating an environment of collaboration, synergy, and ultimately, a space for everybody to experiment, grow, advance, excel and be responsible and accountable for their results. This is why Humility is a Lightning Growth force of Leadership.

A PRACTICAL APPLICATION -- HUMILITY AS THE LIGHTNING GROWTH FORCE

In one of the organizations I facilitate Leadership training, practicing humility has been essential to promoting an inclusive culture — a culture the organization sees as critical to leveraging the diversity of its global workforce.

One of the key strategies they adopted is the "Fishbowl method", used for facilitating dialogue.

At their fishbowl gathering, a small group of employees and leaders sit in circle at the center of the room, while a larger group of employees are seated in the outside of the circle. Employees are encouraged to engage with each other as well as the leaders on any topic, and are invited into the inner part of the circle. During these informal conversations, facilitated a couple of times a year, leaders consistently demonstrate humility —by admitting to employees that they don't have all the answers, and by sharing their own personal journeys, failures, and path of development.

I remember one of the sessions when the company introduced same-sex partner benefits. A devoted religious employee expressed concerns about the new benefits policy in front of a large group of employees. Rather than becoming defensive, a senior leader, highly skillful, engaged the employee in dialogue, asking him questions and probing to understand his perspectives. By responding in this way, the leader validated the perspectives of that employee and others who shared his views. Other leaders shared their own concerns and approaches to holding firm to their own religious beliefs yet embracing the company's values of treating all employees fairly.

Dialogues such as these have made a valuable difference within the organization. Employees have higher confidence in their leaders, are more engaged, and feel more included — despite their differences.

As this example suggests, a humble leader should not be mistaken for a 'weak' one -- It takes tremendous courage to practice humility in the ways described above.

More organizations would be wise to follow the lead of companies like the one in this example; and in terms of personal leadership, where leadership begins, growing our humble spirit will create a ripple effect and long term legacy.

HUMILITY IS THE LIGHTNING GROWTH FORCE IN LEADERSHIP

Esperanza Montalvo is a Communications and Leadership Specialist, entrepreneur and expert in reinvention (she has reinvented herself radically 4 times). From Oil Industry Professional, to Teacher, to Consultant to Entrepreneur. As an International Corporate Facilitator, she has helped organizations get their employees to peak performances – She is now bringing the SAME Tools, Strategies and Methods to every WOMAN who is excited to create something 'New' in their lives and/or accelerate their present growth. Esperanza has published a book, travelled to 27 countries; Is a Mentor and Coach, Trainer, Public Speaker and a peak performance Facilitator within corporations. And most importantly, she is a mother, grandmother, sister, aunt, friend, community volunteer, etc. who takes 100% responsibility for every result and relationship she fosters – In other words, Leadership is a principle she lives by -- That's why she created Leadership with Awareness (LWA); and needless to say, throughout her trajectory, she "has fail and get up, fail and get up, fail and Persist".

ALLI MANG

YOUR FIRST MOMENT EARNS YOU MORE MOMENTS

STAND OUT IN TODAY'S JOB MARKET

We come into this world on someone else's terms but will leave on our own terms. There will be many moments during your life that might be questioned, moments you would love to splice right out, and many more that you'll want to triplicate. Have you ever asked yourself, 'What am I building my experience of life for?' It is quite the existential question, but is the fuse that I want to ignite within you. It is in your best interest to connect deeply to the heart of what makes you feel alive and energized. From that core, you will build purpose and maintain forward momentum in your life – even if at times you seem to be standing still. In the words of Elbert Hubbard, "We work to become, not to acquire."

Time is limited. Believe in your passions and give as much of yourself everyday as if it was the last chance you had to do it. And, don't let anyone try to take away the desires and dreams that live inside you.

Your First Moment is an urgent call-to-action to make a commitment to yourself. This principle applies to everything you do professionally, as well as to what the public has the potential to learn about you. It's about the business of selling yourself: who you are, your expertise, and your reputation – which includes your personal brand. I Opening statements are intrinsic to every part of the interview or pitch.

The opening statement creates the momentum you need to carry out a strong interview. It establishes you as a leader and helps make whoever you are directing your message to show them you can be relied upon to take the baton, and more importantly, that you have unique perspectives that they will benefit from. Giving a strong opening statement is similar in importance to making a solid serve in a tennis match. In music, the opening statement represents the first downbeat in a song. It's about using your career as your platform to become the person you want to be. It's about learning how to act fearlessly, and to become keenly aware of how to set yourself up for optimal success. It has everything to do with you, your decisive mindset and your state of readiness. It addresses how to handle your preparation, how to choose to think and act with intention and positivity, and how to leverage that knowledge to better yourself and your current position. It applies whether you are posting a picture on social media, entering a room, making a cold call, shaking a hand or providing your opening statement in an introductory letter, sales pitch or presentation.

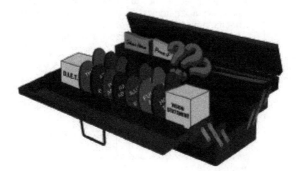

The second part of the title, *Earns You More Moments*, is the score sheet that tells you how well you are doing the first part.

What do the phrases - show them and prove it, 3 questions, the acronym DIET, seven lily pads and a vision statement have to do with your success?

They are the tools you'll use to turn yourself into a marketing machine. The toolbox comprises of everything we have discussed in this book. You will, therefore, be in a constant state of readiness to sell yourself no matter what stage you are in your career. Within a blink of an eye, you will be zoned into exactly what you need to be doing to attend that meeting, lead the presentation or show up for that interview. Once this initial work is done, you will only need to add to it as you grow your portfolio of work and experience. Up next is an at-a-glance review of the tools, followed by showing you how they can be applied.

KEY TOOL	WHAT IT IS AND HOW IT BENEFITS YOU
1. **Show Them, Prove it**	» Your resume and C.V. earned you an appointment to be interviewed. This *show them, prove it* action gives you a forum to illuminate and personalize the cold hard facts of the details on your resume and brings together everything else you have done to prepare. Let's review what the greatest sales technique in the world is: It's connecting on a *heart-to-heart* level with your customers, decision makers and colleague.
2. **3 Questions**	» Start the process by asking yourself, **what is really happening** right now – pertaining to the 'Situation'. After getting a good handle on **what's happening**, you are in a more informed position to decide on **what all of this means to you** regarding the 'Situation'. Once you know **what it means to you**, based on your assessment of **what is happening**, then design a plan of action in order to **do something** about the 'Situation'.
3. **Your Vision Statement**	» The vision statement is part of the "business of you." It establishes in your Heart and your Soul what truly differentiates you.
	» It tells you how what you offer in expertise, experience, and character will benefit others.
	» It *aligns* and *directs* every marketing and promotional decision you make and, in turn, that maintains consistent messaging geared to best serve you and what you've identified as your desired path.
	» It provides a solid roadmap of personal directives that tell you how to conduct your business and how you want to be seen and heard in an authentic way.
	» It controls and solidifies how you want to be introduced and promoted publically and drives you to select the right images, testimonials, hardcopy or softcopy promotional materials, websites, social media platforms, logos, color selections, and copy writing (to name only a few).

4.	**Public Profile Portfolio**	» A public record of your expertise, experience, testimonials, demos, track record, milestones, relationships and contacts, awards, etc. » It forces you to gather everything together in one place, which will allow you to define, refine and redirect your brand (how you want people to see you).
5.	**Seven Lily Pads**	» A checklist based on one of the most effective sales and marketing tactics that focuses your selling message quickly and thoroughly. » It will take the worry out of wondering if you've missed anything during your research and due diligence processes.
6.	**D.I.E.T**	» This acronym stands for *Define, Inspire, Execute* and *Trust*. It is a simplified checklist to ensure that your intention before any meeting or presentation is in line with your Vision Statement. Simple, direct and repeatable.
7.	**At-A-Glance One Pager**	» On one page, chronicle and record all of the above information in bullet point format to quickly and easily recall the most important aspects of your pitch when you have to be *100%* ON.

It will benefit all of your marketing initiatives moving forward. So often, we are caught off guard when it comes to getting our professional portfolio together. The strategies will give you the structure to grab the attention of decision makers in order for you to fly without a net.

KEY TOOLS

1. **Show Them:**

   » **Show Them** how what you bring compares to the competition in a positive and differentiating manner.

   » **Show Them**, what clearly differentiates who you are and how you do what you do.

   » **Show Them** how many ways and scenarios you will benefit them that will matter to them.

» **Show Them** and demonstrate your value. Bring in quantifiable and qualitative examples that illuminate your resume details. (This could include demo reels, your website, apps, games or CD's you've produced, and/or other products you've produced for clients).

Prove It:

» **Prove** that your credibility is unquestionable. This is where your reputation is front and center. Share quantitative details of your past successes, colleagues, customers and companies you've worked with. Details to consider mentioning: yearly sales success, cost control, number of people you manage, number of customers, customer retention, specific education and awards. Share activity that has contributed to your growing expertise and has benefited your past clients.

» **Prove** that your expertise can be relied upon and TRUSTED. Find meaningful ways that sell you as a leader in your field of expertise.

2. **3 Questions**: If you are struggling to make a decision, this process will get you the answers you need in a straight-forward, no-nonsense way. Too often we create pro and con lists of what we should or shouldn't do but it ends up feeling like a chore and many times once the list is created, we never look at it again. The key is the second question – **what does it mean to me**. This is a question you can't hide from. If it means nothing to you – you can stop doing the exercise. If it means something to you however, you are going to discover all you need to know about your concerns to get yourself moving up and on with a plan that works.

3. **Vision Statement:** Show up looking, acting and being the mirror image of what your vision statement expresses. If you were wearing a T-shirt with your vision statement printed on it, everyone would say, "this is you." Make certain that in all manners, especially when conversing, your verbal, written and personal communication is consistent with what you are showing them.

4. **Resume Portfolio:** Pull together and update all your public persona tools, including your public profiles on all social media platforms and the entire content of your website: resumes, demo tapes (if applicable), creative portfolio (if applicable), samples of your work, testimonials, and recommendations.

5. **Seven Lily Pads/Due Diligence:** Helps you build your due diligence work: Hook Them Fulfill A Need, Illuminate The Experience, Rise Above Objections, Rise Above Apathy, Ask For Business, Thank You.

   » While there are always some last minute tasks to do before a major event or interview, it's the longer-term preparation that makes all the difference. Researching the company and the players is essential. As soon as you know there is a possibility of interviewing at a specific company, start collecting background data. Use any assets and your connections you may have to gain as much insight as you can.

   » Whether you are on a first time interview or meeting with a COO at a senior level, you will want to know all you can about the company, its culture and the people with whom you will be interviewing. The reason for this is the knowledge will ground you and allow you to let them know you are ready to 'play in their field.' Part of the business of you and being marketable is to show them you are a strong fit.

» Your practice phase is also a great time to work on eliminating distracting habits, like fixing your hair or looking down at your nails while speaking and using 'ums, "likes' and other disrupters in your speech patterns. Avoid the overuse of generalities and descriptive adjectives, such as "Do you know what I mean?" Without experiencing it for themselves, you're already adopting a point of view for them which may be in your best interest, but not necessarily theirs.

6. **DIET Philosophy** helps to focus your understanding of what makes you unique. In order to make it memorable and repeatable before you go into your meeting or interview, use D.I.E.T. to clearly state within 20 seconds what is going to make you stand out in this meeting and presentation today:

Define – In one sentence, define what makes you truly unique compared to your competition and why others will see that value too.

Inspire – In one sentence, what is your best way to communicate your uniqueness to inspire your audience to see you, hear you and say yes to you.

Execute – Identify the 5 most tangible and provable items to support what differentiates you and makes you highly marketable at this moment.

Trust – Trusting in yourself is the key to executing an exceptional performance. Create one highly personal sentence that you can rely upon to keep your mind focused and your heart fully engaged.

7. **Create an At-A-Glance One Pager** of information that captures all of the above points on one page. At the meeting,

you want to be free to be present and ready for anything that they throw at you and that takes preparation and fast recall. The at-a-glance tool is the vehicle to give that to you.

» This one pager highlights all of the best of you – your vision statement in one line, your personal brand and your sense of value as a professional and all the due diligence you have done to prepare yourself accordingly.

» The one pager is a great tool that can be used to work on speeding up your recall and getting your words out quickly and efficiently. It helps to focus your thoughts before the interview and provides a checklist when you review afterward to ensure you hit all the marks you intended to. Also, you can easily add new information as needed.

» It is one of the most paramount preparation tools, as you have all of the most pertinent information on one page. It includes your due diligence and identifies your marketing position.

We come into this world on someone else's terms but will leave on our own terms. There will be many moments during your life that will be questioned, moments you would love to splice right out, and many more that you'll want to triplicate. This is your day to claim your space in this world and to develop your life in the way you dream. It will continue to grow and flow through you like a funnel. All the answers you need right now are inside you. Your hours and years of work are forever in place. TRUST that all of your knowledge and abilities will always be available to you. Share with the world what your story of life is and tell it with all of your might.

Multi-Million Dollar National Brand Spokesperson **Alli Mang** is an award-winning, results-oriented sales and personal branding expert who helps her clients capitalize on how to sell themselves with optimal success. She is the Director of The Leanne Mang Foundation Inc., in honor of her sister who committed suicide. The foundation provides grass-roots support for those suffering with mental illness with a focus on adolescent suicide prevention.

Alli Mang's other books include: *Sold Out, How to Reach Your Full Potential in Sales; Your First Moment Earns You More Moments – Stand Out in Today's Job Market.* She is also a featured author in the business and motivational book, Lightning Growth.

Visit www.allimang.com for more information.

BUSINESS

ALI M AL-KHOURI

DEVELOPMENT OF SUSTAINABLE ORGANIZATIONS

"Every profession bears the responsibility to understand
the circumstances that enable its existence."

Robert Gutman

Given the popularity and the prevalence of the concept of *sustainability* in corporate culture, one would expect its effective and holistic implementation to either be well under way or on the verge of completion. However, this does not seem to be the case for the majority of institutions and organizations. Further, the effects of *sustainability* barely scratch the surface. The truth of the matter is that, when it comes to the implementation of sustainability, organizations are either just at the very start of the process or in the early stages of its development. For each organization, the base for this progress rests on the fundamental concepts that it has in place concerning proper conduct and/or ethical corporate practices.

There are various implementation references to the concept of organizational sustainability that are also being increasingly used in practice instead of the traditional terms and phrases such as CSR (corporate social responsibility) and corporate citizenship. When it comes to the ways in which the concept of sustainability can be perceived, there are two traditional schools of thought. The first is that it sustainability means continuing to meet targets on an ongoing basis, without jeopardising future requirements (Boudreau and Ramstad, 2005) and, the second, is that it simply means maintaining business operations. (Colbert and Kurucz, 2007)

However, another definition has emerged in recent years for what a *"sustainable organization"* really means, which encompasses the key aspects of the two traditional definitions referred to above. This new term often referred to as the *"triple bottom line"* involves not only commercial concerns, but also those of social and environmental. This term often goes, hand in hand, with the term PPP (People, Profit and Planet), the three components, which refer to the social, commercial and environmental aspects, respectively.

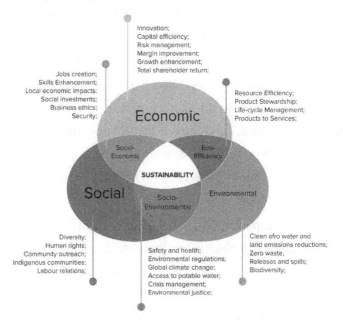

Fig. 1: Triple Bottom Line Model

This refinement of the understanding of organizational sustainability takes into account the fact that, although it is crucial to keep in mind the social and environmental concerns; organizations need to recognize the importance of focusing on generated bottom line profit. This also considers that for an organization to deliver long-term sustainability, it must balance its performance in terms of the equivalent environmental and social 'bottom lines' in order to deliver sustainable economic value to shareholders.

KEY SUSTAINABILITY DRIVERS

The Global Reporting Initiative (GRI) provides a framework for corporate sustainability reporting based on the input from a wide range of civil society organizations, labour groups, businesses, academics, and other experts. This reporting, in general, aims to standardize and quantify the environmental, social and governance costs and benefits derived from the activities of the reporting organizations accordingly. (Brown et al., 2009)

Today, the world's largest companies in all sectors and regions disclose their sustainability performance and impact to some degree. The KPMG Survey in 2013 concluded that almost all of the world's largest companies report on sustainability practices, with at least 62% of them in every sector producing a sustainability report.

Since the impact of sustainable-oriented policies often requires a business to change fundamental aspects of how it operates, this has the knock-on effect of making sustainability targets all the more difficult to achieve. Nevertheless, the trend of sustainable concepts being implemented into every level of organizational structures is showing no sign of abatement. A McKinsey survey on sustainability published in 2014 revealed that businesses no longer question its importance; although not all succeed in implementing it. It listed three primary reasons why organizations address sustainability as depicted in Figure 2.

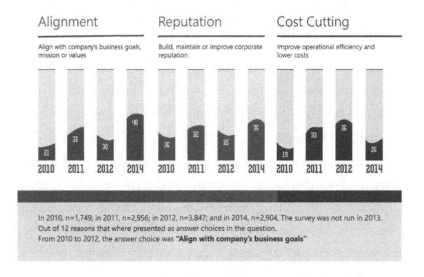

Fig. 2: Top 3 Reasons Organizations Address Sustainability
Source: Bonini and Görner (2014)

According to its proponents, it is widely argued that the benefits of adopting a sustainable approach to business are manifold. With this approach, it is claimed that in addition to the substantial tax advantages and possibilities of attracting talent, strategic and operational risks are reduced, recruitment expenses are cut, staff output is increased, waste and other material expenses are slashed, energy costs are diminished and, last but not least, revenues are multiplied.

The proper implementation of sustainability in an organization means that it must critically evaluate its stakeholder relations, internal operations and its effects on the environment from all perspectives. In order to achieve all this, the culture of the organization needs to be conducive to fully understanding these impacts when developing product lines, especially, regarding issues related to ecological concerns such as toxicity, the prudent use of energy sources and the reduction of material waste. This concern for the greater good inspires employees and promotes engagement in the innovation and creative processes, which in turn has the effect of enhancing productivity and widening profit margins.

New solutions that improve recycling and waste redirecting have the potential to not only reduce costs, but also to increase profits and streamline processes. In fact, a major reason why organizations seek to incorporate a sustainable approach is because they want to set themselves apart from their competitors. The six companies discussed below are just a few examples of this:

» The first is **P&G (Procter and Gamble)**. During the period 2007-2012, revenues of USD 15 billion were brought in by its energy saving and eco-friendly products. The company set a goal to have 30% of its total energy use coming from renewable sources and for its packaging to be cut by 20% by the year 2020. By embracing open innovation, the company is committed to meet these targets by using only renewable energy sources and maintaining its commitment to keep landfill waste to 0% of its total waste components.

» The second example that has a focus on sustainability is **Wal-Mart**, which has been successful in reducing its waste by just under two-thirds. Landfill waste is set to be reduced by over 17,000 tonnes each year. In 2009 alone, they recycled 590 tonnes of aluminium, 54,000 tonnes of plastic, just over 5000 tonnes of mixed paper and just over 2 million tonnes of cardboard. Annually, they expect to save around $20 million and prevent 17,000 tonnes of waste being sent to landfills.

» In response to their customer demand for them to improve their environmental impact, in 2013, **Siemens** managed to bring just over EUR 32 billion in revenue and cut its carbon emissions by just less than 400 million metric tons by launching a range of eco-friendly products and services, with a focus on environmental technology, energy efficiency and renewable energy.

» The fourth example of a company that has reduced the percentage of its products destined for landfill is the **Henkel Corporation** (formerly Dial Corporation) - manufacturer of personal care and household cleaning products. It was able to cut 40% of the amount of material required for containers and packaging as well as reduce the volume of water required to manufacture each product, by devising a strengthened cleanser. This resulted in the corporation's storage, distribution and shipping expenses being slashed.

» The fifth example is the Poland Spring, Deer Park and Arrowhead bottled water, which fall under the umbrella of **Nestlé Waters**. The companies have reduced the amount of plastic in their bottles by just under one-sixth, which has had the knock-on effect of not only cutting production and transportation expenses, but also reducing landfill waste.

» The sixth and last example presented here is that of **IBM**, which claims that it has been able to claw back between USD 1.50 – 2.00 for every USD 1 expended.

It is the well-developed ecological approach and zeitgeist in first world countries that make them conducive for organizations looking for ways to set themselves apart from the competition and improve their performance. Amenable legislation, a well suited market and helpful regulations also aid in this regard.

Developing countries can generate huge income from less expensive forms of social investment, often because the fundamental requirements of its citizenry are left unfulfilled. Moreover, there is a greater potential for these low-income countries to not only expand their clientele through social programs, but to also ramp up their endeavours to achieve sustainability. Although, the situation is clear for developed and less developed countries, it is the middle ground ones which present the greatest challenges to the implementation of sustainable practices. In countries such as Brazil or Russia, this concept still remains in its intermediate phase, which complicates the incorporation of these ideas into organizations and companies. This issue is further exacerbated by the fact that, for the Russian market in particular, the boat has been missed for some vanilla CSR approaches and it is too early in the day for others.

Let us now look at some of the barriers to the implementation of sustainability in more detail.

BARRIERS TO ORGANIZATIONAL SUSTAINABILITY

In Figure 3 below, McKinsey outlines some of the challenges presented when attempting to implement sustainable practices and gain value from them in organizations. These difficulties are often categorized into three generally agreed upon areas. The first is *"resource issues"*, which usually take the form of a lack of expertise, time and funding. The second is *'cultural/organizational issues'*, which generally mean a disconnect between the goals of the senior management and the organization operations. The third and final challenge is represented by *"informational issues"*, i.e. a general failure to accurately account for progress, as well as failures with regard to the issues at hand: a lack of actionable, detailed knowledge on actual performance; a lack of common measurement metrics; insufficient up-front financial payback information; as well as the inability to accurately measure and track results in real-time

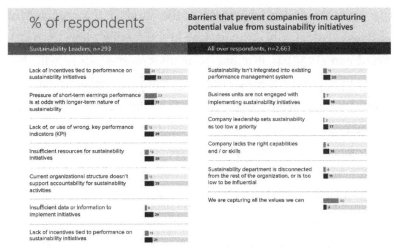

Fig. 3: Barriers to Sustainability in Organizations
Source: Bonini and Görner (2011)

In addition to the aforementioned, another key issue is that each organization is required to tailor and customize its sustainability plans to its own specific requirements and objectives. Any organization searching for a *"one-size-fits-all"* approach is likely to encounter difficulties further down the line.

The long-established practice of organizations to see success and failure purely in terms of their bottom line can make it difficult for them to meet their non-monetary targets, such as those often associated with sustainability. When attempting to apply the triple-bottom-line approach referred to earlier, the social and environmental considerations often receive far less focus than the commercial aspects. Taking this one step further, the lack of attention to the holistic aims of the organization could result in other aspects of its plan not being implemented. Too much focus, though, on the social and environmental issues, at the expense of the commercial concerns, for example, could also spell the end of a company at the hands of a more prudent and less ecologically aware player in the market (Jensen, 2001). Friedman (1970) is just one of many commentators who has long opined that a focus on ecological and societal concerns will always detract from the profit. Eccles et al. (2011) explain that this perspective identifies sustainability as "just another type of agency cost where managers receive private benefits from embedding environmental and social policies in the company, but doing so has negative financial implications."

It is argued that those organizations which are less principled and more willing to accept adverse ecological effects from the manufacture of their products are much better placed than their more ethical competitors to increase profits and growth. In a game of inches, where every inch adds up to give a winner and a loser on the market, these advantages include incurring lower costs, keeping wages down, entering into businesses which are morally dubious and attracting customers who are looking for the lowest possible price. Despite this, however, it is not the ethical concerns that drive the majority of organizations to implement sustainable concepts into their daily practice; it is the potential for profit. This is usually categorized as streamlining, which takes the form of reducing waste and the utility bills. However, this is an important foray into the world of sustainable practices. As a company gains a new reputation for being ecologically oriented, its own self-image as an environmentally-aware company often pressures it to maintain that positive public relations angle.

SUSTAINABILITY ASSESSMENT

When it comes to the assimilation of sustainable approaches into an organization, several stages are involved. In order to overcome potential issues, encourage good practice and maintain accurate records, it is crucial to know at which stage in the process the organization is. The following table depicts a three phase sustainability assessment approach proposed by Hitchcock (2015).

Table 1. The Three Phases of Organizational Sustainability

Phase	Sustainability 1.0: Eco-efficiencies and Risk Reduction	Sustainability 2.0: Competitive Advantage	Sustainability 3.0: Regeneration & Re-invention
Phase Description	» Apply eco-efficiencies to reduce costs. » Ascertain operational effects.	» Create new products and services and increase performance through the application of sustainability. » Implement sustainability into the commercial plan.	» Devote funds to commercial, environmental and societal concerns. » Evaluate the business approach. » Ascertain how to solve global issues.
Common measures	» Observe and isolate challenges to sustainability such as climate effects, employment issues, chemicals and toxicity. » Use procedural enhancements and eco-friendly construction approaches to cut waste and utility expenses.	» Encourage partners to adopt a more sustainable approach. » Incorporate an ego-friendly line into a range of services. » Ensure the periodic publication of sustainability reports. » Implement a metrics driven long-term sustainability strategy.	» Reassess the long-term vision of your business. » Find areas of environmental or social concern, which could take advantage of your main lines of business. » Work out a way to transition to the new plan.

Source: (Hitchcock, 2015)

SUSTAINABILITY 1.0: ECO-EFFICIENCIES AND RISK REDUCTION

The initial stage in the process, known as Sustainability 1.0, is delicate so requires careful management. No public broadcast of the organization's sustainability efforts should be made as yet because implementation is in its preliminary phase. Instead, the focus should be on the most pressing issues at hand, e.g. risk assessment, mitigating effects and dealing with any public fall out. This time also represents the ideal opportunity to make up the ground work required to be comfortable with going public, which involves checking with existing partners to see whether they have more sustainable alternatives available.

SUSTAINABILITY 2.0: COMPETITIVE ADVANTAGE

The second phase of organizational sustainability is termed "Sustainability 2.0". It is at this point that, instead of being more of an afterthought, the idea of sustainability develops into a core principle. Not only does it help to distinguish a company from its competition; it also represents a way of making a good impression on the market, increasing shareholder satisfaction and facilitating innovative solutions. The effects of this newly adopted approach soon begin to take over and the organization's objectives turn towards the social impact of their operations and whether an increased focus on sustainability could help penetrate new market sectors or demographics. The moniker of a "sustainable organization" is adopted wholeheartedly, despite the inherent contradiction of *this not being entirely possible* in a not fully conducive environment. When an organization is in the Sustainability 2.0 phase, it is at that point that a completely sustainable approach becomes the final aim. Considerations such as its commercial edge potentially lost including an eco-friendly and sustainable service begin to emerge as well as other deliberations.

SUSTAINABILITY 3.0: REGENERATION AND REINVENTION

The third phase, which represents the point at which the implementation of a sustainable framework has been more fully developed, incorporates a sharp shock as it becomes clear that a completely sustainable approach is incompatible with the core aspects of their commercial approach. It is at this relatively mature point in the proceedings that the organization's focus becomes directed towards not only providing products and services for their customers, but also a societal or environmental hurdle of responsibility that they are well placed to overcome.

360 ORGANIZATIONAL SUSTAINABILITY

It is tempting for most companies to narrow their efforts for achieving sustainability to the way they manage their resources — for better or worse. There can be no doubt that this represents a central theme for these endeavours, but it would be a critical mistake to focus solely on this area. The concept of sustainability is multi-faceted and not limited to just one or two factors. The issue needs to be approached from multiple points of view in order to ensure its implementation is at its most effective. The concept needs to be broken down into four key areas in order to ascertain progress: the first factor that requires evaluation is the **global environment** (planet's biosphere). The second is more local and relates to **societal and cultural concerns** (community/society/ethno-sphere). The third is more local still and refers to the organization's **personnel, partners, shareholders and customers** (all stakeholders in the company). The fourth, and perhaps the most crucial (the organization itself), is the **operations, values and goals of the company** or institution - the most local aspect to consider. All of these four areas are interdependent. Failing in one would eventually result in an adverse impact on all the others. When taking the last of the four areas in isolation, the company or the institution itself, the company cannot be said to be sustainable in the truest and most holistic sense of the word; if any of the other three areas are unsustainable in some way.

Any management board must also adhere to some key principles in order to ensure this holistic approach is being implemented.

1. Staff trained and utilized sustainably.

2. Staff have sustainable lives; work-life balance formula in an organization so an appropriate balance is struck for their staff in terms of time spent in and out of work.

3. Local, national or global communities which the organization is part of are also sustainable in their approaches.

4. Attaining ecological neutrality in operations with all stakeholders (and suppliers, distributors etc).

5. Achieving growth and generating economic value.

In order for all of the above to be the case; it is vital that wholesale changes are made to the way in which organizations are perceived, led and run by senior management staff.

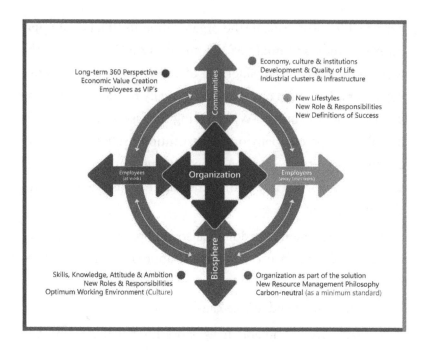

Fig. The 360 Organizational Sustainability Model
Source: (Hollingworth, 2009)

BUILDING A SUSTAINABLE ORGANIZATION

The right mentality and a certain level of doggedness are required on the part of any organization in order to complete a sustainability plan. To begin with, it is important that a holistic approach is taken. Rather than focusing on specific areas, which may appear more manageable and realistic to take on, the benefits that can be gained from well thought out and rational wholesale companywide changes provide the opportunity for management to make intelligent, informed decisions that will generate the most significant results.

The next aspect to take into consideration is the requirement for the sustainability strategy to be well organised and rolled out gradually, giving time for adjustments to be made and consolidated. Since the level of sophistication required for the wholesale implementation of a strategy of this kind is high, a careful and considered step-by-step approach that takes account of the priority issues should be adopted.

The third aspect is the importance of return on investment (ROI). Only with a standard metric can those parts of the organization, which are most in need be properly evaluated. In this way, the most potentially profitable returns can also be identified, thereby, increasing the overall health of the organization. When resources are limited, this represents the best way to ensure that the greatest return is gained from the minimum effort invested.

With the advent of technology, it has now become far easier to gather, analyze and deliver enterprise-wide data to ascertain where the most attractive options for improvement lie. This concept is typically embodied in the form of an automated system for the collection of data, which allows for trends and movements in the company's performance to be tracked effectively and applied with confidence. Thus, the human decision making factor is also minimized, with the cold and rational machine-based decision making process coming to the fore instead, which therefore, generates better results for the organization.

CONDUCT TO MAINTAIN GROWTH

Here, eleven factors must be taken into consideration, which need to be in place, prior to any organization's being in a position to develop and maintain the strong progress that it has made in achieving total sustainability.

1. BUILDING THE TALENT ARMY

Getting the best expertise and talent available is vital in order for an organization to continue to expand and maintain the progress that it has made. Unless this is in place, tail offs in performance are likely. As any good manager will confirm, the organisation's most important asset is its staff, and this is not just a throwaway line. The people in any organization are fundamental to its continued success and growth. As an organization develops, it is natural that its personnel will also need to change. This growth can either be organic or could require attrition or other changes to allow the organizational and people aspects of the organization to remain in synch. This also requires organizations to be introspective and ask themselves some difficult questions to ascertain whether their current personnel are best suited to moving the organization forward in its chosen sustainable direction or not.

2. MAXIMIZING OPERATIONAL EFFICIENCIES

Refinements to productivity processes serve to reduce expenses and to implement a culture that is focused on keeping these to a minimum, continuously striving for new and innovative ways to improve the way it interacts on a department or sectional level internally, as well as improving its channels of communication. This ensures that the 'profit' aspect of the three bottom line principles is dealt with effectively. If the organizational culture in place is well thought out and conducive to the organization's sustainable and efficiency goals, then it is likely that the personnel will implement and follow the processes that best meet this objective. We are judged by the company we keep and, whether we admit it or not, we are driven by its people — for better or for worse.

3. DEVELOPING AN ENTREPRENEUR MENTALITY

The third key factor that needs to be in place is a go-getting, entrepreneurial attitude that has been adopted by the management team. In order to achieve and maintain the organization's sustainable objectives, the experience of the management team must come to the fore as it can allow the organization to take advantage of circumstances that their less experienced colleagues might miss.

4. SOUND DECISION MAKING

Leaders and managers are in place to deal with issues, which is where the 'buck' stops. This requires them to have the courage to deal with issues firmly and prudently. The way these issues are dealt with is crucial in determining the organization's short- and long-term sustainability. In order to respond best to these issues as and when they arise, it is important to have clear processes regarding the organization's operation in place, which would enable it to make the best decisions in the sometimes limited time available. If the opposite is the case, and one works with knee-jerk reactions to unforeseen and unplanned problems; then it becomes increasingly challenging to implement a truly sustainable approach. A measured, rational and carefully considered style is vital in order to ensure that the progress made until that time is continued over the long term.

5. GREAT LEADERSHIP

The fifth key requirement that needs to be in place is that the leadership team needs to be successful and have a wealth of experience to call upon as it creates an impression of security and safety – 'the gravitas' that comes hand in hand with the best management teams transmits to the rest of the staff, who feel confident that their calmness under pressure, calculated decisions and measured long-term projections will bring the organization's sustainable-oriented objectives to fruition.

6. THINKING LONG TERM

The sixth key factor is the need for society to turn from looking solely at its immediate concerns to taking a more long-term and rational perspective on issues and, perhaps more importantly, the funds available for their resolution. This also applies to organizations, which need to ensure that their stakeholders are also similarly focused on objectives of this nature. There are certain industries in which this problem is more prominent, the building trade being one. The short-term appeal of cutting costs by constructing environmentally unfriendly buildings can often trump the long-term benefits of opting for the environmentally friendly option. If the outlook adopted was more long-term, the benefits would be more apparent.

7. COMMUNICATING DIFFERENTLY

A variety of different people are interested in becoming part of sustainable initiatives — these range from students fresh out of university to business people looking for a return on investment. Therefore, any dealings with these different groups need to be tailored to their interests and needs. Approaches need to be refined so that a one-size-fits-all philosophy would be found wanting.

8. EMBEDDING SUSTAINABILITY THROUGHOUT THE ORGANIZATION

The eighth key principle is that a piecemeal approach is going to be counterproductive. The very best results have always been gained from a holistic, top-down implementation as opposed to ad hoc attempts at resolving efficiency issues. It is only when a sustainable mentality permeates all levels of a company or an institution that it can actually be effective.

9. IMPROVING MANAGEMENT SKILLS

In any organization, a constant challenge is trying to work out how experience and expertise can be transferred to other employees. However, if the management team in place is sufficiently able, this task can become less onerous and challenging.

10. RISK TAKING

The tenth key principle that needs to be in place is that risks must be taken. Taking the safe option all the time is guaranteed to stifle invention and innovation, which are prerequisites for maintaining growth. Thus, this often requires a change in mentality. In a rapidly changing market, an inability to generate new solutions and paradigms because of a reluctance to take a chance can sound the death knell for any pretensions of becoming a truly sustainable organization. As the popular saying goes, "there is no 'I' in 'TEAM'" and that could not be more true when it comes to implementing a sustainable approach in any organization. It is vital that everyone has everyone else's best interests at heart, with the long-term health and prosperity of the organization taking centre stage. Only together can these objectives become reality.

Some of the risks that need to be taken may involve investing in obscure or fledgling forms of technology, and sometimes at an almost prohibitively high cost. It is, of course, far easier to afford popular mainstream options that are less sustainable, but at what actual cost to the organization? This is a key question to consider.

11. DISRUPT OLD BUSINESS MODELS

Although the proverb "if it ain't broke, don't fix it" indeed has some merit, the attainment of sustainable operations is only possible if old ways of thinking are challenged and improved upon — this is the eleventh and final principle. Where no improvements can be made, these processes should be further developed and supported. It is only possible to remain constantly one step ahead of the competition when an organization has managed to fully incorporate sustainability into its ethos. This requires bravery on the part of its management team, and having the gumption to embrace options that have been ignored by the market. This culture is self-sustaining in that it can generate huge opportunities for innovation and employee morale.

CONCLUSION

It is thus clear that the holistic nature of an organizational sustainability approach is what allows an organization to focus on each and every aspect of its commercial, cultural and societal considerations. This idea has become increasingly popular over the last ten years or so. The benefits are obvious, with customers, staff and other stakeholders becoming more valuable to the business. Organizations search for ways in which to streamline, enhance marketing and hiring and increase their access to sustainable resources, but through the medium of sustainable and ecologically friendly methods. These have the consequential effect of driving innovation and new approaches to product lines as well as providing improved organizational efficacy. When following this principle, organizations are better placed to meet their long-term targets while addressing their immediate challenges. There can now be little doubt. The impact of sustainability on all our lives, not to mention the impact of the leading organizations throughout the globe, is here to stay and becoming steadily entrenched. Time and tide, indeed, wait for no man.

REFERENCES

Jensen, M. (2001). Value Maximization, Stakeholder Theory and the Corporate Objective Function. Journal of Applied Corporate Finance 14(3), 8–21.

Eccles, R.G., Ioannou, I. and Serafeim, G. (2011). The Impact of Corporate Sustainability on Organizational Processes and Performance, [Online]. Harvard Business School Working Paper Series 12-035 (14 November). Retrieved from: http://hbswk.hbs.edu/item/the-impact-of-corporate-sustainability-on-organizational-process-and-performance

Friedman, M. (1970). The Social Responsibility of Business is to Increase Its Profits. New York Times Magazine, 13 Sept., 32 (33): 122-126.

Colbert, B. A. & Kurucz, E. C. (2007). Three Conceptions of Triple Bottom Line Business Sustainability and The Role of HRM. Human Resource Planning, 30(1): 21-29.

Boudreau, J. and Ramstad, P. (2005). Talentship, Talent Segmentation, and Sustainability: A new HR decision science paradigm for a new strategy definition. Human Resource Management, 44(2), 129-136.

Bonini, S. and Görner, S. (2014). Sustainability's Strategic Worth: McKinsey Global Survey Results, [Online]. New York: Mckinsey & Company. Retrieved from: http://www.mckinsey.com/business-functions/sustainability-and-resource-productivity/our-insights/sustainabilitys-strategic-worth-mckinsey-global-survey-results

Bonini, S. and Görner, S. (2011). The Business of Sustainability: McKinsey Global Survey Results, [Online]. New York: Mckinsey & Company. Retrieved from: http://www.mckinsey.com/business-functions/sustainability-and-resource-productivity/our-insights/the-business-of-sustainability-mckinsey-global-survey-results

Hollingworth, M. (2009). Building 360 Organizational Sustainability, [Online]. IVEY Business Journal, 73(6), 2. Retrieved from: http://iveybusinessjournal.com/publication/building-360-organizational-sustainability/

Fust, S.F. and Walker, L.L. (2007). Corporate Sustainability Initiatives: The Next TQM? Understanding Emerging Corporate Sustainability Practices Through The Lens of Total Quality Management, [Online]. White Paper Korn/Ferry International. Retrieved from: http://www.kornferry.com/institute/download/view/id/16762/aid/207.

KPMG (2011). Corporate Sustainability: A Progress Report, [Online]. KPMG International and Economist Intelligence Unit. Retrieved from: https://www.kpmg.com/Global/en/IssuesAndInsights/ArticlesPublications/Documents/corporate-sustainability-v2.pdf

Brown, H. S., Jong, M. d. and Lessidrenska, T. (2009). The Rise of the Global Reporting Initiative: A Case of Institutional Entrepreneurship, Environmental Politics, 18 (2), 182 - 200.

Professor **Ali M. Al-Khouri** is the vice Chairman of the Arab Federation for E-Commerce, a technical arm of the Arab Economic Unity Council, League of Arab States. He is also working as a Director-General in UAE Ministry of Interior.

He has more than 100 publications from books and peer reviewed journal articles, and participated in the development of many international reports for United Nations, World Economic Forum, and European Commission. He has been honored with tens of local and international awards for his contributions to practice and body of knowledge.

Dr. Al-Khouri is a professor and fellow of the British Institute for Technology in London. He is also a member of many teaching faculties in British Universities. He is also a member of several academic committees, and also as an advisor to EU, UN, and WEF.

JESSICA LORUSSO

A KEY TO SALES SUCCESS

**What is the one difference between a successful
business and failed business?**

SALES PERSISTENCE

Again and again, sales persistence has proven the difference between success and failure in sales growth. Historically there are numerous examples of people who though hopelessness and impassable obstacles have overcome those many sales challenges to obtain tremendous business success.

Today there are some products and services that we would not be using or be very different if it was not for the patience and persistence of the people creating them.

DO YOU SEE A LIGHT BULB IN THE ROOM?

Thomas Edison filed his first patent application not for a light bulb design but for the "Improvement in Electric Lights." On October 14, 1878, after many test designs and many test materials, Edison improved on his initial light bulb design.

"Genius is one percent inspiration and ninety-nine
percent perspiration"

Thomas Edision

The next U.S. patent for Thomas Edison's continuous improved light bulb design was in November of 1879. After much more improvements, mistakes and downright failed attempts, along with many variations on materials used, the discovery of the carbonized bamboo filament marked the first step of commercially manufactured light bulbs. In 1880, the Edison Electric Light Company began selling their newest improved light bulb to consumers.

> "I have not failed. I've just found 10,000 ways that won't work."
>
> Thomas Edison

NO ONE WILL MAKE MONEY SELLING JUST CHICKEN IN A RESTAURANT.

Colonel Harland Sanders at the age of 65 took his saving and his monthly social security cheque of $105 to begin to franchise his chicken recipe and concept to what we now call KFC. With the belief that restaurant owners would clamor at the business concept and fried chicken recipe, the restaurant owners would see an increase in sales. After driving around the country sleeping in his car, he knocked on 1009 doors and said "I've got a great chicken recipe and I think if you use it, it will increase your sales." Of those 1009 potential restaurant owners all of them said "NO." To sell the first "Kentucy Fried Chicken" franchise is took Colonel Harland Sanders to ask his famous question to potential restaurant owners 1010 times.

"One has to remember that every failure can be a
stepping-stone to something better…"

Colonel Harland Sanders

THERE IS NO MONEY IN CHILDREN'S BOOKS.

"It is impossible to live without failing at something,
unless you live so cautiously that you might as well not
have lived at all - in which case, you fail by default."

J.K. Rowling

After twelve different publishers rejected J.K Rowling's
manuscript she was accepted by Barry Cunningham from
Bloomsbury Publishing. He was quoted in saying that "she
would never make any money from her book." JK Rowling is a modern "rags to riches story", in just five years her
life has changed from practically penniless and on welfare
to multi-millionaire with sales in excess of £238 million.
Thomas Edison, Colonel Harland Sanders and JK Rowling all
inspire us to go after our ambitions and obtain our targets. They
give us hope to that our dreams are possible. Sometimes we
forget that your ultimate prize comes at a cost. The cost may
be time, money or resources or a combination of two or three.
When we do not want to pay the cost for our success, failure
comes into play.

PERSISTENCE AND DETERMINATION

GET THROUGH IT.

Your sales goals are achievable when you apply determination and persistence. Even after investing a large amount of energy and resources into your venture, more often than not people give up and quit. It is very possible that they may almost complete their project, however as soon as it gets to be a challenge and it is not enjoyable the decision is to quit. Can you imagine if Thomas Edison said at the 9,999 light bulb design "that's enough this will never work" the light bulb would not look like it does today. Remember your frustration is in the moment and it will pass.

TAKE THE T OUT OF CAN'T

Persistence and determination requires an attitude vaccination. Yes we need to cultivate a positive attitude toward persistence. We also need to inoculate ourselves from other people. These other people are negative towards your endeavor and will tell you that whatever you are doing it can't be done. Stop the influence of the naysayers. They tell you that you are wasting your time, money and/or resources on your dream. Then you will start to thinking that the naysayers are correct. At this point you will start to convince yourself that you must stop your ambition goals and more on to less risk but with no ultimate prize. Unless you win the lottery, you must do the work necessary and use persistence and determination to reach your sales targets. The second negative influence is the people who care. They genuinely care for you and do not want you hurt or they are hurt by the sacrifice you must make to achieve your targets. The danger is that these caring people will ask you to stop or put in less effort into your endeavor or not pursue your dreams at all. You must be determined, do not listen to naysayers whomever they are friend or foe. Forge ahead with your plan of action and ultimate success.

PERSISTENCE AND COURAGE

"Keep going and get through it my goal is just ahead."
44% of salespeople give up after one follow-up.
[Source: Scripted]

It is troubling that, 44% of salespeople give up after one follow-up. When you look at how many times that our successful inventor, entrepreneur and writer needed to make improvements on a design or contact for sales success you realize that you are not giving the sales process a fair opportunity. Getting past the gatekeeper takes courage and is one of the challenges many sales professionals face in their careers. In fact knowing how to handle the gatekeeper is an important factor to your success.

It is sad that many sales professionals dread the gatekeeper who may be the receptionist or an administrative assistant. These gatekeepers put you through a process called screening, where they must assess whether your call is useful enough to connect with your potential buyer. Believe it or not the process is a lot of pressure for them. Your call could be the best opportunity for the company however he or she does not know that. What if he or she is wrong and your offering is not what the potential buyer perceives as necessary. From the superior's point of view the gatekeeper is not doing his or her job in preventing unnecessary distractions. The superior then sees the gatekeeper in a negative light. In turn the gatekeeper then doesn't put any calls through.

You may be asked to write or email instead. Here is a 2016 sales statistic about email opens from Tellwise **"An average buyer gets 100+ emails a day, opens just 23%, and clicks on just 2% of them"**. With a 2% email click rate your email probably will not get viewed. The solution is to change your mindset of the gatekeeper to initial decision maker. He or she has to power to press the start button or to press the delete button on your interaction with that person or people you need to reach in the organization. Make this initial decision maker feel important, feel appreciated and feel respected. You want the initial decision maker to have a positive attitude towards you. More importantly the initial decision maker must perceive you as "worth the risk" to put your through to the potential buyer. It may take a few interactions with the initial decision maker to get to the next level decision maker. Just like a base ball game you can make a home run if you are not willing to run to first base.

PERSISTENCE AND PATIENCE

63% of people requesting information on your company today will not purchase for at least three months – and 20% will take more than 12 months to buy.

[Source: Marketing Donut]

People buy when they are ready to buy. It may take a few days or it could take years to actualize. New projects take time to develop, buyers must process the information and prepare to execute then finally implement that project. Not being available to them when they need you puts you at a large disadvantage. It is paramount that you schedule regular contact using various methods with them. Staying in your potential buyer's radar will help you to remain top of mind.

PERSISTENCE AND NURTURE

80% of sales require 5 follow-up phone calls after the meeting.

[Source: The Marketing Donut]

It takes time to cultivate and nurture relationships to build trust and credibility between your potential buyer and your organization. You must convince the prospective buyer that you and your company are the best option for him/her. When you are not available or not in the right place at the right time, that buyer will look for the same product or services elsewhere. The situation is harmful to your bottom line when you have already prepared that potential buyer and did most of the ground work for that sale. Now that sale is going to the competing business.

PERSISTENCE AND DISCOVERY

70% of people make purchasing decisions to solve problems. 30% make decisions to gain something.

[Source: Impact Communications]

Take the time to understand your potential buyers' needs and desires. Most sales professional do not have a systematic method of questioning and understanding what the needs and desires of the potential buyer is. Some sales professionals have the mindset that that their careers are just glorified orders takers.

Loss Aversion is a theory that states people fear loss and tend to avoid losing something, rather than gaining something for example losing items it is more powerful than finding an object. Be persistent in your fact finding mission of what is important to the potential buyer.

Ask questions about:

» What will happen if they do not take action?.

» How will the situation affect them?

» Why do they need to solve their concern?

A professional sales person understands that for continued sales success and to nurture a long term relationships solving potential buyer's problems is a more impactful sales strategy.

PERSISTENCE AND DISCIPLINE

In 2007 it took an average of 3.68 cold call attempts to reach a prospect. Today it takes 8 attempts.

[Source: TeleNet and Ovation Sales Group]

With so many opportunities for potential buyers to receive information it seems common place for many potential buyers to just delete our emails or do not return our calls when we leave a message. After we call to follow up the potential buyer will tell us they did not receive the information or message. . The biggest draw on people energy is their time. The bigger challenge for the sales professions is that your potential buyers do not have enough time and energy to attend to adequately and give attention to everything they see, hear and read and most of it gets processed in the trash bin. The amount of cold calls it takes to reach a potential buyer is now increasing and will continue to get worse. Recently I read that in 2016 it now takes 18 cold calls to get a response from a single potential buyer.

It takes 18 dials to connect with a single buyer

(Source: ttp://blog.hubspot.com/sales/surprising-statistics-on-sales-prospecting-that-will-change-the-way-you-look-at-cold-calling-infographic) (source: TOPO)

If you look at a new statistics the process of cold calling potential buyers is becoming more challenging then every before. In fact because of the increased amount of daily cold calls those potential buyers are tougher to communicate with.

For a moment, put yourself in the potential buyer's shoes. What is the situation that the potential buyer is in? Could he or she be working on a deadline? Maybe they are reacting to a catastrophe that just happened. Maybe his or her ego is leading their decision and their mindset is that they are much too important to talk to the likes of you. Whatever the situation is that, you are perceived as "no priority status." The act of persistence will help you cut through the cold call fog. Equally as important you must have the discipline to make the nineteenth cold call to get the attention you are asking for.

PERSISTENCE AND COOPERATION

Only 11% of salespeople ask clients for referrals, although 91% of clients are open to provide referral.

[Source: Dale Carnegie]

Why is "Word of Mouth" advertising a more powerful form of advertising compared to any other forms of adverting? The answer is TRUST. Simply put word of mouth advertising is so effective, because the potential buyer has a longer term relationship and will trust the recommendation from that person rather than a stranger. In fact 92% of people will trust recommendations from friends according to Nielsen Global Trust In Adversting Survey.

There is great potential business growth, in utilizing a referral strategy. The problem is that most sales people do not ask for referrals from there happy loyal clients and most business do not have a referral system in place. Did you know that **73% of executives prefer to work with sales professionals referred by someone they know (IDC)**

Decide who are your loyal customers? Those loyal customers are happy to refer someone who would need your service. Most people are happy to help. Even a person who does not uses your products and services will know someone who does. To be successful with a referral strategy, implement the act of persistence to continually ask for the referrals. If you can ask for a sale then there is no excuse not to ask for a referral. Think of it as an extension of closing the deal.

PERSISTENCE AND PURPOSE

"Like a poor marksman you keep…missing…the target. Kaaahhhnnn!!!"

- Admiral James T. Kirk

You can't have persistence if you don't know what you want. There must be a purpose and a plan to actively work towards. Once you have decided what you want create a plan to get there. Start with the end in mind. Decide what actions are required to get your results. Don't get overwhelmed by the plan. Break your plan down into smaller tasks and schedule them with deadlines to keep you moving forward. If the plan is not giving you the results you wanted this is a clear indication that you must readjust. Continuously improve helps you see your result faster. Always, measure your results. If you don't know if you are working towards, you cannot apply continuous improvement and if is more difficult to see results.

Is a task a priority? Decide if any task that is part of your plan, a priority? If the task has nothing to do with your plan then you cannot participate in it. You have two choices delegate or ignore it. Doing tasks that do not coincide with your purpose is a great way to derail your success. Use persistence to continuously act and improve on your goals and plans. **"If you fail to plan, you are planning to fail",** rumored to be said by Benjamin Franklin.

PERSISTENCE AND FAILURE

Success consists of going from failure to failure without
loss of enthusiasm.

Winston Churchill

Richard Branson is one of the UK's highest profile billionaires. Richard Branson made his fortune with the Virgin Group that is made up of 400 companies. He equates his business success to is attitude towards failure and his companies, "Some business opportunities where fruitful and some just flatten out." Virgin Coke is one example of one of his business failure but that did not stop him because Richard Branson always say "Business opportunities are like buses, there's always another one coming."

Do not be embarrassed by your failures, learn from them
and start again.

Richard Branson.

The best time to cold call is 4:00-5:00pm. The second best time is 8:00-10:00am. The worst times are 11:00am and 2:00pm.(Source: InsideSales.com and Kellogg School of Business 3)

Cultivate a good telephone manner. Learn proper telephone etiquette. You only have one chance to make a first impression. After you have reached the potential buyer and you make etiquette blunder even if it is innocent, you may have lost a chance to sell and you did not even know it. The challenge with telephone conversations is that you cannot use facial expressions or body language to help you enforce your message. The one thing that you have is your voice. More importantly we can only convey the importance of our offer with the <u>tone</u> of your voice. When we do get through on the telephone to a potential buyer the key to an effective telephone conversation is what we say and how we deliver that message. The solution is to use energy and feeling.

PERSISTENCE AND KNOWLEDGE

"By seeking and blundering we learn."

Johann Wolfgang von Goethe

Failure does not mean defeat. With failure there are four opportunities. The first is experience. Failure gives us a deeper understanding of what happened and helps us find the meaning and the lesson from that failure. The second opportunity is knowledge. Once you have learnt the lessons in the failure, you can adopt continuous improvement to the situation. The next time that it happens your will be much more prepared. The third opportunity is resiliency. The rate you take and the energy need to bounce back from your failure. With every failure there is a loss. The loss could be emotional or loss of money, time or resources. You must pay these loses first before you can figuratively say "You are back on your feet." Growth is the last opportunity. If we allow ourselves we can develop more strength from the failure. Use persistence to bounce back and learn from your failure and you will continue to experience and develop strategies that will work and propel you forward to the next success or business opportunity.

PERSISTENCE AND RESPONSIBILITY

When you consider that 80% of prospects say "no" four times before they say "yes", the inference is that 8% of sales people are getting 80% of the sales.

(Source: Markeing Donut)

Take 100% responsibility for the action of persistence in your professional life. You are the only person who creates the actions and results in your life. You can choose to great success or rock bottom failure. You are in charge of your experience.

The average sales person only makes 2 attempts to reach a prospect.

[Source: Sirius Decisions]

If you look at the data, do not get discouraged by a potential buyer's "No" response because the No is what can be called a "Not Now" response. Calling a potential buyer until he or she answers the phone is a better strategy than after the second voicemail you decide to let it go. Being responsible in saying it's my duty to keep going and look for potential buyers to help, is a must better strategy than just giving up. At the first sign of any obstacles or naysayers don't make any excuses to why you are giving up. Blaming the circumstances or blaming others for your results and your experiences will only allow for failure.

Take control and take responsibility for all your actions use persistence to set higher standards for yourself. Only you can choose to be, a successful sales professional.

PERSISTENCE AND SUCCESS

> Nothing in this world can take the place of
> persistence. Talent will not: nothing is more common
> than unsuccessful men with talent. Genius will not;
> unrewarded genius is almost a proverb. Education will
> not: the world is full of educated derelicts. Persistence
> and determination alone are omnipotent.
>
> Calvin Coolidge (Source: http://www.brainyquote.com/
> quotes/quotes/c/calvincool414555.html)

Persistence is one of the most important elements that will help you to be a successful sales professional. A project or opportunity will not come to fruition if persistence is not applied. Persistence is one of the qualities of high achievers. High achievers are successful because they commit to a project and work through any challenges until that project is completed.

Remember when you were learning to walk. We made every attempt to walk and fell down a lot of time we cried and may even got a few bumps and bruises. That was OK. We were learning. We had to walk because we would be so much more mobile and then have more opportunities to do things. We didn't stop at the first sign of trouble. We made mistakes but we corrected them and continued on with our improved method. If we got hurt well that's what kisses and Band-Aids are for. We persisted and we succeeded.

Instead of looking at the negative side to our sales calls, why not apply our childhood walking attitude to our sales success. Persistence is the quality of continually doing the tasks necessary despite of any challenges ahead. Potential buyers will test you and people close to you will tell you to "Just give up." The outstanding prize comes when your refuse to give in. You will be amazed after all your hard work that you came out the other side the just like a CHAMPION.

SOURCES:

https://en.wikipedia.org/wiki/Colonel_Sanders

http://www.bulbs.com/learning/history.aspx

http://www.scotsman.com/lifestyle/that-magical-day-when-barry-met-harry-1-1068487

https://en.wikipedia.org/wiki/J._K._Rowling

https://en.wikipedia.org/wiki/Loss_aversion

https://en.wikipedia.org/wiki/Richard_Branson

Jessica LoRusso's MISSION is to teach entrepreneurs to build their dream business that works.

She knows that applying efficiency principles in your brand, your sales, & marketing, your finance, your client experience and your team is the cement that strengthens your business. Jessica helps to take the stress out of entrepreneurship and helps you move from chaos to calm.

Jessica is an accomplished business director with expertise in overseeing sales, marketing, training, customer service and business operations with 16 years in establishing and growing businesses to become market leaders. Skilled in strategy and business system development she helps structure businesses to thrive.

Jessica sold her thriving business Zealous MediSpa in November 2014 to pursue her strength and passion of innovative business systems strategy and showing others how she made a million dollars in just one year. Her love and expertise in developing and executing strategic business plans has shaped her new company Powered by Jessica for the purpose of helping entrepreneurs thrive in their businesses.

Finalist for Manitoba Women Entrepreneur of the Year Award (Building Business and Excellence in Service Categories) for three consecutive years. Winner of Rookie of the Year, Winnipeg Chamber of Commerce.

Jessica is powered by three values that she practices every day –Enthusiasm, Generosity, and Excellence.

TERRI LEVINE

TURBOCHARGE YOUR BUSINESS AND INCOME

If you own any type of business, you are always looking to grow your revenues and profits. Often, business owners spend a lot of time, and money, and energy working to make their companies more profitable. Sadly, many business owners don't have the right strategies that are proven to actually increase their revenues and profits. They waste a lot of time, money, and other resources.

Imagine your business doubling or tripling its revenues and profits. How does that make you feel? What will happen in your business and your life as a result of the increase in revenue and profits? Maybe with more income you can take a major vacation or pay for private school or buy a new home... maybe you can have less stress, work fewer hours, spend more time working out and being more present with your family, or attending church or serving your community.

My passion, as a business consultant and Chief Heartrepreneur™, is to help business owners turbocharge their revenue and their profits and to also show them how to actually working less and enjoy their lives more.

There are many ways to get your revenues and profits increased. I focus only on the ways that are authentic and that align with who you are in the world of business and that work with your own internal guidance system. I mentor my clients, who are business owners, just like you, to grow their business-es using reverse marketing and reverse selling and I share with them 300 low and no cost ways to market that drive their prospects right to them. Reverse marketing is the process of having ideal prospects come to you. Ideal prospects call you, fill out contact forms on your website, they come to your place of business, and they then ask to buy your products and services. This is very different than traditional sales and marketing which has a lot of cost, takes a lot of time and then has you pushing, manipulating, overcoming objections, marketing AT people and selling TO people.

Would you like to know how you can turbocharge your business, increasing your revenues and profits and put in place the reverse marketing and selling concepts?

Ok, here we go. I will reveal the turbocharge formula that I share with clients of the Heartrepreneur™ Network and then mentor clients to implement. You can join the Heartrepreneur™ Network here to find out more: http://heartrepreneur.com/the-heartrepreneur-network/

Get ready to rocket your business and explode your revenue and profits!

THE TURBOCHARGE FORMULA

STEP ONE - IDEAL CUSTOMERS

The first step in the formula is to know exactly who your ideal customer really is. Often, business owners tell me they know this and when I ask them to describe this customer the picture isn't clear. I want you to have an exact customer in mind. Maybe one you have already had purchase your products or services or one that you really want to have as a customer. Get clear what about them is ideal. They are the ONLY customers you want to attract with reverse marketing. If you aren't very clear you will attract less than ideal prospects and then you either will have a lot of non-buyers taking up your time or you will have buyers who have complaints or cause problems.

ACTION:

Write down every specific characteristic of your ideal customer. Include every small detail you can think of and what makes them perfect.

STEP TWO: LOCATION

Think about where your ideal customers are hanging out. Are they watching YouTube Videos, are they members of clubs or organizations, do they read certain magazines or journals, do they attend specific conferences or conventions?

ACTION:

Write a list of all the things they do, places they go, media that engage with, and people they hang out with. Make certain you include on-line and off-line activities.

STEP THREE: BIGGEST BENEFIT

Make certain you are clear on the number one thing that keeps your ideal customers up at night. What is the result they want to achieve? The goal they want to accomplish or the problem they want to solve. People make purchases that are based on solving their biggest problem or attaining their biggest goal. How does what you are selling do that for your ideal customers?

ACTION:

Don't guess what the biggest problems or goals are. Go and ask at least 5 prior customers and if you are new in business and don't have 5 customers, go do a survey of prospects on Facebook, or with www.surveymonkey.com or with Google Forms. Be certain you have identified the biggest problem or results.

STEP FOUR: CORE UNIQUE POSITIONING STATEMENT

Create a Core Unique Positioning Statement. This is a statement that tells in one short sentence how you are the one and ONLY company who can solve this specific problem for this specific audience. If you can add a guarantee, even better. This is not your unique selling proposition or elevator pitch. This is a statement used in reverse marketing to bring ideal customers to you.

ACTION:

Write your Core Unique Positioning Statement following this formula:

I am/we are the ONLY (now state what you do - example: health and wellness company) that helps (now state who your ideal target customer is - example: women who have trouble sleeping) to (now state the obstacle they will overcome or goal they will achieve - example: quickly fall and stay asleep with all natural ingredients) (and if possible end with the word guaranteed).

Putting this together a Core Unique Positioning for this company would be: We are the ONLY health and wellness company that helps women who have trouble sleeping to quickly fall and stay asleep with all natural ingredients - guaranteed.

STEP FIVE: MAGNETIZE

Now, you get this statement out there using the list from action step number two. You might use Facebook ads, attend networking events, have a booth at a conference, etc. This statement works to magnetize your ideal customers right to you.

ACTION:

Create a list of your top five places to begin sharing your Core Unique Positioning Statement. In addition, use this statement on your email signature file, letterhead, business cards, social media profiles, website, blogs, etc. This is how you integrate this statement into your marketing.

STEP SIX: FREE SAMPLE

Make it easy for people to contact you after they hear this statement because if it resonates you want to give them a free sample or free trial - no strings attached. You might have them get a free demonstration, free sample, free audio, free book, free session, free trial size package, etc.

ACTION:

Decide what you will give away for your free, no strings attached sample and offer it everywhere you can, both on-line and off-line.

STEP SEVEN: OFFER

When your ideal customers take you up on the free samples you simply offer them your products or services that can benefit them. You don't need to convince them, sell them, manipulate them or overcome objections.

ACTION:

Your reverse sale sounds like this:

How did you like the free massage? Of course, that is only a taste of how we can de-stress you and aid your body to get healthier while your mind gets calmer. Would you like to have a longer massage and experience our full service?

NO NEED TO SELL - EVER AGAIN

With this formula you have attracted only ideal customers using low and no cost marketing and brought them right to you, using reverse marketing. Once they are identified you have provided them a free taste of your products or services and now all you do is ask them if they want more of your products and services. If they say 'yes', great. you have a sale. If they say 'no', great. You gave a sample away and nothing more.

The turbocharge formula does bring more ideal customers while greatly reducing your time, energy, financial expense and marketing frustrations. The formula also allows sales to happen naturally and authentically and uses heart-to-heart, conscious and authentic selling. This is how to increase your revenues and profits in the 21st century! I call this being a Heartrepreneur™ - a business owner who does business with integrity, marketing and selling with heart.

Terri Levine: Chief Heartrepreneur® and Founder of the Heartrepreneur® Movement

Dr. Levine is the bestselling author of Turbocharge How To Transform Your Business as a Heartrepreneur™ and is known as the business mentoring expert with heart. Terri was named one of the top ten coaching gurus in the world by **www.coachinggurus.net** and the top female coach in the world. She assists businesses worldwide to create the right inner mindset and outer actions for business growth. As a keynote speaker, Terri has inspired hundreds of thousands of people through her high content,memorable, and motivational speeches. She has been featured in the media on platforms such as ABC, NBC, MSNBC, CNBC, Fortune, Forbes, Shape, Self,The New York Times, the BBC, and in more than fifteen hundred publications.

She also operates **www.heartrepreneur.com**, mentoring business owners to turbocharge their business to create more revenues and profits while learning to be Heartrepreneurs. Terri is the co-founder of **www.businessconsultantinstitute.com**, training business consultants to create super profitable consulting businesses.

LEWENA BAYER

LIGHTNING GROWTH: SUCCESS STRATEGIES FOR TODAY'S LEADERS

SOCIAL INTELLIGENCE- THE NEW SCIENCE OF SUCCESS.

JUST LEAVE YOUR SHOES ON.

"Just leave your shoes on," says Aunt Janet, as you and your family enter her front hallway. But you know your Aunt. And just by the way she's standing, you can tell that she would really rather you took your shoes off. Unfortunately, your 13-year old son takes Aunt Janet at her word and before you can catch him, he bounds through the doorway and settles feet first, germy, muddy shoes and all, onto Aunt Janet's couch. By her forced smile and heavy sigh, you sense that Aunt Janet is not impressed. And so, as soon as she turns her back, you tell your son to *Go right now, quickly, and take off your shoes!*" Confused, he insists (and not very discreetly) that Aunt Janet said he could leave them on. So now you're embarrassed and apologetic, your son is confused and defiant, and Aunt Janet is tight-lipped and disapproving. It's going to be a great evening!

Sound familiar? It's amazing how misreading a small tonal cue can set off a whole avalanche of emotion and miscommunication. Fast forward five years and that socially awkward 13 year old is now 18 and trying to navigate his way through his first job interview. Unfortunately he didn't make a great impression because he misinterpreted the prospective boss's friendly tone as an invitation to be "friendly" and so he told a couple of jokes he maybe shouldn't have told, and he offered an overly familiar fist pump and a *"Thanks buddy"* instead of a handshake and more reverent *"Thank you Mr. Boss"* on his way out after the interview.

Aunt Janet would likely chalk her muddy couch up to "kids these days" having no common sense. And she may be right in that common sense isn't as common as it used to be. But both the prospective boss and Aunt Janet would be wrong in assuming that it's just young people who are lacking in it. You don't have to look very far to see people of all ages and backgrounds, and at all stages in their professional careers who have seemingly lost their senses – well...their common sense anyway. The fact is, it is in the work world where presumably grownups with polished interpersonal skills and honed social savvy are leading the pack, where we see some of the lowest social intelligence being exhibited. Having said that...

Have you travelled for business lately?

Been to a restaurant with a client?

Attended a public sporting event with your work colleagues?

Driven to a client site?

Sat in on a workplace meeting?

Talked to a human that could drag him/herself away from a device long enough to actually look at you?

Call it social skills, call it courtesy, call it common sense, whatever you want to call it; fewer and fewer people seem to have it. And this is particularly problematic in the workplace where having "it" can mean the difference between merely surviving and thriving.

This elusive "it" is comprised of behaviors such as:

» paying attention

» focusing on someone or something other than oneself

» connecting with others in a meaningful way

» being aware of our surroundings

» thinking about what might be appropriate in a certain context

» consciously adapting behavior to show consideration and respect for others

» considering the impact of our words and actions

» seeking to understand expectations for social behavior in different contexts

» exhibiting common courtesies; meeting general social expectations

Because these behaviors are not see as much anymore, choosing to exhibit them is a smart thing for anyone who perceives him/herself as a leader to do because it makes him/her stand out- in a good way. This cluster of behaviors are habits that socially successful people engage in. And collectively, when exhibited consistently, this social ease, this ability to navigate social settings successfully, is called *Social Intelligence*.

Without question, high <u>social intelligence is an attribute that is CRITICAL</u> for leaders who want to succeed in the new world of work. Social Intelligence goes beyond general social skills. And although related, social intelligence is not the same as "common sense". For most of us, common sense means having good judgment in practical matters. The problem is that what constitutes good judgment varies depending on the context. Social intelligence underpins our ability to have good judgment and so common sense is what happens when you actually use your Social IQ.

First, the bad news:

» Aunt Janet is correct about many young people (leaders of the future)

» Having lower social skills- but it's likely technology to blame, more than poor parenting. (Of course- sometime poor parenting is a contributor too.) Research out of UCLA College, shows that many people are looking at the benefits of digital media in education, and not many are looking at the costs like decreased sensitivity to emotional cues, loss of ability to understand the emotions of other people and the displacement of in-person social interaction by screen interaction seems to be reducing social skills. Building on this, Psychiatrist Dr. Clive Sherlock says changes in courteous behaviour are evidence of society becoming more selfish and a 'lack of respect' and that technology is encouraging people to be more 'involved in themselves/Read more: http://www.dailymail.co.uk/news/article-2255843/The-younger-generation-really-ARE-ruder-study-shows-likely-tip-postman-say-hello-strangers.html#ixzz3KEaNulRy

And now the good news:

» According to Multiple Intelligence Theory (Gardner et al), unless there is a physiological issue, all of us have capacity for high social intelligence. Rather than seeing intelligence as dominated by a single general intellectual ability, multiple intelligence theory proposes (and research validates) that there are up to eight "modalities" that make up our intelligence. These modalities include different types of intellect. For example, each of us has capacity for some or all of these modalities to be developed. This includes, aesthetic, emotional, social, kinesthetic, musical, logical, spatial, and linguistic. Multiple intelligence encourages us to respect and value more in people than the results given by a single dimension IQ test. In some roles, areas, and professions, standard IQ measurements may not be of much use at all. (http://www.mindtools.com/pages/article/newISS_85.htm)

» A Harvard – Stanford study concluded that one's success in the workplace is based on 85% social skills and less than 15% technical skills. So if you're in business, boosting your social intelligence (and the Social IQ of your team) can impact success, and the bottom line.

» Civility Experts Worldwide Inc. research shows that there are measurable impacts to civility and common courtesy when you improve social intelligence; including social radar, social knowledge, and social style adaptation.

SOCIAL SUCCESS – 3 KEY INGREDIENTS

There is a growing understanding that in the new world of work, technical skills and book smarts are simply not enough to be a great leader. To meet the demands of increasingly diverse, ever-changing workplaces – where collaboration may well be considered currency- the civility, sensitivity, thinking skills, cultural competence, and communication skills that collectively create high social intelligence, are absolutely essential to success for anyone who wants to retain a leadership role for the long haul.

Social IQ includes a cluster of behaviors such as, being aware of your surroundings, considering what might be appropriate in different settings, and paying attention. These are three of several habits that have been identified as behaviors that socially successful people engage in.

Collectively, and when exhibited consistently, these behaviors are perceived as "social ease" and this ability to navigate social settings successfully, is called *Social Intelligence*. Social Intelligence goes beyond general social skills. And although related, social intelligence (SI) is not the same as "common sense". For most of us, common sense means having good judgment in practical matters. The problem is that what constitutes good judgment varies depending on the context. Social Intelligence underpins our ability to have good judgment and so common sense is what happens when you actually use your Social IQ.

There are many reasons why social intelligence has declined. These include, among other things, parenting style shifts, generational and cultural issues, trends, demographic shifts in labour and talent pools, and reliance on technology. The reality is, some people acquire strong academic knowledge and credentials but they never move beyond the social awareness of a 13 year old. And, if someone happens to get a job in spite of low social intelligence, he/she is likely not even aware that there is a competency gap in this area, or he/she knows about it, but doesn't care. This is mistake because a leader's inability to interact successfully can have devastating consequences on his/her ability to keep a job.

Outlined in the chart below are some examples of how Social IQ can impact us at work.

	Indicators of low Social IQ	Impact (degree of impact varies with context
Individual	» Inability to read verbal and tonal cues » Inability to exercise restraint » Communication faux pas. e.g., Interrupting, ignoring	» Low confidence » High stress » Incivility
Team	» Failure to see value in contribution of others » Inability to adapt to change » Increased miscommunication and/or lack of communication	» Ineffective teamwork » Low resilience » Poor performance » Lack of service orientation
Organization	» Failure to identify demographic » Shifts both internal and external » Inability to create an empowering environment » Difficulty fostering "fit"	» Difficulty recruiting and/or low retention » Poor engagement » Lowered productivity

The good news is that psychologists have identified that Social Intelligence (unlike other intelligences) can be improved. We can actually teach people to be social intelligent. According to Karl Albrecht, researcher and author of *"Social Intelligence-The New Science of Success"*, *"...in the simplest terms, this is the ability to "get along with people," which - it is assumed - people learn as they grow up, mature, and gain experience in dealing with others. Unfortunately, many people do not continue to learn and grow as they age, and many people never acquire the awareness and skills they need to succeed in social, business or professional situations. It is quite clear that adults who lack insight and competence in dealing with others can make significant improvements in their SI status as a result of understanding the basic concepts and assessing themselves against a comprehensive model of interpersonal effectiveness".*

The process for building Social IQ is three-fold and involves:

a) determining need/expectations for exhibition of Social IQ on the job (or related to a specific social scenario)

b) assessing social competence

c) building competence in each of three aspects of Social IQ

Assessment need not be complicated, for example, many of us can identify social incompetence just by watching others. For example, have you ever watched someone say to a woman with a larger belly, *"When is your baby due?"* only to discover that woman is not pregnant? Have you ever watched a pre-teen's posture change as she is directly approached by a more assertive classmate? Have you stood uncomfortably and listened as a co-worker told an entirely inappropriate joke but was oblivious to the tight-lipped smiles of the listeners? Or have you ever watched The Big Bang Theory on television and watched Sheldon struggle in almost every social setting? These are all examples of low social intelligence.

There are also paper-based and other types of assessments you can use to identify low Social IQ but in our work at Civility Experts Worldwide, we've found that self-analysis is the very best approach. When you provide individuals an opportunity to identify their own strengths and weaknesses related to social skills, they are in fact using and building social skills in the process of going through the process.

There are three aspects of Social IQ – and you need to have skills in each area to be social competent.

1. Social Radar- this is your level of awareness and the extent to which you can pick up on and correctly interpret tonal, contextual and nonverbal cues. You learn the meaning of these cues by watching and engaging with others. And this is a continuous process because our environments and the people we interact are continually changing. When you work or live in diverse settings, being aware of, and interpreting the meaning of these cues is an experiential learning process. While you can gather some insights from books and other sources for example, you could read somewhere what it mean when someone from Italy flicks his/her fingers, with palms down, outward from just below the chin? But, you can't be sure that explanation applies to all Italians, in all situations, or where that gesture might be applied. And you can't assume that the gesture means the same thing when exhibited by a Spanish person in a different context, or a Chinese person who is in Italy, etc. The most effective way to build Social Radar is to be present- to pay attention. You have to teach yourself to eliminate distractions and to focus on what is going on around you. (It's very difficult to do this if your eyes are constantly glued to a handheld device.)

2. Social Style- this is the "approach" you use to interacting with others. What is your style? Is it passive, or introverted? Are you assertive or gregarious? Are you formal or informal? There are many ways to assess social style and this may be influenced by how you communicate, elements of your upbringing or culture, your personality,

your age, and even your gender. Once a person can identify his/her style, he/she needs to become skilled in identifying the social style of others as well as the social style that is appropriate in any given setting. And then, he/she must be able to adapt his/her style accordingly. If this were as easy as it sounds, we wouldn't be experiencing the temper tantrums, road rage, inappropriate behaviors such as bullying, and the general lack of restraint that we see more and more these days.

3. Social Knowledge- refers to both the written and unwritten rules that apply to any given situation. Written rules include codes of conduct, legislation, regulations, contract obligations, etiquette etc., where the unwritten rules include the social nuances, the unspoken expectations and invisible boundaries that exist in our homes, communities, social settings and in the workplace. In some instances, we may even include values, ethics and cultural norms in the unwritten rules category.

As you might guess, it's difficult to gather social knowledge if your social radar is low, and it may not matter how much social knowledge you have or how strong your social radar is if you don't have the ability to adapt your social style. All three skills are intertwined and all three are required to be deemed socially "competent".

BUILDING SOCIAL IQ- BEST PRACTICES

Once a person understands that he/she is lacking in social intelligence and presuming he/she has also identified which one or more of the three social intelligence aspects (Social Knowledge, Social Style or Social Radar) he/she is lacking in, the next step is to engage in strategies and learning to build social intelligence in those areas.

Where possible, it is always recommended to start with Social Radar. If your social radar is high, you will more able to notice when people are upset or not responding in an expected way and then you can choose to adapt your behavior or offer some repair if you've offended.

Examples of repair behavior include:

» Offering an exit handshake (to make up for a weak or limp handshake when you first met)

» Apologizing- verbally or in writing

» Toning down, e.g., your attire, the volume of your voice, the level of your assertiveness

» Extending common courtesies, e.g., making introductions, offering comforts such as food or beverage or acknowledgement of some kind

» Adjusting your use of shared space, e.g., moving away or moving closer, standing or sitting, shifting your posture, squaring your shoulders etc.

One of the best ways to build your social radar is to practice "active presence". Active presence is the opposite of what Karl Albrecht, *Social IQ- The New Science of Success*, calls "absent presence". Absent presence refers to being physically in the room but mentally and sometimes even emotionally absent. Being actively present means you have to be able to set aside distractions and focus. You have to actually pay attention, listen and engage with the people and setting in the physical space. This sounds easy but it's not something many people can do without practice. There is an intentional effort exerted when one is present. I find the best way to learn to be actively present is to start doing the following:

- » Unplug. Take a digital detox. Start with 30 minutes, then an hour, then a half day, and if possible work up to 1 day/month. Or, set aside time e.g., 8pm onwards in the evenings during the week where you shut off the phones, radio, television and just enjoy the quiet. Putter around the house, read a book, have a conversation with a family member, garden, build something, draw, cook- do anything that doesn't involve you electronics and/or media interaction.

- » Meditate. Even if you can only muster a few minutes a day, become more aware of your own thoughts, the energy around you, the smells and noises etc., can help you hear your inner voice better and your intuition will become stronger. Once you have a better sense of yourself, it will be easier to get a sense of others.

- » Become a people watcher. When you are out and about- at a stop light, at the doctor's office, waiting for colleagues to show up for meetings, browsing the grocery aisle etc. watch people. Study their gestures and body language in different situations, listen to how the tone of their voice shifts etc.

- » Engage in face to face interaction. These days with our busy, stressful lives it's very tempting to withdraw from social settings. We tend to eat dinner in front of the television, text instead of phoning, conference call instead of meeting in person etc. Force yourself to engage in face to face interactions in new settings with new people and be present- it's amazing what people will tell you through their body language and gestures if you are paying attention.

Once you've mastered social radar, the next step is to build your ability to adapt your social style. If you'd identified that you don't quite know what your social style is or how to adapt it, you might benefit from taking a self-assessment to identify your personal social style. There are many great sources for this, as examples:

» www.socialstyle360.com

» www.smallworldalliance.com

» http://www.16personalities.com/free-personality-test

» http://www.myersbriggs.org/

Basically there are four core social styles: Analytic, Driver, Amiable and Expressive and the extent to which you are Responsive or Assertive help determine your style.

Low Responsiveness
(Controls)

Low
Assertiveness
(Asks)

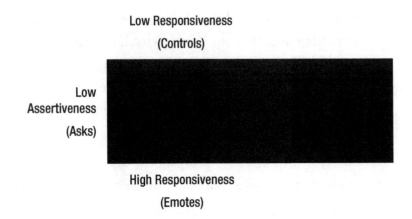

High Responsiveness
(Emotes)

*Chart from http://changingminds.org/explanations/preferences/
social_styles.htm*

Knowing what your style is helps you to understand how others may perceive you relative to their own style. And then you can make choices about how and when to adapt your style to be more effective socially with an individual or a group in a specific context such as in the workplace. As an example, a leader who is a "Driver" that is not very emotional and potentially assertive who offers a gregarious or energetic greeting at a workplace event might be perceived by someone who is "Amiable" and so expressive emotionally and more passive, as being rude or inappropriate.

If a person has knowledge of his/her social style AND has high social radar, he/she would pick up contextual cues upon entering the workplace event and he/she would them immediately adjust (in this case tone down) his/her style- and in doing this before interacting with others who have a different social style, avoid potential misunderstandings, appear approachable, and build trust- all of this is important for earning respect as a leader.

Lastly, if a person has self-assessed that he/she has ability and willingness to adapt social style, and he/she is working to build social radar but still having difficulty in social settings, the next step would be to employ strategies to build social knowledge. Social knowledge refers to both the written and the unwritten rules that apply in a specific context. Best practices for increasing social knowledge include:

» Continue to build Social Radar: set aside time daily to do a digital detox (even 15 minutes), practice mindfulness, engage in social interaction etc.- all the best practices suggested for building social radar contribute to social knowledge. As you are paying attention you can learn a lot of unwritten rules. Unwritten rules include applications of written rules that people usually only learn by experiencing different situations and contexts. Unwritten rules also include "exceptions" e.g., allowable breeches of the rules based on age, gender, or rank etc. And unwritten rules include what constitutes what people actually do in certain contexts (what we don't talk about) versus what they say they do (what they should do).

» Read or study to learn about written social rules for different contexts and cultures. Workplace codes of conduct, policy manuals, government rules and regulations, legal rules, and etiquette and protocol guidelines all represent "written" rules. The only way to learn all these rules is to actively engage in the review and learning of them. Keep in mind that cultural norms and related etiquette change ongoing.

Be sure to use current sources and be sure to differentiate between fact and opinion. Further, even when you have acquired a wide range of social knowledge, try not to make assumptions or judgments about the rules.

» Choose civility: Practice the 4 E's rule (created by Civility Experts Inc.). Let's face it, the idea that amidst chronic change, you could learn all the social knowledge there is to know, is a completely unreasonable notion. This is why the four E's rule is very useful. The four E's rule is that *everyone in every situation gets exactly the same respect and consideration every time.* In following the four E's rule, you tend to behave in a way that reflects an attitude of kindness, equality, and civility. As a result, even when you don't know the written social rules, and/or you potentially break a rule, people will forgive you because your overall demeanor is of civility and respect.

» Ask questions. Maybe it's a lack of confidence or communication skills, maybe it's worry about making mistakes or looking ignorant, but it seems many people these days would rather ignore an issue altogether or trust the internet for answers- rather than simply ask another person a question. If you aren't sure what is appropriate or expected in a social setting, why not ask? The reality is if you are unsure, there are likely others who are unsure. Asking polite questions is a way of conveying interest and showing others that you understand the social rules apply to you. Be brave, start a conversation.

As you can see from the best practices outlined above, build-ing social intelligence- which as a reminder Harvard studies showed accounts for up to 85% of your long-term success in life and work, is not difficult to do. However, it does take discipline, energy, and commitment. As a leader, investing in yourself in this way is a success strategy that could result in impactful, and measurable returns.

For 17 years **Lew Bayer** has been internationally recognized as a leading civility expert. With a focus on social intelligence and culturally-competent communication, the team at Civility Experts – which includes 83 affiliates in 24 countries has supported 100's of organizations in building better workplaces. . In addition to her role as CEO of multinational civility training group Civility Experts Inc. **www.CivilityExperts.com**, Lew is Chair of the *International Civility Trainers' Consortium*, President of *The Center for Organizational Cultural Competence* **www.culturalcompetence.ca**, and Founder of the In Good Company Etiquette Academy Franchise Group **www.ingoodcompanyetiquette.com**

With the release of her new book, *The 30% Solution*, slated for release early 2016, Lew will be a 10-time published author. Lew donates her time as Director of the National Civility Center, and she is also a proud Mentor for *The Etiquette House*, a member of the Advisory Board for *A Civil Tongue,* a national magazine columnist, and has contributed expert commentary to over 60 online, print, and television publications. Lew is one of only 5 Master Civility Trainers in the world, a distance faculty member at *Georgetown University Center for Cultural Competence*, a long-term facilitator at the *Canadian Management Center* in Toronto Canada, a Master trainer for the *Canadian School of Service*, a certified Impression Management Professional and a certified Culture Coach® who also holds credentials in Intercultural Communications, Essential Skills, and Occupational Language Assessment.

Lew is a 6-time nominee for the RBC Canadian Woman Entrepreneur of the year. She was previously awarded Manitoba Woman Entrepreneur in International Business and she was the first Canadian to receive the prestigious AICI International Civility Star Award.

DIANE A. CURRAN

BUSINESS LIGHTNING BUGS, SPACE CAPSULES & BADMINTON

Let's begin in the dark. In business, our competition never sleeps. There they are again, sparkling everywhere on the Internet even after lights out, grabbing coveted viewership on our favorite social media platforms.

Zippy, zinger-filled headlines flash into "content-rich" posts. They offer wisdom in three or four bite-size bullet points, linked to the latest data on consumer or industry trends made pretty with colorful infographic charts. Or how about a 20-question quiz that instantly divines your unique strengths? Just pick your favorites from our multiple-choice page-clicking screen test!

Social media success looks as swift and simple as catching lightning bugs in a bottle.

Can growing a business be as carefree, clever, and fast as the innocent firefly? Their bioluminescent tails are designed to attract mates to make merry with, and prey to feast upon, at dusk. Easy!

BUSINESS: HOW DO YOU BOTTLE LIGHTNING AND GROWTH TOGETHER?

You can read "Lightning Growth" as a convergence of opposites.

Let's start by distilling lightning and growth into two sets of bullet points to consider. The two words arise in quite different realms.

We can explore lightning and growth as the tangible elements of nature: earth, sky, water and fire. Or we can use the symbolic language and metaphor we are so fond of in stories and opinions. Either way, we find ourselves pondering:

WHAT IS LIGHTNING?

Sudden

Brief

Discharging

Unpredictable

Uncontainable

Transformative

WHAT IS GROWTH?

Incremental

Developmental

Increasing

Maturing

Valuable

Transferable

LIGHTNING STRIKES

People physically hit by lighting who live to tell the tale describe it in the strongest direct terms: "The lightning felt like a heavy metal object hitting me over the head. My muscles seized up, especially around my neck and shoulders." Another survivor said it was "like a professional baseball player hit me with a bat full-swing." [1]

(Given the challenges of recovery after such an experience, some find welcome personal support in a grass-roots organization founded by a strike survivor with a website at lightning-strike.org. The National Weather Service offers safety education at www. lightningsafety.noaa.gov)

We can understand that the forces of nature are not to be trifled with, although we tend to imagine ourselves invulnerable and invincible by default. This invincible mindset tempts us when imagining the thrill of "lightning" striking our own business life.

HOW MIGHT BUSINESS LIGHTNING STRIKE?

One of your social media videos suddenly goes viral and you get 100,000 views, or better yet, a million unexpected hits! Susan Boyle's 2009 audition on Britain's Got Talent rose virtually overnight to 1, 2, then 3+ million views. As I write this, it has 198 million views, and will inevitably exceed a stratospheric 200 million views. [2] She even got the career she said she'd "never been given the chance" to create, with the irascible Simon Cowell's support.

Perhaps you release a little App, it catches fire virally, and you get interviewed by one media outlet. Suddenly the whole medis swarm jumps on the bandwagon in a mere few days. Think 2016's summer fling with Pokémon GO!

LIGHTNING? THE FLASH OF "OVERNIGHT" SUCCESS

Does lightning ever strike twice? Well, the old saw says no, yet one industry seems to defy the odds regularly, known for its many overnight successes: the entertainment industry.

My favorite quote on the subject is from the late Estelle Getty, who played Dorothy's mother Sophia on *Golden Girls*. In real life she was younger than her TV daughter Bea Arthur. After winning her first Emmy amid seven nominations for her wizened and witty portrayal, she quipped, "After 50 years in the business, I'm an overnight success." [3]

Are there other industries or professions with this same long-time-coming overnight success dynamic? Yes, indeed.

In the creative arts, there are young prodigies but also sudden senior superstar writers, painters, musicians.

In sports, there are players who are not champions in their youth yet become extraordinary coaches "suddenly" seasoned by wisdom and the grit of life experience.

In business there are serial entrepreneurs who may have eked out a living for many years with various ventures, then suddenly hit it big with their latest start-up that catches fire in the mass market with a unique concept, great timing, media fascination, or all three.

TRANSFORMATION IS UNCONTAINED BY TIME

We expect lightning to project a sudden, brief, unpredictable discharge of energy. Yet we chase after such a peak experience, hoping to gain something inside it that will last: transformation.

We often roll up our sleeves to work on changing our circumstances, expectations, or habits. However, the seeds of relapse are contained in any such effort. We even have a saying for it, "The more things change, the more they stay the same."

Yet transformation is entirely different. Those struck by physical lightning, like those who report near-death experiences, speak about a permanent shift. Life felt and looked one way before that moment, and shifted forever in and beyond that moment.

In business, the concept of "disruption" exhibits this quality of permanent shift. Just as the butterfly can no longer revert to being a caterpillar, neither can a business or industry shift be reversed. When the Wright Brothers bested other contemporary inventors with the longest, if not first, early flight (39 minutes aloft!) on October 5, 1905, the aviation industry was born and a new transportation race was on.

On January 9, 2007, Apple changed the telephone industry forever with its very first iPhone, a one-button wonder. I was among those at Macworld in San Francisco when it was first displayed inside a glass-domed monolith on the exhibit floor. It was literally hypnotic. We could not touch it, but the shift was immediately palpable as geeks by the thousands queued up for a quick, reverent glimpse of an uncontainable future made present.

Now before we fly into the world of space capsules, the other half of our opposites mash-up—growth—deserves some time in the sun.

CULTIVATING GROWTH

While lightning discharges electricity, often burning itself into the ground, growth gathers up raw materials from the soil, creating a precise alchemy of seeds, minerals, water and sunshine to produce plants, crops, trees. We measure business growth in customers, product mix, or industry stature.

Growth is incremental and developmental, lending itself to planning and tracking.

THE LONELINESS OF THE LONG DISTANCE RUNNER'S HIGH

Used to be that marathon runners had very little company as they raced their 26.4 mile feats of endurance in rain, sleet, sun or snow. Then running got so popular and the field so crowded that prestige races had to initiate "flights" of start times to give all entrants a fair chance to win, or at least better their own records.

Marathon runners (especially ultra-marathoners who often run multi-day races) train against themselves. They pursue the satisfaction of a new personal best. Growth is patiently measured in lengthened, efficient strides, refined breathing, and minutes or seconds shaved from completion times. But it's not all grit and gristle. Those with a consistent training regimen are intimately familiar with both the second wind (a sudden up-tick in performance with less effort) and the runner's high (the euphoria associated with endorphin release) which make an otherwise solitary slog appealing and rewarding. There's even talk of an elusive third wind.[4]

Marathon businesses may achieve steady-state strength (like the Martha Graham Dance Company, 90 years and counting) or scale up from mom and pop kitchens or garage experiments into corporate behemoths (like Kentucky Fried Chicken or Apple, or that little ol' bookseller Amazon's multi-industry empire.)

INSPIRATION MAY STRIKE, BUT GROWTH IS GRADUAL

In the world of food we could call gourmet food trucks lightning, and grocery stores ultra-marathoners that persist to create growth. How so?

Food trucks alight for a few hours, then batten down their awnings and drive off to the next location, with or without a posse of other food trucks in tow. They are nomadic, inciting spontaneous demand, thriving on sizzling originality.

Grocery stores are community pillars where you buy staples like rice and beans, milk and bread, and other dietary and household commodities. They have little room for errors in experimentation with historically razor thin profit margins. The grocery industry as a whole is a mature, long-standing symbol of local business. Even at the chain level their strong suit, or value, is stability and familiarity.

As a point of reference, convenience stores are examples of incremental growth, too. Restaurants may move in and out like nomads, becoming stable only if locals patronize them at a steady predictable pace. Chain restaurants exemplify the "increasing" and "transferable" aspects of growth if they learn how to generate sufficient, reliably "clone-able" customer loyalty.

GROWTH ADDS VALUE

Typifying professionals, contrast the country doctor versus the big-city medical specialist. The M.D. who sets up practice in a remote village or town signals a willingness to treat people instead of conditions, growing their practice by cultivating generations of families, and relationships filled with trust and personal connections. The urban specialist chooses a narrower path of study and advanced board certification early. They shine with rare diagnostic knowledge or narrowly focused medical/ surgical skills, but are typically accessible only via a structured system of authorized referral.

Professionals like attorneys, therapists, interior designers, personal trainers, coaches or marketing consultants, and many others, may take on a very diverse range of projects early in their career to establish themselves. Yet as they grow, they begin to specialize after discovering not only whose needs they can best serve, but what they most love to do, and which rarefied skills they wish to pursue and cultivate to grow their value.

HOW DOES BUSINESS MERGE LIGHTNING WITH GROWTH?

What does it take to merge such polar opposites?

A. Inspiration & Lightning Bugs: Matching Light with Heat

B. Commitment & Space Capsules: The Power of Perseverance

C. Alignment & Badminton: Test and Track, Again and Again

World cultures have long mythologized lightning. Among the many gods assigned power over weather, Westerners know Zeus best. But Zeus is a generalist, with lightning bolts only one of many powers (loyally assisted by his brother Poseidon of the oceans.) We know the Norse god Thor, but he is a big thunderbolt fan, packing more noisy heat than light. In Japan, Raijin presides over storms, thunder and lightning (originally in a gang of eight) to protect the Dharma of the Buddha.

These days, we're tempted to assign this power to one Mr. Danny Zuko, whose "Greased Lightning" energy andflying car is iconic in 1978's much loved film *Grease*. Danny was love-struck by lightning himself when he spied the innocent Sandy, and sparks flew as they grappled with the obstacles of young love to triumph with a big musical finish.

INSPIRATION & LIGHTNING BUGS: MATCHING LIGHT WITH HEAT

A plant's needs are basic, including sunlight for photosynthesis and earth for its mineral/chemical building blocks.

A business needs light and heat too. It needs both lightning and growth—a vision and mission—or it can wander into unwanted territory. It needs regular flashes of visibility to couple with energy that attracts growing attention (and purchases!) from its desired audience.

EPIPHANIES ARE LIGHTNING

Like lightning, business epiphanies occur without regard for time, schedules, or convenience. People who've been overtaken by an inspired, intuitive, or ingenious idea say it lands suddenly with an unmistakable jolt to conventional thinking. It's impossible to ignore, and often arrives "full-blown" in remarkable detail.

CAN A BUSINESS COMMAND LIGHTNING TO STRIKE?

We want the answer to be yes. I am going out on the skinny branches to exclaim yes it can! I'll share my own discoveries about what it takes to build muscle for such "inspiration on demand."

» *Embrace* not knowing as an empowerment in life

» *Give up* waiting to feel motivated and get started now

» *See* past failures as breadcrumbs on the path of adventure

» **Jot** a quick note (or stick figure sketch) the minute an idea hits

» **Keep** an "Aha! File" of idea snippets, even the puzzling ones

» **Allow** idea snippets to germinate like the seedlings they are.

These six simple secrets will build both receptivity and the capacity for attention necessary to fish for and net free-floating epiphanies on demand from the ethers of imagination. Artists embrace the blank canvas as dance partner, not foe. Writers learn quickly that an insight often dissipates in casual conversation, rarely able to reconstitute itself later on the written page. And inventors lock themselves in the lab to protect concentration and explore it when it peaks.

Business owners and professionals who cultivate curiosity and a creative, inventive mindset will find they already have a vast library of insights about their own industry, practical working knowledge, and untapped expertise they may have ignored. The mind is just waiting for a (relaxed, not forceful) signal that it's okay to sparkle with new patterns of thoughts and ideas.

COMMITMENT & SPACE CAPSULES: THE POWER OF PERSEVERANCE

Getting out of your own way is essential for inspiration and for achievement. How many of us know we are our own worst enemy? I can see a forest of hands going up, mine too.

There is another powerful antidote to creative blocks that can be activated instantly and engaged for measurable results at any time: Don't grapple with resistance or obstacles alone. Assemble a team.

Even if you are a Solopreneur going it alone, having a kitchen cabinet (informal advisors committed to cheering you on yet willing to offer constructive reality checks) or a more formally staffed team is essential. No business is an island.

How much power can a team provide? When President John F. Kennedy announced on May 25, 1961 that the United States of America would put a man on the moon in under a decade,[5] he could as easily have said we'd have cows jumping over the moon, it was so inconceivable.

But NASA invented, designed, engineered, tested and launched the Mercury, Gemini and Apollo manned missions, and we did exactly that on July 20, 1969. President Kennedy's vision became reality with a committed team who persevered, then persevered further at remarkable speed, a unified team in the face of every obstacle; and fulfilled on an extraordinary memorial to their felled visionary leader.

ALIGNMENT & BADMINTON: TEST AND TRACK, AGAIN AND AGAIN

As I was contemplating the qualities of speed in life and business for this book, even before I thought about flight and space travel, which alternately breaks sound barriers, then floats in seeming stillness, I found myself wondering what the fastest sports using balls might be. Tennis anyone?

Nope, it's not tennis serves or even baseball pitches breaking 90 mph, nor soccer or a host of other ball sports. It's badminton, with its strangely shaped, lightweight shuttlecock made of cork and feathers. It routinely clocks in over 200 mph in professional play. [7] So much for sweat-free teatime rituals of lazy conversation.

ALIGNMENT. GETTING WHAT COULD GO WRONG TO GO RIGHT

Badminton shuttlecocks share a unique property with early U.S. space capsules. The NASA Mercury capsule was designed in an almost identical shape, so "it would automatically right itself during reentry, even if the onboard control system failed" [6] in order to protect astronauts lives and the craft itself.

Modern badminton "shuttles" are marvels of precision. Slow-mo video that shows how *they right themselves* to travel cork-side first (no matter how they are hit) is eerie and mesmerizing. The optimal racquet angle to hit a badminton shuttle is 71.6 degrees, and it doesn't happen by chance. Pros spend many hours to create the eye-hand-body coordination needed to achieve this alignment while playing at a 200 mph pace. Whew!

Inventors, business owners, communications experts, and anyone with a vision and mission bigger then themselves are equally primed to right what could go wrong. They formulate best-concept tests, track results, then analyze objectively what did-or-did-not work. Next, they realign or reformulate their goods on offer to add what's missing that would make a difference.

When ongoing commerce includes re-testing and feedback solicitation as a quality control measure (for products and services) then quality upgrades and industry leadership become available.

Lightning is sudden adventure. Growth is a committed journey. Combine them with care, and you'll have the energy for inspired, sustainable business success and satisfaction.

FOOTNOTES:

1. "They were struck by lightning, and lived" by Alene Dawson, Los Angeles Times, August 21, 2015 http://www.latimes.com/health/la-he-getting-out-lightning-club-20150822-story.html

2. Susan Boyle - Britain's Got Talent 2009 Episode 1 - Saturday 11th April, UKAdvertChannel on You Tube https://www.youtube.com/watch?v=RxPZh4AnWyk

3. Estelle Getty, 'Golden Girls' Matriarch, Dies at 84, By Bruce Weber, The New York Times, July 23, 2008 http://www.nytimes.com/2008/07/23/arts/television/23getty.html?_r=1

4. "The Zen of Running: Catching Your Third Wind" by Jason Saltmarsh, Huffington Post, February 18, 2014 http://www.huffingtonpost.com/jason-saltmarsh/running_b_4797956.html

5. "The Decision to Go to the Moon" National Aeronautics and Space Administration NASA History Office http://history.nasa.gov/moondec.html

6. "How the Spaceship Got Its Shape" By Andrew Chaikin, Air & Space Magazine, November 2009 http://www.airspacemag.com/space/how-the-spaceship-got-its-shape-137293282/?no-ist

7. "The world's fastest sport isn't the one you're thinking of" by Adam Wernick, PRI Science Friday, January 7, 2015 http://www.pri.org/stories/2015-01-07/worlds-fastest-sport-isnt-one-youre-thinking

Diane A. Curran is a branding and marketing expert with a focus on igniting ideas. Author of The Marketing Deck: Deal Yourself a Big Idea, she created an innovative deck of cards and book series for readers to play their way to new marketing momentum, with games and events that engage people at any level of business experience or curiosity. Steeped in the creative arts from her earliest memories, she is equally passionate about the role and power of marketing as high performance communication. With four decades of marketing and creative projects for thousands of marketers shaping hervision, she knows the pulse of modern marketing propelling our future.

JASON MACKENZIE

LIGHTING GROWTH

You lay your head down on the pillow the night before the biggest product launch of your career. You know you'll sleep soundly. The way your team is firing on all cylinders is a joy to behold. Tasks are getting done on time. When a problem arises, the team surfaces it right away and comes together to overcome it. No one feels the need to hide their struggles. They feel total ease in telling you exactly what they need. Better yet, they hold your feet to the fire if you don't live up to your commitment to them. There are many days it feels like you could go golfing and no one would miss you. You love being a leader because it means helping people be their best. There's no better feeling in the world.

You can facilitate this type of cohesion and performance with your teams. You can become a leader that inspires loyalty that extends far beyond regular business hours. It's easy to create relationships across your organization which make traditional boundaries a thing of the past. People will go out of their way to help you. They'll do it because you've wholeheartedly done the same for them. All of this and more is possible. All it takes is rethinking what it means to be accountable to one another.

As leaders there is a universal challenge we've all faced. We're about to convene our weekly project update meeting. We feel the familiar gnawing in the pit of our stomach. The project is late; people are behind on their work. It's the same thing, meeting after meeting. They only person who feels any sense of urgency is you because your boss is breathing down your neck. You can't yell at everyone but you don't know what else to do. This cross-functional team is wholly dysfunctional. Only half the people show up for any given meeting and most of them don't report to you. They can clearly see there is a red circle beside their name. Why don't they take accountability seriously?

As a new leader I lived this experience more often than I care to admit. I struggled mightily to put my finger on what I was doing to create it. As a brash, self-centred young leader my first response was to blame everyone else. As I grew into a more mature and seasoned leader my first response was still to blame everyone else. I know what Bill Murray's character in Groundhog Dad went through. I was too afraid to turn the mirror inward because I was afraid of what I might see. There was no way I was going to ask for help. Asking for help meant I didn't know how to do my job. I'd be exposed as a fraud. So I kept doing what hadn't been working because it was the only thing I new how to do. Except I pushed people harder and harder and grew more aloof.

My leadership awakening came from a place I least expected but now seems obvious. I made some dramatic steps in my life that changed the way I interacted with the world. One of those was overcoming a titanic battle with alcohol. That decision created the space for me to finally grieve the death of my wife. I realized I had been living a life based on fear. I was afraid of finding out I hated living a sober life. I was afraid of being rejected if I deviated from the alpha male stereotype. I was afraid to discover I had already reached my potential. Not one of those fears came true. I realized, at forty-one years old, that I had been imprisoned in a cell of my own making.

The more deeply I understood this the more I felt compelled to share my story. I knew I couldn't be the only one who had been living this way. I started to tell my story and something completely unexpected happened. People started sharing theirs with me. I was shocked at what people were telling me. I realized they felt safe talking to me because I showed the courage to take the first step. They knew I wouldn't judge them because I was honest about the things I had done. I showed them my humanity and they reciprocated by showing me theirs. I created relationships that were different than what I had known before.

Allowing myself to be vulnerable was transforming my personal life. I decided to do the same thing at work. This should have felt risky because I was a senior leader in my organization. I felt nothing but peace. I shared the impact of my wife's death and battle with alcohol in a newsletter that was distributed around the world. I shared my morning routine of meditation, affirmations and gratitude around our facility and offered to speak to anyone about it. I started sharing more of myself with everyone. Most importantly of all, I started listening. It's incredible what the decision to listen can reveal to you.

I transformed as a leader. I became effective in ways that had always seemed elusive to me. I started to forge relationships everywhere in my company regardless of the department or position on the food chain. I felt free to acknowledge what I didn't know and when I needed help. I started to realize people were human beings before they were employees. Accountability became a two-way street and I realized it was about much more than a red or green dot beside your name.

I want to share the concepts and actionable strategies I have learned and used successfully. When you embrace and implement these you will become a more open and transparent person. You'll show your authentic self and draw people into your orbit. When people feel safe they are willing to push their limits further than they thought possible. We're accountable to each other as human beings first and foremost. That's the accountability that fuels the highest levels of personal and professional performance. Never forget that.

NURTURE THE WHOLE PERSON

"Don't bring your personal problems to work." That tired phrase has been trotted out by HR departments and managers forever. Where did we get the idea that separating personal from professional was possible in the first place? A compartmentalized employee will never be as great an asset, to the company or their family, as a whole human being.

Get to know the people you work with on a personal level. Show an interest in their lives outside of work. Know how many kids they have and what their names are. Know them well enough to be able to see if they are struggling with anything. If they are then gently reach out to them and let them know you are there if they need you.

Of course you have a responsibility to your company to make sure that people are living up to their obligations. Creating an environment where people know you care about them opens up a much greater suite of options than might otherwise be available to you. People, often from outside your immediate team, will come to you and ask for help when they need it. Knowing you've created that space for them is one of the most satisfying things a person can feel.

CULTIVATE VULNERABILITY

Stop living under this illusion that you are different because you are a leader. Focusing on what makes you different puts up walls between you and everyone else. It's the similarities we share that bind us together and make us stronger. It takes someone to have the courage to lay down their shield first. Leadership means going first.

Humans have been story-tellers since time immemorial. We relate to stories because it's in people's stories that we see echoes of ourselves. Share yours. Talk to people about the challenges you've faced and the mistakes you've made. Explain the lessons you've learned and how you've applied them to create a different future.

Sometimes the hardest person to be honest with is ourselves. If you can't then its impossible to be honest with anyone else. How can you relate to someone else's struggles if you refuse to acknowledge your own? The world is full of people hiding behind personas. When you cast yours aside people start seeing you as a powerful breath of fresh air. People love to breath fresh air.

EXPAND THE DEFINITION OF LEADERSHIP

One of the most harmful myths we perpetuate is that leadership is for other people. People who are better and more capable that us. As a leader, your job is to make sure everyone else knows they are a leader too. When they realize that they will take an increased level of ownership over their choices.

Teach people a more fundamental definition of leadership. It means to make the choice to make a difference in people's lives. Helping people see what they are capable of is leadership. Helping them understand the butterfly effect their actions can create is leadership. Saying "Thank You" is leadership. Listening to them without judgment is leadership. Offering to help is leadership. Asking for help is leadership.

We are all leaders. We all have a role to play in shaping our world and shaping our work environment. We may occupy different spots on the corporate totem pole. That means nothing more than we have different roles to play in making sure the things that need to get done, get done. Leadership is not for other people. Leadership is for everyone. Teach and model this behavior and watch the people around you stand taller.

OFFER HELP AND DON'T FORGET TO ASK FOR IT

Leaders can develop a fatal tendency to circle the wagons around their own sphere of influence. We want to protect our team from attack from the outside. Even when the outside is inside the same company. We tell ourselves that reflexively protecting our underlings is a sign of strength. It can be but it can also prevent you from understand what is really going on.

Practicing empathy will take you miles further than reacting defensively. Listen to what the other person has to say and understand why they are saying it without judging it. It could very well be that they simply need help with something. They might not know where to get it or they might be too scared to ask. Many people fall victim, like I did, to the fear of asking for help. Many leaders' greatest fear is appearing weak. If they open up to you about needing help, help them. Do everything in your power to help them with their issue like they were your most important customer. When people see you are the type of person who goes out of their way for others your personal power will increase drastically. Remember though, when you offer it, do everything you can to deliver on your commitment.

When you need help, ask for it. Every single one of us needs help and we need it often. When you ask for help you'll quickly discover something amazing. People will help you. You'll build relationships with them at the same time. These relationships will help you get more done now and in the future. People love to be of service to one another because it makes them feel important and needed. Your asking them for help is a way for you to give them a gift that costs you nothing. For more information, I suggest you refer to the Esteem layer of Mazlow's Hierarchy of Needs.

REDEFINE ACCOUNTABILITY

All of the above strategies help support an expanded definition of accountability. Let's focus on the most foundational aspects of what it means to be accountable. It's much more than defining SMART goals or creating Visual Management boards although those are critically important in the right context. Our accountability to each other as human beings underpins everything else we do.

We are accountable to doing everything we can to support each other in being our best. We have the power to make a contribution to people going home at the end of the day feeling happy and fulfilled. The choices we make about how to interact with each other flow through all areas of our lives. Your behaviour at work will affect how a co-worker interacts with their children. It can impact how they sleep or how they feel about themselves. Make the choice to be kind and foster cooperation. Do no harm.

We're accountable to creating an environment of openness where we can all express ourselves freely. We should all feel confident and secure that we can express our opinion and it will be listened to and considered. Disagreement should be encouraged as a tool to sharpen our collective and individual thinking. If someone needs to be called out, then let them be called out in a non-threatening environment. When there is nothing to hide from there is no reason to hide. This is the environment in which everyone can thrive. We are accountable to sustaining and nurturing it so we can be the best expressions of ourselves.

A team committed to elevating each other as human beings first can't help but perform at a high level. They will put each others' interests ahead of their own. They will sense when someone needs help and will freely offer it. In turn they will be able to openly receive help when it's offered. The deeper our relationships the greater the sense of accountability we feel to one another.

As the leader of your team you must walk the talk. Explain to them that you want nothing more to enjoy watching them perform at their very best. Talk openly about how you want them to walk out the door with their head held high, proud of a job well done. Help them see that when you hold them accountable to delivering on time its about more than the specific task.

It's your job to give them what they need to succeed, to remove roadblocks and to help them get the job done. When they hold your feet to the fire to live up to your commitments you'll know you're winning.

YOU WANT ME TO DO WHAT?

I can hear what you're thinking because I though the same thing. "You want me to talk about my life and what I'm struggling with? You want me to ask people for help? Even the people on my team – the ones I'm supposed to lead? To top it off, I'm supposed to roll over when Dave from Finance complains to me about my team – again? I just want people to get things done on time! Besides, I'll get eaten alive if I do any of these things"

No, you won't. You'll realize that everyone is waiting for someone to go first. You are vastly stronger and more effective as your whole, authentic self than you are as the persona you are trying to project. There will be people who judge you. Don't live your life in fear of them. You will be amazed when you discover the judgment you fear turns out to be almost non-existent.

People will spend far more time asking you what you are doing. They will come to you with their deeply personal issues and share them openly because they trust you. You'll learn more about their day to day lives and the challenges they are facing. You'll start seeing endless opportunities to help them. And you will because helping people feels far better than fighting with them. With every barrier you knock down you will become more of a force in your organization.

People from across the organization will want to work with you because you get results. Everyone wants to be associated with the winning team. Your wins will be based on mutual benefit, human to human relationships and trust. You'll discover people going out of their way to help you where previously you ran into constant roadblocks.

Treat people as human beings rather than employees. Cultivate vulnerability by being more open about your story. Find the courage to share the authentic version of yourself. Work hard to help people understand that we are all leaders if we choose to be. We all have an incredible amount of power to change people's lives. When you see an opportunity to help, offer it freely. Realize that asking for help only makes you better. It's an act of kindness because it gives someone else a chance to be of service.

These actions will fundamentally change what accountability means in your company. Your teams will be tighter and support each other in performing better. People will go above and beyond to help each other. Getting things done on time won't be a burden. It will be an opportunity to work together to achieve a shared goal. People will hold each other accountable to the level of performance they know they're capable of. You will start achieving results together that you once thought impossible. The leader goes first. What are you waiting for?

Now sleep soundly. You've got a round of golf to play in the morning.

Jason MacKenzie is an expert on peak human performance. He's a father, speaker, author and coach. He teaches audiences around the world how cultivating vulnerability will liberate the strength, wisdom and courage we already possess.

He is a survivor of his wife's battle with bipolar disorder and subsequent suicide and has overcome a decade-long battle with alcohol. When he stopped running from grief and fear he became the husband and father his family deserves.

His driving purpose is to help lift those who want more from their lives to increasingly higher levels of personal and professional performance. Jason is a strength-finder and works with you to help you ask powerful, affirmative questions about what's best about you and your life. He'll help you dream about the future and then guide in you in carrying the best of yourself forward.

His mission is to show you that you are inherently successful and then stand back and watch you fly

STEVE LENTINI

SUCCESS STRATEGIES FOR TODAYS LEADERS

MANAGING THE CULTURE FOR GROWTH

Having managed sales teams and for the last 18 years trained, coached and consulted many companies in the area of sales what my experience has taught me about lightning growth is this; Managing the Culture is critical for growth and especially during challenges that any growing company will experience.

When the Biosphere 2 was built in Oracle Arizona, the idea was to demonstrate the viability of closed ecological systems to support and maintain human life in space colonization. (one intended use anyway).

When trees of many different sizes and shapes began to die, testing was done to see why. Everything was tried...new food, fertilizer, water, more sun and less...nothing seemed to solve the problem. Trees would grow to a certain height and then topple over. One windy day, a worker noticed immediately what was missing...**the wind!** What they discovered as they varied the speed of the airflow into the building, the trees swaying back and forth, developed deeper stronger roots. Small roots would break with the sway, and eventually new roots would develop off of the broken root and grow even deeper...much deeper.

It doesn't matter what the industry or size of the company, modern or mature...challenges will come and the question is,

will your team withstand the hi winds? It's your culture that will determine if your company will survive and it's your culture that will help provide lightning growth. Will you assist the company in developing deeper roots? Will you assist your employees in what's required to grow deeper? Do you want employees or

What follows are my observations and stories from working with successful sales and company cultures and from working with cultures that were out of control. From what I have experience you can determine for yourself what direction to take. The question is this;

WILL YOU DO WHAT IT TAKES TO MANAGE YOUR CULTURE?

In 1982, I sold my distribution company to a large family owned company. Initially it was a big shock to my system. The culture was all about sales. Support departments were the brunt of criticism mostly when things went wrong. Sales typically did not take any responsibility in helping the company perform productively. The company leadership as well had a responsibility as it seemed like the family did not know what to do, how to even address managing the culture. I'm not sure they even knew how out of control it was.

If something was out of stock, it was purchasing's problem. Instead of the sales team helping purchasing perform better and win, with usage projections when new customers were added, or an existing customer began to purchase new items the company stocked, purchasing was beat up.

The same was true for the warehouse and customer service. If mistakes were made ... the out of control sales culture made the team around them wrong.

In my 16 years with the company, growth was emphasized over anything else and the culture suffered. There was never, not once, any training about how to support one another in winning. We all had the same goal and yet it seemed like we operated in different worlds. Never was a meeting held say monthly, to talk about team and how each department was critical to the company's success. Only the sales team held meetings with leadership except for meetings about what mistakes were made and or how a departments performance could be improved. Since the largest pool of revenue was for sales compensation, the support departments had employees that were hired for the least amount and expected to produce the best. On top of that, new hires found out quickly, that team was not a part of the language in the company...it was Sales and All Others.

In later years the company did eventually reconfigure the sales compensation to hire and train better support staff and eventually had more focus on team. The result; the company is a success today.

Example 2.

A family owned company with a sales team of about 40 and a total staff of about 160. When I got there the company had not been profitable in 7 out of 10 years or there about. The leadership team was family and a collection of people considered to be "key people" on the team.

The culture was out of control. From day one, various people warned me about who to watch out for and who to avoid...and there was a pool going on about how long I would last, based upon others who had taken the job.

The "key people" on the leadership team, leaked information

to certain individuals on the sales team, on any critical issues that were discussed in leadership team meetings. There was a sycophant atmosphere involving a former sales manager who had this group around him, regaling them with tales of his great success and his ideas of how the company was so bad...along with how he could do it better. The tales involved too, how the family that ran the company did not know what they were doing. The truth was, of all his ideas, he never went to the family with any great ideas and what he did know about, and truly was an expert on, complaining and making others wrong around him.

This example, led to the same behavior in others on the sales team. It was not unusual to hear sales people shouting at support staff in the office in front of others. Support staff eventually took on the same behavior between departments and between individuals in departments.

Management was totally indifferent to addressing any of the culture issues. It became a silent under current in the building even though it was also the elephant in the room.

Everyone knew it was there and yet did nothing about it, except to complain among themselves and to others who could do nothing about it. It seems no one went to management except to say what an "ass" so and so it and others would just agree.

It seems incredulous even as I write it and I experienced it firsthand.

Eventually the company experienced extreme financial challenges as the sales force was over compensated, even at the expense of a reasonable company profit. Instead of implementing common sense cures, I was told, "we cannot change any of the sales team compensation as we promised them."

Eventually the compensation issue was dealt with by the new owner of the company. The company was sold at a fire sale price. A sixty-year-old family business was lost to an out of control culture that said "don't mess with the sales team."

What would you prefer? A reasonable profit and a team environment with clear boundaries that say certain behaviors are not acceptable nor tolerated, or a fire sale to a competitor?

Indifference equals acceptance in any situation and especially when out of bounds behavior is tolerated. It says silently ...we are ok with this.

Having a culture that is managed for individual respect with equal contribution from sales and sales support departments is critical to lightning success.

Leadership has a responsibility to check in the on the culture by being proactive with training and also the message about the "why" the company is in business. The team shares the same goals although they have differing responsibilities. What is the shared goal? Express it often, especially in management meetings. Open meetings to employees by invite or just open some of the meetings to help support employees experience some of the challenges faced by the company. Sales meetings need to have support people attend as well with open discussions about the shared goals. Each sales team member should experience all of the support roles from time to time...every year, once a year or at least every two years. This help sales teams understand the challenges that support teams face from customers and challenges between departments.

Managing the culture is key to the lightning success of company and especially for todays' leaders.

Culture was not even talked about when I entered the work world. It was "do the work and shut up." Support employees were just that, employees and not people. Todays' leaders have a responsibility to provide growth for people they employ. As our employees grow deeper roots and become better people, they make a larger contribution to the company and customers take notice. They like doing business with adult companies, with adult people who run them.

A part of any culture is the vision and language that is spoken and I don't mean politically correct language ...and that is a part of what's required today thanks to our new world. I am talking about a positive vision and language as compared to the negative. Small minded thinking has no part in the culture of a lightning growth company. As John Maxwell says "leaders need to think today of limitless possibilities." Limitless thinking can be taught and continually coached. Whether is signage or a training program quarterly or a monthly newsletter, reminding our people of the power they have if they can imagine anything. Encourage limitless thinking in every meeting and address every challenge with "let's focus on the solutions to our challenges... what we focus on ...increases."

When a leader hears limited possibility language, that is the time to coach staff with "hey, what happens if we look at this with limitless possibility thinking?" Challenge all the people to test it in their own lives. I have seen complete teams learn to challenge and push back against negative, limited thinking.

Imagine what effect a group of enthused, positive, limitless thinkers would have on your company and the growth?

Besides managing the day to day operations and sales...it is an excellent investment in time and energy and it does take both... to manage your culture for lightning growth. Something that 20 years ago was not talked about much.

Beginning with the end in mind, ask yourself, "what is the culture that you want to encourage and nurture? Once you decide, consciously work towards that end...every day. Is it a positive culture that encourages personal growth and responsibility, accountability? Do you encourage everyone taking the steps in the extra mile in helping the company reach its shared goals? Do you remind everyone that even the smallest thing done well, with good intentions make a difference? Even if its cleaning up after yourself in the employee kitchen or in the restrooms? No matter where folks work, do you remind them that they are putting out an energy everywhere that says "this is who I am...?"

We are always harvesting something we planted...cause and effect. What is the effect you desire and what is the cause that will bring that desired result?

Everything we think, do and say is planting a seed for a future...? Isn't that enough of an argument to get you to look at your company's culture if you do not already do so?

Lightning Growth will include Culture Success Strategies and the work that goes into managing it....

Be well

Gratefully yours, Steve Lentini

Steve Lentini is Entrepreneur and Businessman with 40 years in sales and management and author of sales and leadership books and articles. Steve is a Key Note speaker and an engaging trainer.

Having consulted with a wide variety of companies across many industries, including Software, Healthcare, Service and Distribution...Steve is very qualified to address any sales challenge.

DAVID RYBACK

STRATEGIES FOR LIGHTNING GROWTH IN SALES

1. **Excite the Customer:** First of all, **excite the customer**. What's unique about your offering? What's your "secret formula"? How can you present your product/service/talent in its most attractive, but also provocative, fashion? What makes it different than what's already available in the marketplace? The first task is to answer these questions so that you have the best to offer from your own perspective.

2. **Dominate the Market:** There's something about the enthusiasm that comes with first entering the market. So this is the time to dive in without any hesitation whatsoever. **Imagine dominating the market** with all your energy and vitality at this point. Even if your offering has been around a while, the fact that you are new to the marketplace is where you can find your energy. Imagine dominating the market and let your energy carry you.

3. **From Your Heart:** The one challenge you need to master is your "elevator speech." Keep it down to 30 seconds or less. If you need more time for it, there better be a good reason for that tradeoff. Never rush it. Keep it at a natural pace and **let it flow straight from your heart**. Those hearing it will judge it with discernment as to whether you're really authentic about your offering. Keep fine-tuning those words until you hear "Tell me more"

whenever you deliver it. Those are the magic words that will tell you that you've finally mastered it: "Tell me more."

4. **Research:** Here's a word you may not like: "**Research.**" Before you reach out to your first client, find out all you can about that organization. There are 3 modes:

a. Internet and e-mail

b. Phone calls

c. Face-to-face

Find out all you can about the client's needs. Take the time and energy to field-test your offering to discover what the responses are to it. The proof of the pudding is in the eating and the proof of your offering is in the customer's/client's reaction to it. This research is indispensable. Don't allow for any surprises. Know the reaction to your offering through research BEFORE you enter the market, not after.

5. **Choose a Niche:** Once you've completed your research, you have a choice to make—cover the marketplace or focus on a specific niche. To assure your success, **choose the niche**. Select what you consider a responsive niche and put all your resources behind that initial push, like a sharp laser beam.

6. **Empathy:** Become familiar with the concept of emotional intelligence (EI) and apply that to your sales approach. The component of EI that needs attention is **empathy**. To what extent can you put yourself in the customer's/client's shoes? What is it that s/he needs? How does your offering fill that need better than the competition? How does the user of your offering see that need being met? Forget your agenda for a moment; let yourself really get

into the mindset of the receiver and do so wholeheartedly, being as critical or cynical or suspicious as anyone might be when first confronted with something new. Only then will you know your offering from a broader perspective and know better how to sell it.

7. **Make the Connection:** Sometimes a new offering needs to be explained to its new users, especially if innovation is involved. The more innovative, the more education may be necessary. The new users will run the gamut of being open or closed to your offering. Those closer to the closed side may need some instruction, at least connecting the dots to illustrate how the needs can be better met by your innovative offering. Consider yourself an educator to **make the connection** between a unique offering and how it satisfies a need better than anything else.

8. **Bottom Line: Focus on the bottom line**, which is typically manifested in money or time saved. Whatever the superior benefits of your unique offering, ultimately it needs to be demonstrated in higher income and/or time saved. Without demonstrating this bottom-line benefit, you make it harder on yourself to prove the success of your offering.

9. **Integrate New Information:** Learn as you go. You have chosen a niche market to begin with. As you begin to penetrate that market niche, the questions will get tougher. Take all the information you've gleaned in talking with higher levels of authority and **integrate that new information into your sales pitch**. Keep fine tuning so that your perspective becomes both broader and deeper.

Only then will the higher levels appreciate what you have to offer and be able to support to their associates. The new information includes what you've learned about how your offering may meet the needs of the organizations you're selling, all this learned as you listen to your customers/clients.

10. **Your Cutting Edge:** As you do all the above, **discover your own cutting edge**—the best combination of the personal resources you bring to bear—and integrate all you've learned above with your own personal uniqueness. Explore what it is that makes you different from others, for good or bad, and convert that into a uniquely personal approach that is entirely your best self. This will not be easy—finding your own WOW factor—but it will help put you over the top. Here are 8 ways to accomplish that:

a. This first one can be both the most challenging and the easiest, depending on how you choose to approach it. It takes Item 6 above to the limit in terms of caring about your customer as if s/he were a beloved relative. This may come easily to you or it may present a great challenge. Your best bet is to let go and just imagine him/her to be that beloved close one. **Have her/his welfare as a top priority.** Not long ago, I was in the process of finding the right surgeon for a procedure that involved a fair amount of risk. One surgeon listened to my concerns without rush and finally said, in a comforting voice, "If you were my brother, I would tell you not to have the surgery." I had the surgery anyway and the outcome was successful, but this man really listened and gave me his personal assurance that at least one surgeon heard my concerns. He was the one I chose. Allow yourself to "love" your client.

b. When beginning your presentation, **begin with what is most familiar to you**. The initial part of your presentation is what makes the most impact. Start with what is most comfortable for you and allow your authentic, more comfortable self take the first lap.

c. To add to that, **just be yourself as much as possible**. It makes the whole process incredibly easier.

d. Back to the emotional intelligence framework, **be as aware as possible** of the clients'/customers' need for your offering, and engage them with the specifics that speak to their needs.

e. Continuing along that line, **give your clients the breathing space** they need to react once in a while. Without losing the momentum of your presentation, allow yourself the flexibility to engage with the customer rather than dominate the interaction. Be in the moment—the client's/customer's moment. Allow the interaction to become a subtle dance rather than a one-person show.

f. Don't hesitate to **allow humor** into the situation, naturally (even if you have to practice some jokes in private and try them out on associates beforehand).

g. The best time to ensure the other's participation is anytime, but particularly when you feel you've passed the tipping point of your presentation. If the client seems to be taking over, don't panic. It's what you want to happen. **The best outcome is allowing the customer**

to begin to close the sale.

h. When it's all over, **ask for feedback**. This gives the other a chance to be a player in the transaction and creates a sense of shared responsibility in the making of the decision. It helps to build the relationship for future business.

Some helpful tips to accomplish the above items:

1. **Practice:** You've heard the old phrase, "Practice makes perfect." This applies to effective sales as much as it does to anything else. Selling is a skill that involves persistence in the face of constant rejection. The more you can practice your delivery, your engaging interactive involvement, and the subtle movement toward the close, the more natural it will come across. It's like any talent that takes a lot of practice. Those best at it make it look so easy. **The secret is the practice.** The payoff is the ease of ultimate delivery. Whether it's acting on Broadway, top-level sport competition, or speaking on the platform, what looks so easy to accomplish comes with lots of work beforehand. So perfect your sales by taking a disciplined approach to practice.

2. **Honest Feedback:** Along these lines, if you want to feel comfortable addressing groups in your sales endeavors, it wouldn't hurt to attend some Toastmasters sessions to **get honest feedback** on your delivery style. The information you get will be incredibly valuable as you **fine tune your talents for more effective selling.**

3. **Make it Second Nature:** Though you'll be spending time

practicing, that doesn't mean you have to memorize your presentation. **Just practice your presentation enough** so that it becomes second nature to you. Make sure to include

a. Personal stories that were meaningful to you

b. Details of incidents that help move your stories along

c. The emotions involved, particularly fear, as that will stand out from the rest, and all this with

d. Emotional energy

4. **Develop an Arc: Develop an arc for your presentation,** starting with a startling or fascinating beginning, a building of tension as you develop and engage your "audience," and then ending with a strong finish.

5. **Enhance Rapport:** One way of doing this is to engage your "audiences" with questions and challenges. **Enhance the rapport with them through interesting interaction.**

6. **Your Prospect's Point of View:** The best approach is to make the prospect feel that it's his/her idea to enhance the understanding of your offer. **Help the prospect understand the value of your offering from her/his point of view.**

7. **Learn to Care:** What matters most in all this is your ability to hold on to your sense of authenticity, that you really do care about your prospect. The best way to assure this is to really **allow yourself to truly care**. This is the key to all of this. Nurture this value within yourself over time. It will make your job more than a job, into a calling. Instead of draining you, your selling will be enriching you with each new relationship. Your ultimate goal is to serve

your prospect and that becomes a fulfilling venture from day to day. Here are some recommendations to make this part of your new value system of selling:

e. Whether or not you make the sale, **make sure your prospect gets something of value** from your presentation, something of real value. It might be a piece of useful information, an offer to be available for future consultation, even a small gift.

f. If you know you're going to **leave your prospect with a gift**, then that allows you to feel more confident through your presentation. You know that, whether or not a sale is made today, there will be an opportunity for your prospect to thank you for that gift, making your next meeting that much more anticipated.

g. **Include some insight into the prospect's needs**, whether it relates directly to your offering or not. That obviously helps show your caring for the prospect.

h. The essence of engagement is drama, and the essence of drama is conflict. How can you include some conflict in your own personal story of yourself involved with what you are offering? Maybe it once saved your day. Perhaps it helped you in a difficult personal relationship. **Don't be afraid to go deeper into your own feelings.** Tell a story of how your offering made a real difference, resolving some personal conflict in your own life. If you have to change some of the details to "protect the innocent," or to enhance the drama, you can use a bit of poetic license, as long as the essence of the story is real. Don't lie about the essence. And never lie about the emotional drama—that is the core of what makes the story authentic.

i. "Follow your bliss," said mythologist Joseph Campbell. **Dig into your inner soul** and capture the personal meaning and purpose of your sales career. Engage your emotions and inner spirit in the venture of making a calling of your service. Let your sales career be a personal opportunity to reach greater heights of meaningful service. Aim to please your prospect at the highest levels and you yourself can enjoy a high calling while making your sales grow like lightning.

Finally, let's take a look at how some sports legends made their efforts succeed, and how you can learn from them.

The greatest hockey player, Gordie Howe, who recently passed away, and football great, Johnny Unitas, both had the same philosophy: For great confidence, just practice, practice, practice.

Michael Jordan told us that his intense play came from intense practice. So practice with your own style of intensity and the outcome will be demonstrated in your sales numbers.

Some final notes on how to reach your prospects electronically:

1. Use testimonials in your website whenever you can. Nothing works like hearing other people talk about your good points.

2. Always start your copy with the benefits for your prospects.

3. Quickly develop a newsletter to send your prospects, to allow them to read about your expertise.

4. Use headlines and sub-heads liberally.

5. Use the first paragraph or two to get the essence of your message across. No need to write "How are you doing?"

6. Have you noticed how I enumerated all my recommendations? Did that make it more appealing to you? If so, it might also do the same for your prospects.

Good luck—no, it's not luck: It's practice balanced with focus and authenticity. Remember: You can be an overnight sales genius, but only if you put in the dedicated hours of work recommended here to make the "overnight success" possible. It's all in your hands, no one else's. So, instead of saying "Good luck," I'll say "Farewell," which literally means "Do (what you do, in this case, sales) well." But I do hope to see you sometime.

David Ryback is the author of *Putting Emotional Intelligence to Work* as well as *Secrets of a Zen Millionaire* (winner of the Georgia Author of the Year in its category). He is a recent recipient of the Kay Herman Legacy Award by the National Speakers Association. He is an international speaker who touches hearts and forges success in sales and leadership. He can be reached at **404/918-7800** or **David@ EQassociates.com**.

AKASHA GARNIER

COLORFUL LESSONS: FIND THE KEYS TO YOUR STRENGTHS AND YOUR BRAND

When I was approached to write a chapter for Lightning Growth: Success Strategies for Today's Leaders, it was very close to my first book launch for Secrets to Shine Through the Noise, so I had to balance the ideas of presenting and growing my own product at the same time.

I had learned some excellent strategies and time-savers from Justin Sachs, the CEO of Motivational Press, so I was honored to be part of this book to help plan, recognize and acknowledge brand growth.

We all have our journey stories, don't we? Is there a story you tell yourself about why you are not going after your goals? I admit I had my own reasons.

Have you wondered why some people are discovered, while others are lost in the fray and can't take that next step? There may be some obvious answers like more marketing budget or who they know. Yet, that's only part of the puzzle.

How then do winners stay on top of the game and achieve lightning growth?

DISCOVER HOW TO BE THE CLEAR CHOICE OVER YOUR COMPETITION.

Your story is what connects you to the customer and makes you memorable. When you resonate with your audience and clients that let you shine through as the best choice. And it's what will get your customers to buy from you over and over again. Add those key elements and you'll find yourself standing out from the competition. Customers purchase perceptions and reputations, not Product X. They buy the promise of what you'll deliver. They buy likeability. And they'll continue to buy when they like your story and brand.

You have the chance to use the power of branding to your greatest advantage.

Your brand, or reputation, is one of the most important factors in your life. This applies to your personal brand, or your professional brand. It determines how people react and listen to you...it even determines how much you sell and how expensive your product is.

Your brand image is so important that it cannot be left to chance.

I speak from personal experience during my own journey, and also to the fact that my recent web project just received platinum and gold MarCom awards. The Marcom Awards "honor excellence and recognize the creativity, hard work and generosity of marketing and communication professionals" according to their website. After working hard and smart on some digital projects, we are happy to receive recognition. It's not just about the hardware. Sure, consist winning of awards helps open doors. Marketing can sometimes be nebulous, and these industry awards represent measurable success. The other practical piece is equally important: Winning these awards opens more doors and gives me healthy options.

My agents have offered freelance branding projects to help with a day job as I as carving the path to my dream job of being a best-selling author. I believe in working smart. Having rent covered and going on a sailing adventure as a reward for hard work eases my mind. And it's easier to write with a peaceful mind, trust me. I even believe that writing well is a muscle that we can train; I warm up and meet goals at my day job, then focus on getting my own writing done in my spare time. (Just keep a healthy work/life, get-paid-what-you're-worth balance. Remember that a job that requires unpaid overtime is not ideal if it is going to halt progress toward your dream job!)

As I was expanding my writing portfolio and earning money to travel for my travel thriller series I worked with some creative agencies. One of my first projects in Chicago was writing for a paint brand found at two of the main big box home improvement stores.

Actually, this project brought together two of my talents when we took our newly formed marketing team out sailing on Lake Michigan with an authentic wooden tall ship.

Our team sailing outing was a gorgeous day, like living in a sunshine, puffy-cloud postcard of the Chicago skyline. We went out for some team building, and as an event manager, I was nominated as hostess with the mostess.

We were a new marketing team, and had focused on deadlines instead of connections.

This day ushered in a fresh perspective, with a creative way to get to know each other.

One of the games we played as an ice breaker was "What's your Elan?" (This was meant as "élan" as in "vigorous spirit or enthusiasm", and as the new premium paint brand dubbed Elan.)

Everyone on the team had already chosen a color from this collection and was invited to share their first job. I held up a color sample and shared the job and the rest of the team guessed which teammate it was. The stories were playful and memorable. We certainly got to know our teammates in a creative way. Many team members kept their color swatch and pirate bandana on their desk for the rest of the year.

Now think about how this applies to you.

Do you still have a favorite color? Has it changed from your last answer (even if it was grade school)?

A color may have been one of the first ways that we expressed ourselves as individuals.

We were declaring who we were then, and now.

Fresh perspective activity>>>

Take an objective look in on your own story and home.

What would you say about the person living here based on the clothing?

The organization?

The refrigerator?

Set a timer. Rush write for 15 minutes (hand writing or typing both work, just keep the editor side of yourself away for 15 minutes, and don't stop).

After 15 minutes, review your answers.

Do these answers feel accurate? Are you surprised by this snapshot of your life?

What change could you make?

This same paint client provided a colorful branding lesson. When the project began the paint product had a very generic style with no customer recollection or awareness; they were now ready to create a name for themselves.

They are ripe for a rebrand or relaunch. In non-marketing speak that means that if you talked to a customer after visiting a big box store and asked them about the brands of paint they remember looking at, they people that we spoke with could not remember this one. To them it didn't exists. So we set off to change that.

When I went into better defining the paint client's brand I asked questions and benchmarked their completion.

I asked them "What makes you distinctive? Why are you doing this rebrand?"

When I asked their "why" it was weak at first. It basically boiled down to "Nothing sets us apart. We're just putting out a product to compete with our competitor's top of the line release.

OUCH. How can I help them with an answer like that?

Now think about your brand (your business, product or yourself).

We're helping to refine, reshape and re-launch what sets you apart.

Do a 10-minute brainstorm on: What sets me apart?

Yes, sometimes this question taps new ideas and produces different answers compared to "what makes me distinctive?". I call these revelations "light bulb" moments. And I've heard from many readers about their revelations after doing these exercises.

I work with several JV partners, so I invite you to reach out to me with answers and with ideas on how we could help each other's lightning growth (Akasha@Akashagarnier.com). Join my mailing list at Akashagarnier.com for "6 Pro Secrets to Shine Through the Nosie":

1. Use creative and business strengths to live a life on purpose, determining outcomes in advance.
2. Learn why many people end up at destinations they didn't consciously choose.
3. Understand how to reroute this outcome by developing a written life plan that articulates what they want in each of the major life domains.
4. Define, refine amplify your personal and/or business brand to shine through the noise.
5. Celebrating small successes along the way to rejuvenate the journey.
6. Color yourself intrigued with inspirational coloring pages based on the upcoming thriller series.

I work with community organizations, most recently with members of Teen Cancer America, The Who's charity, helping to raise awareness and to build a teen cancer unit in every state.

I have consulted on TCA's social media projects including 5 #ROAR4TCA's and in donating images from <u>Secrets to Shine Through the Noise</u> to Color with Care, a coloring book for teens going through cancer treatment. I wrote <u>Secrets to Shine Through the Noise</u> as a source to gain knowledge, power, and skills to make positive changes, and then to share the stories of lessons along the way; it's also intended to help inspire and give back to the community with my promo partners, Teen Cancer

America and Nando Milano Trattoria. I donate 10% of proceeds from <u>Secrets to Shine Through the Noise</u> to Teen Cancer America; Nando Milano is donating an additional 10% to those who buy the book and dine at Nando Milano Trattoria Chicago or Champaign, IL.

I think of this chapter and my book as a love letter to my starving artist self. I was working 3 jobs and trying to fund films when I first moved to LA in my 20's. Eventually I met mentors who helped me see what I was capable of – they recognized my shine before I did. Now I've become a branding expert, and have helped people become distinctive with their personal and professional brands. It's exciting to hear the feedback and I look forward to watching "Shine Through the Noise" evolve as a film and community.

As I finish this chapter, I hear choruses of "It's the end of the world as we know it", by R.E.M. in the background. Yes, it is a new world order. The Chicago Cubs have shaken the 108-year-old curse, and on-going brand jokes about being loveable losers. Whether you are a baseball fan or not, the story is heartwarming. They came back being down 3 games and took time to regroup during the rain delay.

That was the perspective they needed to refocus and get the runs and outs they needed. The city of Chicago was elated, united and renewed when they held on to the ball for the last out.

Your journey may not involve 108 years, or goats...but there will be hills and valleys. Here's my key to lightning growth: make time to do these exercises to help identify some of your current inner and outer noise.

Inner noise: This can be whatever keeps you feeling stuck... or the story you tell yourself when going back to a job you don't like. Or the feeling that there's not enough time, and you'll make a change another day.

Outer noise: This often involves your competition, or industry or the opinions of others.

I truly believe that once you quiet some of your inner and outer noise, you 'll be better poised to achieve growth. This improved stance sets you up for success, and clears some of the obstacles in your path.

So remember, wherever you are on your journey...believe it's worth the trip!

Cheers & fair winds!

Akasha Lin Garnier

Akasha first started writing Gothic stories to entertain her Halloween party guests in St. Paul, Minnesota. She went to college in Minneapolis where the radio station nominated her to be Production Director and "the voice of WMMR". Akasha enjoyed a wide range of musical influences from The Beatles, The Who, Prince, U2, Pearl Jam, Madonna, The Replacements, Lady Gaga and house music. She then honed in on a show featuring dance music hosted with a friend from her honors writing class. Fortunately the first PR proposal she ever wrote said 'yes'! Voila, First Avenue of "Purple Rain" fame sponsored her award-winning radio show. Akasha continued to round out her writing, PR and producer skills in alternative radio, event and film production.

Akasha's proud of her work as a writer, producer and activist; she balanced branding work as writer and producer in Minneapolis, Los Angeles, New York, Chicago, London, Paris/Cannes, Maui and Hawaii. She excels at helping clients shine with 15 awards/accolades since 2007. Akasha also enjoys giving back through her promo partners, the main partners are The Who's charity: Teen Cancer America and her Italian family's tasty restaurants, Nando Milano.

Akasha was invited to write a motivational book based on her branding expertise, love of travel and ability to inspire with the right blend of business and creative skills: Secrets to Shine Through the Noise (August 2016 Motivational Press release). "Shine Through the Noise" helps amplify personal and professional brand value with an action-able plan. Akasha will celebrate the book's release in a few select cities, and then finish negotiating her travel thriller series for release in best-selling book and film form.

#ShineThroughTheNoise #ItsWorthTheTrip

Sign up for Akasha's A-list for special offers, invitations, inspiration and updates on the travel thriller book and film series: http://www.akashagarnier.com.

Secrets to Shine Through the Noise illustrates Akasha's award-winning abilities as a brand expert, writer, filmmaker and producer to help readers harness business and creative skills; readers and clients have been able to shine through personal and professional noise using these secrets:

» What do we mean by "shine through the noise"?

» We talk about content heavy websites and how that can dull a brand. What branding pro secret do you have to share with our audience about improving their web presence?

» What social media secret could you share with our audience to help them get millions of impressions in under a month?

» We talk about harnessing the power of business and creative skills to help people shine through the noise.

» What's your noise, or Kryptonite?

» What best practice can you share about this?

MOTIVATION

CYNTHIA JAMES

RADICAL SELF CARE: A PORTAL TO SUCCESS

By Cynthia James (Bestselling Author, I Choose Me: The Art of Being a Phenomenally successful Woman at home and at work)

Let me start with a few definitions so that we are on the same page.

Radical: *Change or action relating to or affecting the fundamental nature of something; far-reaching or thorough: a radical overhaul of the existing framework.*

Care: *Effort made to do something correctly, safely, or without causing damage*

> » *Things that are done to keep someone healthy and safe; things that are done to keep something in good condition*

Self-care: *Includes any intentional actions you take to care for your physical, mental and emotional health.*

A few years ago, I sat in a meeting where people shared what they wanted to do with their lives and identified the focus of their intention. One woman said, "Well, I'm putting my attention on radical self-care." I could see perplexed looks on the faces of many in the room so I asked her to explain what that was.

She shared that it was putting herself first, no matter what. Radical self-care was embodying the truth that putting oneself first is the key to healthy living, relationships and full expression.

An amazing conversation broke out in the room as person after person declared that they had no clue how to do what she was describing.

I looked at her and thought, "Wow, that has been my journey over the last several years; learning how to take care of myself, learning how to self-nurture and how to have balance in my life." I remembered taking a class about self-nurturing. I was in a masters program for Spiritual Psychology and this class was mandatory. When the assignment was given, I wondered, "Do I know how to do that? I know how to take care of other people. I know how to work hard and take care of my job and my colleagues. But, I'm not sure I know how to take care of myself." That entire class was revelatory. It really was a course in Radical Self-Care... meaning that 'I' had to learn to come first.

This is an interesting concept because so many of us have been conditioned to take care of others. Women, especially, have caring for others linked to approval, being loved, important and validated.

When you have become adept at being a caretaker and placing others needs beyond your own, there appears to be no other options. This is especially true if your identity is interconnected with the needs of others.

A first reaction in thinking about radical self-care could be the fear that the people in our lives are going to be upset, annoyed or withhold their love. In the work environment, putting yourself first has the possibility of leading to chastisement, not being promoted or even being replaced.

You are right. Things will change. You will be asking people to adapt to a new way of operating with you. They won't understand and will use creative methods to bring you back to the caretaker role. They will give you subtle reminders that you have taught them how to treat you and get what they want from you. The pressure will make it easy to say okay and slip back into the old pattern of doing for others rather than doing for yourself.

There is also the reality that people like to be in control. The thought of letting others make their own decisions and take responsibility for their choices can catapult someone into major resistance because they have always been the one to handle things. They have always been the go to person in crisis and times of need.

When I work with clients I share this. "I have discovered over the last several years that the more I take care of myself the more time and compassion is available for others. I find that I have more energy and the vibration of every aspect of my life is higher."

Getting to this kind of clarity takes time, inner exploration and committed initiative. Here are some ways to know that you are NOT practicing radical self-care.

» Negative self-talk consumes an enormous amount of your time and energy. That includes judgment of your self and others. Your mental acuity is affected and mood swings can be the norm.

» Inability to speak authentically shuts you down and drowns your expressing what you need in the moment.

» Failure to admit that you are exhausted and/or ill and shouldn't take on one more responsibility.

» Eating habits that do not serve you. Sugar, tons of carbs, caffeine overload, fast foods and late night eating are all signs that you are out of control.

» Not exercising or supporting your body with movement is anchored by a list of excuses why you don't have time to do what you know will give you more energy and honor your body.

» Emergence of old anger patterns become present at inappropriate times and hurt the people you care most about.

» Doubting what you know supports you and questioning your intuition.

» Surrendering your power to someone else that clearly does not have your best interest at heart.

» Playing small to keep the peace while creating resentment and non-supportive behaviors.

No time to be still and rest and too busy to spend time with yourself.

» Here is the first thing to remember. You are the most important person in your life. I am not saying that your spouse, children, parents, siblings and friends are not important. I am saying that there has to come a time to surrender to learning what you need and want before others. Your self-care or lack thereof models for others.

I remember being a single mom working 50-hour weeks at my corporate job, caring for my teenage sons and my aging mother and grandmother and trying to maintain a creative outlet. I would go to work at 6:30 a.m., work until 6 p.m., and make my way to the theater to rehearse. This went on for four weeks of rehearsals, one week of previews and an opening to a lovely reception by the public. I was ecstatic. I was also exhausted because there was no down time. I spent weekends making sure food was okay for the week, shop with my mother and grandmother and do errands for them and my kids.

» The challenge was that I was unwilling or didn't know how to ask for help. I believed that I had to do it all. The result was my children and family members expected me to show up whenever they needed something. There was usually some dramatic occurrence that had me rushing to my car to rescue whomever was calling.

I remember thinking to myself that I needed to slow down and rest. But my ego engagement in "being the one" kept me moving at warp speed. One day, I fell getting out of bed. My husband rushed me to the doctor. After many tests and finally seeing a chiropractor we discovered that I had a torn "psoas" muscle. That is the muscle that helps life your leg. No one could believe that I could have been walking around with this and not have felt the pain. I didn't feel it because I was so focused outside of myself. I had shut down my connection to my body and it's needs.

I believe that we all need clear goals and structures to support radical self-care. Here are four steps that might assist you in "choosing you."

Conscious communication creates clarity – True communication is a two way street. It is the giving and receiving of information but it starts with you. Here are some questions to ask yourself before you enter into conversations or send an email that you might regret.

» How do I feel?

» What do I want?

» How is my past coloring my present?

» What am I getting out of trying to be right?

» What do I need to say?

» What agreements have I broken?

» Am I making the other person wrong?

» Am I trying to control this person or this situation?

» Where have I withheld the truth?

» How can I be of service to this relationship and myself?

Movement is a healthy sign of aging – You do not have to be a maniac about working out. However, consistent movement maintains health. Latest statistics:

a) Fewer than 5% of adults participate in 30 minutes of physical activity each day; only one in three adults pursues the recommended amount of physical activity each week.

b) Only 35–44% of adults 75 years or older are physically active, and only 28-34% of adults ages 65-74 are physically active.

c) More than 80% of adults do not meet the guidelines for both aerobic and muscle-strengthening activities, and more than 80% of adolescents do not do enough aerobic physical activity to meet the guidelines for youth.

d) Children now spend more than seven and a half hours a

day in front of a screen (e.g., TV, videogames, computer).

e) 28% of Americans, or 80.2 million people, aged six and older are physically inactive.

Here are some benefits of consistent movement:

» Less colds

» Reduced anger and depression

» Better sleep

» Lowers rates of heart disease

» Lowers blood pressure

» Improved levels of concentration and focus

» Increased oxygen to the brain that may enhance its ability to learn

» Alterations to neurotransmitters

» Structural changes in the central nervous system

Attention to nutrition nourishes the body – In order to live a fully expressed and thriving life the body needs vitality.

Here are some interesting statistics on *nutrition* from the President's Council on Fitness, Sports & Nutrition:

Food safety awareness goes hand-in-hand with nutrition education. In the United States, food-borne agents affect one out of six individuals and cause approximately 48 million illnesses, 128,000 hospitalizations, and 3,000 deaths each year.

Typical American diets exceed the recommended intake levels or limits in four categories: calories from solid fats and added sugars, refined grains, sodium, and saturated fat.

About 90% of Americans eat more sodium than is recommended for a healthy diet.

Reducing the sodium Americans eat by 1,200 mg per day could save up to $20 billion a year in medical costs.

Food consumption increased in all major food categories from 1970 to 2008. Average daily calories per person in the marketplace increased approximately 600 calories.

Since the 1970s, the number of fast food restaurants has more than doubled.

More than 23 million Americans, including 6.5 million children, live in food deserts—areas that are more than a mile away from a supermarket.

Simple steps to become conscious about eating:

» Pay attention to portion control.

» Drink 6-8 glasses of water a day.

» Monitor salt and sugar intake.

» Stop eating late at night.

» Remember protein bars are not meals and are usually high in sugar.

» Sodas contain huge amounts of sugar and additives.

» Eat more protein, vegetables and fruit.

» **A centering or spiritual practice reduces stress** – There is a lot of conversation about mindfulness these days. I believe that mindfulness is the art of learning to be present in each moment. Anyone can do this. It is not about religion or a certain spiritual practice. It is about a willingness to learn how to become still and listen to the powerful voice of intuition. It is about being intentional to bring your whole self to every experience and interaction.

Here are some thoughts on what might support you in this area:

» **Use affirmations**; Statements of what you are willing to receive. They do not have to be true in the moment. The more you say them the less power negative thoughts and self talk have in your life. Here are some examples.

» I am fully equipped to handle anything today.

» Today, I bring my best self to my work and to my life.

» I radiate joy and peace wherever I am.

» I am healthy in mind, body and spirit.

» I am destined for success and I claim it now.

» Love expresses through me in every relationship.

» Money is my friend and I am open to receiving extraordinary wealth.

» **Meditate** – There is not one way to meditate. Some feel it is shutting down your mind. From my perspective that is impossible. In meditation, the mind quiets. For some it is practicing in sitting meditation. For others, it is listening to quiet music, walking in a quiet forest or simply focusing on the breath. I suggest you explore different forms and see what works for you. Here are some things that are important.

1. Be away from technology while you practice

2. Have a quiet place where you will not be disturbed

3. Do it consistently (mine is first thing in the morning)

4. Music or guided meditations might assist

5. Use a mantra (a word or phrase that brings you back to center)

6. Focus on the breath – breathe in to a count of 5 and exhale to a count of five until you feel yourself begin to relax

» **Journal your feelings** - research suggests expressive writing can support therapeutically. It may also offer physical benefits to people battling terminal or life-threatening diseases. Studies by those in the forefront of this research—psychologists James Pennebaker, PhD, of the University of Texas at Austin, and Joshua Smyth, PhD, of Syracuse University—suggest that writing about emotions and stress can boost immune functioning in patients with such illnesses as HIV/AIDS, asthma and arthritis.

» Write 2 pages in a journal in the morning before you go to work. This can be random thoughts or ideas about the way you want to express

» Try keeping a small journal in your bag or office and just writing down feelings around stressful moments when they occur.

» Write immediately following a time of meditation or contemplation.

» Journal your dreams and goals. Be specific and dream BIG.

Today, my interaction with other people and the interaction with my career are from a healthy standpoint rather than from need—need to be validated, need to be in control, need to feel important, need to be loved.

You have the chance to learn how to take care of yourself. You can discover what nurtures you. For me, it's hot baths with candles, walks, meditation, and reading great books that feed my soul. It's turning on music and dancing around the house. It makes me feel joyous and alive.

Take time to determine what you need to feel cared for and comforted. Begin by building an intentionally nurturing schedule. If you can't start daily, try weekly. What are you willing to do once a week to nurture yourself? What are you willing to do to feel better, healthier, more conscious and balanced? Once you have made the choice, make that time sacred, without interruption. It may be uncomfortable at first. It will feel like you are in a void or in limbo because it's foreign. Do it anyway, for you will discover a place of health and balance that opens portals for new and exciting possibilities in your life.

You deserve radical self-care and the world is waiting for you to be your most powerful and healthy self.

Cynthia is a transformational specialist and one of today's brightest and best loved inspirational leaders, guiding people to make changes at a deep level for lasting healing. Cynthia excels as a speaker, coach, singer, and multiple award-winning author of What Will Set You Free and Revealing Your Extraordinary Essence and #1 Bestseller for I Choose Me: The Art of Being a Phenomenally Successful Woman at Home and at Work. Cynthia James embodies the quote "I am not what I have done. I am what I have become;" and, she leads others to do the same. Her own life was transformed as she transcended a violent and abusive childhood. Through education and personal healing, she created the foundation for all her programs.

Ms. James has facilitated hundreds of workshops, seminars and keynotes, including: Omega Institute, Celebrate Your Life, Woman Arising, the Gift in Shift, the Colorado Behavior Healthcare Council, the Women's Success Forum, the Children's Hospital, Spirit One Seminars, LeadingAge, and many others. Cynthia's most recent programs and tools include: Advanced Awareness Coaching, offering depth, focus and results for high level business leaders; and, Affirmative Living, which includes a meditation CD, Passages, and an APP for iPhones and Droids, 100 days of Affirmative Living, in English and Spanish.

Cynthia was once a working Hollywood actress, co-hosted a radio talk show, a television talk show in Los Angeles, and appeared in the movie, Sacred Journey of the Heart. She is a former Miss Minnesota Universe, sought after as a radio guest and is a contributing blogger for YourTango.com. Thousands follow her monthly inspirational videos and her monthly newsletter and blog. Cynthia has uniquely combined the creative arts with innovative therapeutic techniques to bring powerful personal growth, healing and expansion to individuals of all ages, cultures, and lifestyles. She facilitates the message of her award-winning books, What Will Set You Free and Revealing Your Extraordinary Essence, worldwide and as a workshop to women in prisons. Internationally, she has led workshops in England, Switzerland and Ireland; and, she has led a myriad of pilgrimages to various spiritual locations in France, Peru and Italy.

In 2012, Cynthia created and facilitated the internationally successful Venus Transit University, reaching over 8,000 people. In 2014, she and her husband of 16 years, Carl Studna, created and co-hosted Bridging the Gender Gap Teleseries, focusing on developing trust and understanding between men and women. Also in 2014, her Extraordinary Living Project was selected to be a Commitment Maker by the Clinton Health Matters Initiative. In the same year, she founded her Extraordinary Living Foundation whose mission is creating sustainable health for women in mind, body and spirit. In 2015, Cynthia and her business partner, Jean Hendry, created the Women Creating Our Futures conference featuring nationally and internationally recognized speakers, life coaches and artists guiding hundreds of women to build the life and future they both desire and deserve.

Cynthia holds two Master's Degrees, the first in Consciousness Studies from the Holmes Institute, where she was awarded the honor of distinguished alumni. The second is in Spiritual Psychology from the University of Santa Monica.

ALICE STEFANIAK

OPPORTUNITY PATHWAYS

"But there was a difference between being stuck and choosing to stay. Between being found and finding yourself."

Martina Boone, Compulsion

"Staying locked into an image of how things are supposed to be can blind us to the grace of what is."

Elaine Orabona Foster, In Movement There Is Peace

Inertia...drawn into a black hole...leaving the world behind ...wandering...all signs of being in a rut. The not-sure feeling of how life is moving at a chaotic speed and leaving us behind is a common one. The real-sure notion that we are spinning on *our* axis and making a difference is a state we crave and cherish. So where are you now...on the road again or lost in space?

Hopefully by the time you are done reading this chapter you will learn the art of creating options for yourself and how coaching may help you attain the feeling that you always have somewhere to inscribe your heart and mind.

WHY OPTIONS IN COACHING

When I think of the most engaging parts of coaching that I experience, it is when people are depth-diving to discover their most limiting options and finding ways to expand or create more possibilities than they ever considered.

How does this happen and why is this part of coaching? Well, coaching has as one of its goals—to expand horizons, destabilize limitations, and offer a panoramic view of life so that we can actually experience more of it.

Different people have said it in distinctive ways: some people ask for a coach experience because they are stuck or seem limited in their imagination of what they might do in a certain situation that is imploding around them. Other people want to be part of the coaching experience because it may give them tools to use when they are starting a daunting new project that is confounding them. Still others want coaching because it shores up their confidence and is an encouraging experience whenever they feel like procrastinating about a new decision.

What I also see is that coaching allows someone besides YOU to look inside of your head and view things from another angle. Coaching also allows you to see what you might not want to talk about because you are simply not ready to take that leap into the dark. In other words, the invisible elephant in the room is all too visible to the coach but the client has become very quiet when we tiptoe near that visibly-hidden topic.

So whether you are stuck, frozen in place, terrified, lacking confidence or just want to stop talking about the issue or the question being posed, coaching at its best is relevant, welcome and produces results.

VUCA??

One of the factors that allows coaching to specialize in creating options is the awareness of what the military coined as VUCA after the fall of the Soviet Union and the rise of the various regional wars, terrorist activity, and break up and realignment of various countries throughout the world. In short, V stands for volatility –that explosive word that insinuates that changes in our world are often unpredictable and have not been seen before. U stands for uncertainty that is caused by the volatility and the what we often call disruptive changes. C stands for the complexity involved when we look at the multivalent and seemingly endless causes and factors. And A of course, stands for ambiguity –the chaos that surrounds us our work and community that is unexpected yet revelatory (Slocum, 2013).

Tom Peters used to call VUCA chaos and many others at the executive level have envisioned VUCA for years but are now talking more about it with their whole staff. Instead of making decisions in a more calculated and long-term vision the descriptors of VUCA say we need flexibility and quickness in decision making. Being an adaptive and agile company is considered a plus.

What does this mean in terms of coaching? Oftentimes, what I see as a coach is the reactions to the VUCA environment named by fears and worries of the person in front of me. If you are not aware of how management is dealing with the volatility of each day and the fact that certain processes at work can become obsolete in a few weeks, or that the talents that you bring are no longer needed, or that suddenly you are being trained for something that you were not hired to do, and there is pressure to get things done that are not fully explained—-you are experiencing VUCA.

What is interesting is that the 2016 Super Bowl experience was an illustration of VUCA on many levels. The whole season for the Carolina Panthers was one of extraordinary gains and wonderful results especially for the quarterback, Cam Newton. What he and his team had accomplished was a wonderful exhibition of his talents and the unified team experience that worked with him to bring them all to the Super Bowl. On the other hand, the disruptive and chaotic experience of the Denver Broncos with two different quarterbacks, Manning and Osweiler and a powerhouse of a Defensive group also arrived at the same Super Bowl. What might have been an easy guess at what might result with these two very different teams instead became an interesting VUCA experience.

For instance, the fact that Peyton Manning was eventually the quarterback who would lead the Broncos –also an unknown to the very end of the season—made for an interesting and unpredictable result for both teams. In fact, for days after the Broncos won the game, there were discussions and creative explanations for what happened and why the Broncos won while the Panthers and especially Cam Newton were bewildered and beaten. The variables of both teams and the mistakes made by both teams led to a very unusual result in scoring, storytelling, team philosophy and perceptual discomfort.

There could have been more plausible experiences that people could have seen happening but instead there were more options available that were favorable to the Broncos and problematic for the Panthers. So the options were expanded by simply watching each decision by the players every time someone moved on the field. They were not always explicit choices that players made but that is what makes the choices even more difficult to explain later. The collision of forces and certain selective actions by various players made the ambivalence very hard to explain especially for those players who counted on winning. So that definitely was a VUCA experience in miniature.

So what do people do with this type of environment in terms of options, flexibility and strategies for the future?

METHODS FOR CREATING OPTIONS

BRILLIANT QUESTIONS

One option that coaching has taken very seriously is the power of asking good questions. Not only questions that are insightful and reasonable, but questions that make people look at the world from unusually discerning and sometimes extraordinarily perceptive perspectives. McNulty has this to say:

Get curious, and get out of your comfort zone. VUCA is a condition that calls for questions — lots of them. Penetrating questions that ferret out nuance. Challenging questions that stimulate differing views and debate. Open-ended questions that fuel imagination. Analytical questions that distinguish what you think from what you know (Ed McNulty, October 27,2015)

STRATEGIC IMPACT

Another approach for coaching is to suggest that the client or people in a corporate group attend a set of university courses about strategic foresight. An example is the graduate studies program at the Ontario College of Art and Design. The courses say that they want to "positively impact society, enhance business success and manage organizational change" by "teaching complex problem finding, framing and solving, to envision and develop sustainable futures" and "to think holistically - exploring, challenging and finding meaning in order to reframe and guide both present and future actions" (OCAD University, 2016)

What was interesting is that this is the recipe for coaches who are leading people through the labyrinths of life. We always end up talking about complexity, organizational change, reframing ideas and envisioning the future. So strategic foresight courses might be one of the recipes to take people through their paradigms and visions of how they navigate life.

MIND MAPPING

One of the tools that I use to invite strategic initiative to help people navigate the chaos is to do some mind mapping. It is a great tool that allows people—who are interested in new options—to see the results of their choices. Mind mapping takes

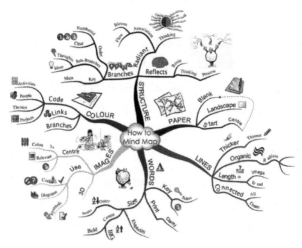

the issue, puts it in the center of the map and extends many branches around that center. The branches sometimes look like thickets and tangles rather than simple suggestions. I emphasize thickets and tangles because there is nothing straight and narrow about today's ideas and visions.

To give you an example, we might look at a person who wants to stop procrastinating and do creative work on a project. When I put that in the middle of this person's mind map, we had about 10 very crowded and multipronged branches around the center that addressed the issue of procrastination and the desire to be creative. Some of these branches were astonishing even to the person who was doing the mind map. He thought he knew exactly why he was procrastinating. Instead it turned into a powerful revelatory exploration of why he worked nights and got the most work done during the evenings he spent away at the office. Working at night at the office became more of the central aspect for that him. It was a pattern that happened early in his life when he did not want to come home and take care of crying children while his wife went off to work in the evening. That pattern no longer existed now—his wife no longer worked evenings and his children no longer were crying babies, but he had found a safe nest to work without stress that only complicated his procrastination at other hours of the day.

So mind mapping can often help people discover some of the old patterns of life that continue to sap people's energy today or make them revert to unhealthy practices that create more ambiguity about a project. Once we have the mind map, we explore the driving motivations—the stories that keep the problem from being solved. We also start reframing these perspectives into new outcomes.

Now the person in coaching has two densely populated maps—the original mind map of the problem, and now the added motivations for solving or reframing the problem. We might now have one or two solutions that would work and we then build a third map of who, how and when the problem will be solved in a step-by-step roadmap. We can even have someone start the map from the final step of success and know all the intermediate steps before everything is solved.

As someone who works with people in various scenarios, what remains constant is the work that is done to map out, discover new frames and build a step by step map toward completion. The problem may change and the motivators will definitely change, but the process can always work on how to get from A to B. The other thing that never changes is that we work as a team on all three mind maps since the questions and the brainstorming we do together frees up the person rather than burden him/her with a tedious job. And it affords time to brainstorm and dream while I make the map.

DECISION MAKING

There are lots of ways that we can familiarize people with the process of decision making when they are in the midst of making choices or rearranging priorities. It is important to ask the person what he/she hopes to do in his/her life over a period of time. That question may never be asked in the heat of the moment when an actual decision is being made because too much is happening.

So let's look at job decisions. When people are making a decision, they may think about many things that are related to the job rather than the actual job being offered. They may think about the salary that is offered or the positive relationships that may develop because of the job. On the other hand, a person is may consider the kind of company they are going to invest their energy in, the type of effects that this job has on people and how it serves the community or relates to their family's perceptions and needs.

A chart might be made with these priorities as well as the alternatives that are considered about their talents. Then there is the issue of whether the job will be held for a significant amount of time, as well as the problematic aspects of the job—job stresses, environmental stresses, personal creativity, future potential, etc.

Besides all those factors, a person needs to know that there are alternatives available, and whether they are actually suitable alternatives or merely thoughtful dreams.

The decision to move ahead can be made through several processes. The coach can do some role-playing to practice a job interview with questions that involve some of these factors. Another option is to make sure that the person making the decision has some immediate feedback. This fits in with the theories of James Rest who believes that the community in which a person lives needs to have some input on serious decisions. He believes that each person then consults with this group who knows the client and his/her values and philosophy of life. When that person has to make a decision, that group reviews the problem and identifies competing explanations that might have some consequence.

I also may offer the coaching client other decision-making plans like the Gofer plan that was devised by Leon Mann when he worked with teens. He gave them five steps: that became the initials of GOFER: consider your **goals**, that lead to your various

options, see what the **facts** tell you, **evaluate** the positive and negative effects of the decision, and **review** how you will make the decision (Byrnes, 2013).

Another thing to know about decision making is that the person you have before you is often only an expert in certain areas of knowledge and practice, so decisions are often made that relate to the person's areas of expertise. That can be pointed out to the decision-maker. It is also clear from some theories of decision making that people who have expertise will rely on this experience they have already gained to influence the decision.

So that is why experts are often brought into a situation so that we have their advantageous experience present in the process. We see that so often in television dramas or in the postmortem review of an accident or situation that plays out after a tragedy. Various experts give their opinion about what happened and how it should not happen again.

What is important in decision making is the realization that there are many good models for making decisions and that each decision that is made has many good alternatives as well. The person needs to realize that he or she has certain priorities and values, that he or she has chosen from alternatives, that he or she knows that there is other option that will equally be acceptable, and that he or she knows that no decision is foolproof. There are many stages of awareness in a decision making process: there is the awareness of the conclusions that come to the fore, the awareness of the biases that enter decision-making, the awareness of how emotions are part of the process—all this makes the person who comes to coaching be a little more expansive and able to understand the limitations of the moment.

———

What a client in coaching also faces is the fact that there are reactions to any decision made. An interesting experience that I sometimes do with clients who are suffering from postmortem decisions that were deemed bad or unfortunate is an exercise I've borrowed from Ira Progoff's journal workshop named "The Fork in the Road" (Progoff, 1975). I have them imagine that their decision is one of the forks in the road that they take through life and that there are equally other forks that they could take to get to another instead of where they are now.

Then I ask them to try another path rather than the one they chose and relive what might happen in as much detail as they can. The results are often quite enlightening and very often quite amusing to the person sitting in front of me. What choices we make and what choices we don't make are the results we see in ourselves now and the values we chose to get there. What will they be like for each of you reading this today? You might try it after you read this article and see what happens.

We've covered a lot of ground on learning how to deal with options, being in a rut, living in a VUCA world, and making decisions. Enjoy one of my favorite quotes and happy reading!

this was a quote from google images . . . no author

WORKS CITED

Byrnes, J. (2013). *The Nature and Development of Decision-making: A Self-regulation Model.* Psychology Press.

Ed McNulty. (October 27,2015). *Leading in an increasingly VUCA world.* Columbia Business School.

OCAD University. (2016). *Ontario Institute of Art and Design University.* Retrieved from Strategic Foresight and Innovation (MDes): http://www.ocadu.ca/academics/graduate-studies/strategic-foresight-and-innovation.htm

Progoff, I. (1975). *At a Journal Workshop: The Basic Text and Guide for Using the Intensive Journal.* Dialogue House Library.

Slocum, E. (2013, October 8). *Six Creative Leadership Lessons From The Military In An Era of VUCA And COIN.* Retrieved from Forbes: http://www.forbes.com/sites/berlinschoolofcreativeleadership/2013/10/08/six-creative-leadership-lessons-from-the-military-in-an-era-of-vuca-and-coin/#3f4f1f343b2a

I am a transition life coach, author and founding coach for a new company called Exoteric. My hometown is Chicago but I fell in love with the Denver area when I studied for my Ph.D. Since then I moved back and hope to continue my adventures here. My journey started at DePaul University, continued at Villanova University and then I received my doctorate at the University of Denver/Iliff. After all that, I followed my inner pilot and was accepted as a coach for certification at the University of Texas at Dallas.

My life experiences continue to lead me toward leadership positions, advisory and consultative arenas, and creative opportunities. Working with many mentors over the years, I found that life is a creative symphony of challenge, adventure, and empowerment. My coaching business is called Dream Cue and there I am the interior designer I've always wanted to be.

ALLISON SUTTER

THE MOTIVATIONAL MECHANISM

Once upon a time, life was amazing. You did what you wanted, when you wanted and had no problem finding the time, energy, inspiration, motivation, creativity, ideas, or resources to get stuff done. Then, you turned five.

That's when the trouble started.

That was the year you learned how to shift from away your natural, inner motivational mechanism to needing motivation to come from an external source. It was a pivotal year in your life and you probably had no idea what was happening.

That's the year you learned the difference between what you wanted to do and what you had to do. It all went downhill from there.

Is it any wonder that we have a perceived motivational drought in a large portion of our population?

There are always those who break away from the pack and figure it out. Perhaps they aren't able to articulate what happened but they knew it was the right choice by how it felt. It's likely they attributed their sudden energetic recalibration to their new response to life's general ennui. They simply decided, unapologetically, things needed to change. The result was a thrilling reconnection with their inner, natural motivational mechanism.

We call these strange beings the lucky ones, the gifted ones, the ones who have it all. We talk about how they seem to have an unnatural ability to sustain focused activity for long periods of time. Many of these strange creatures can even focus on, and complete, projects they don't enjoy. We find this mysterious.

In this chapter, you're going to uncover the mystery of the motivational mechanism and how to access your own.

WHAT'S FLOW?

Have you ever had times when you're totally in the flow? You're focused, creative, and having fun. Time stands still. You don't notice it's been eight hours since your last meal or that your bladder's been full since noon. The kids? They've been calling your name incessantly. They finally gave up and made dinner themselves.

You were so in the zone you didn't notice a thing. You become no body, no thing, in no time. What created this pleasurable, sustained focus?

This state we call flow is you slipping onto your natural state of motivation. It's not that people aren't motivated. It's only and ever a question of what they're motived to. Humans don't lack motivation or need it be inserted into their experience. All humans are born with a natural, fully intact, fully functional motivational mechanism. Until they're talked out of it, of course.

If you want your life experience to be different, it's helpful to become aware of what's happening internally when you're experiencing an outpouring of motivation. It's also helpful to direct a little bit more attention to what's going on internally, and externally, when you're not. All is being made clear to you, in time.

Humans being are naturally creative. We want to do, be, and have more. Keep in mind it's not really the end product we seek to experience. It's much more the unfolding process we desire. The experience we want is the creative one.

This is the motivational mechanism in it's truest form: joyful, creative expansion. Tapping into your natural motivational mechanism is one of the most thrilling aspects about being human. It makes you feel alive.

WHY DON'T I FEEL MOTIVATED?

When you were little, people left you alone for the most part. Because you were short, harmless and took naps often, they let you build fairy houses, fly imaginary airplanes to the moon and wear feathery boas and glittery tops to perform major surgery. They rarely asked you to do things you didn't naturally find exciting because of your inclination to say no.

It wasn't a soft no either; it was a hard no.

In this protected state of youth, you had no problem being motivated to create. In fact, nap time was typically when your second wind hit. No one needed to tell you to stay focused, create, imagine, or keep going. There was no carrot or stick needed to motivate you. You had the endurance of a million wild horses. You were they poster child for motivation.

Then, the tall people in your world had an idea. They thought it would be good if you learned to follow the rules and play well with others. This was where things went awry. No longer were you able to build the way in which you were inspired to, or problem solve in ways that felt natural. Now, you had to do it Their Way.

Things were different from that day forward. There were things you wanted to do, which you had no problem doing. There were things you had to do, Their Way. This didn't feel natural. You began to notice doing it Their Way felt hard. It felt forced, boring, and uninteresting. You resisted, hard.

The tall people took notice of this and began to ask you, repeatedly, to do it Their Way. In fact, in order to get you to do this thing you had never naturally done before, they resorted to cajoling, prodding, promising, and praising.

Some tall ones even punished.

You noticed that the other short ones who did it Their Way immediately got smiles, hugs, and kind words. Who doesn't want that?

The ones who didn't got time outs, stern faces, and more homework. What was the world coming to?

Being the forward thinking short one you were, you could see where this was going. In order to keep the peace, you joined the other Good Ones and made it work. As time passed, however, the tall ones needed to add more and more promises, praise, and punishments in order to get you to comply. The more you tried to do it Their Way, the less you used your natural motivational mechanism. The freedom of youth faded.

Along the way, you even heard rumors of The Ones Who Didn't being called *unmotivated*. Shivers ran up your spine. Was this rumor true? Were they really that bad? You made a mental note to yourself: Avoid, *The Ones Who Didn't*, at all cost.

This continued, as it did for many of the other Good Ones, for years. One day, you noticed it felt as if you'd lost your ability to find your way back to your motivational mechanism. This made you very sad. You felt discouraged, hopeless.

However, not all was truly lost. Reading was the one place in this world left you felt could never be touched by Their Way. You loved reading as a child; it's still your safe place today.

On the way home from work, you visited your favorite book store. You stumbled upon a book with a brain in a light bulb on the cover. It looked interesting so you took it home. Your boss wanted you to do a presentation on motivation and leadership next week. You weren't that excited about the assignment but maybe this book would have some good ideas?

Following your still active, but much ignored, inner motivational mechanism, you started to read. What you found blew your mind. Could it really be true? Could there actually be a way out of Blahs Ville? Was there really a secret, inner doorway leading directly to that indescribable, intoxicatingly delicious sense of creative freedom and motivation you used to know?

HOW DO I RECONNECT WITH MY NATURAL, INNER, MOTIVATIONAL MECHANISM?

While it might have seemed your destiny, to live out a life doing it Their Way, this couldn't be farther from the truth. In fact, your motivational mechanism is alive and well. It needs no jump start, no cajoling, no carrots on sticks. No one else needs to be involved in the reconnection ceremony.

The secret to motivation is to understand it exists within, not without. The idea that someone can motive you is incorrect. They can prod, threaten, trick, instill fear, push, reward or punish you, but they cannot motivate you.

Motivation is defined as: *the general desire or willingness of someone to do something.* Synonyms for motivation are: *enthusiasm, drive, ambition, initiative, and determination.*

These are all inner characteristics of an individual. There's never been a way to insert these attributes into another person, but we can access them within ourselves, at any time.

When you think back to age five, you never had a problem with motivation. You still don't, today.

It was only when the tall people forced you to do it Their Way that things went screwy. It felt like you lost access to your inner power, but you didn't.

When you look over the landscape of society today, there exists a rare and unique breed who've maximized their inner motivational mechanism. How did they do it? Daily attention to what brings them joy, the release of resistance, and a focus on what's good with whatever they're doing at the time.

They follow their highest level of excitement, in any given moment, taking it as far as they can take it until they can take it no farther, daily. They protect this God-given creative inner power at all costs. They show you what it's like to access natural motivation through the power of their example.

What do they call themselves? Small business owner, entrepreneur, writer, leader, artist, musician, actor, activist, and sometimes, even still, five year-old. These are only a few of their nomenclature.

The secret to reinvigorating the magnificence of your motivational mechanism is to:

» stop doing it Their Way. Start being divergent.

» stop doing the stuff you don't want to do. Do more of the

stuff you want to.

» care less about what others think of you. Care more about what you think of you.

» ignore the negative chatter in your mind. Give more attention to the ideas that feel exciting.

» give this process of reawakening your inner guidance, your motivational mechanism, time and space to get stronger. Nurture it as you would your first born child.

Your natural, inner sense of motivation didn't die. It's still there. You just don't recognize it anymore.

It didn't change. You did.

HOW DO I MOTIVATE MYSELF TO DO THE THINGS I DON'T WANT TO?

You already know the answer to this question, silly. You can't motivate yourself to do the things you don't want to. You don't want to do them. No amount of coaxing, cash advances, or carrots are going to motivate you do to the precise thing you don't want to. When you're forced to do it, you experience resentment, anger, and frustration.

Further, you can't motivate other people. You can poke them with insults, prod them with guilt, shock them with fear or ... inspire them with hope. You must recognize, however, that the first three choices are not the same thing as inviting someone to activate their inner motivational mechanism with positivity.

Motivation comes from the inside, not the outside. Inspiring others from a place of hope and unconditional love is the best way to guide them to that inner place of eternal motivation.

Companies pay large sums of money for outsiders to motivate their employees. To what end? Teachers devise tricks to motivate students. Is this helpful? Parents attempt strategies to motivate kids. Don't you see? It goes on forever until someone understands and takes a stand.

For the sake of my sanity and yours, hear me, if you can.

You can't motivate another person to do anything. Motivation is an inside job.

Instead of motivation, when someone is trying to get another person to do something they don't want to do, what usually transpires is guilt, fear, anger, resentment, frustration, or anxiety between one or more of the parties involved. When people coax, or insist, each other into doing something they don't want to do under the guise of motivation, it never ends well.

External motivation is not a sustainable, or enjoyable, pattern of living. It's not even truly motivation. It's trickery. You will always need bigger and bigger prizes to give away with this approach.

Living your life from a place of alignment is the best way to motivate. Others will feel your magnificence and want to know your secret.

HOW DO I GET DONE THE THINGS I NEED TO GET DONE WITHOUT USING EXTERNAL MOTIVATION?

Instead of trying to motivate ourselves to do things we don't want to, or other people to do the things we don't want to for us, let's try a different approach.

Let's assume a few things.

First, that every person on this planet has all the motivation, ideas, energy, stamina, and creativity they need, for any task, already in place and available to them.

Second, that when said person practices something called inner alignment, all the necessary reservoirs of motivation, energy, stamina, and creativity become instantly available to them.

Third, that it's the individual's responsibility find their way to these reservoirs. No one can do it for them.

Fourth, understand there are two journeys in life: an action journey and an emotional journey. They are not the same.

Fifth, that when a person wants to access the motivation, ideas, energy, stamina or creativity to complete a task, it's more effective and efficient, when said person aligns with their inner stream of well being, first. Mental and emotional alignment first, then inspired action. Using this formula, motivation is unleashed naturally from within. Inspiration, motivation's natural playmate, surprises us with a guest appearance every time.

Let's say a tall person, either at work or at home, asks you to do something. This task feels exciting so you jump on it right away or at least at your earliest convenience. Since the emotion that stimulated your body into motion was excitement, you harbor no resentment, anger, or self-pity from this action. This is a win-win situation. It produces the best possible results in the most effective way. You've opened the vault of your motivational mechanism and all it's jewels spill forth.

Now let's say a tall person, either at work or at home, asked you to do something, This task feels laborious so you put it off. Or, you do it but you harbor resentment, anger, or self-pity. Since the emotion that stimulated your body into motion is negative, life suddenly seems to suck. This is a lose-lose situation. You don't complete the task in the most effective or efficient manner and it takes you longer than usual. There was also something about the result that you had to go back and fix, or that just didn't work at all. This is a lose-lose situation.

This time let's pretend that a tall person, either at work or at home, asks you to do something that you don't want to do. You feel annoyed by even being asked and you feel you have to comply.

Instead of taking action right away, you take a few moments (hours, days or weeks) to get yourself into a better feeling place. You've been studying this thing called alignment for a few months now and you're learning all kinds of fun, new ways of thinking, feeling, and being. It really seems to be working.

Instead of doing this task with resistance, and needing to be motivated with an external source, you take the time to find inner calm, peace, and certitude before you lift a finger. You're new mantra is, "Get happy and then ..."

This situation started out as a lose-lose but quickly transpired into a win-win.

You've slowed your habit of being spurred into action with negative energy and are willing to make the inner mental and emotional shifts before moving forward. With practice, you've been able to tap into your ever present motivational mechanism in a way that makes the tall people in your life, at work and at home, smile.

The best part of this story? You're smiling, too. You've proven to yourself there IS a way to live in this world of tall people, but follow your own rules for thriving.

Your take away? Motivation is not something that needs to be inserted into any person's experience. No one can give this attribute to you, or take it away. With the right training and practice, you can learn to access the same motivational mechanism, energy, stamina, and creativity, you had when you were five years-old.

You feel motivated, inspired, and energized vowing to teach the tall ones, through the power of your example, what's possible. They will get it, in time.

Win-win-win.

 **Allison Sutter, M.Ed.,** is a best selling author and contemporary spiritual teacher. She's well known for her ability to seamlessly blend spirituality and practical self-help information making it relevant to daily life. Her second book, titled *Accelerate Your Mojo: 7 Simple Steps to Ignite Your Intuition, Shake off Fear and Unleash the Real You,* is due out in the spring of 2017. Allison's on-line courses currently serve students in twenty-two countries. She resides with her husband and three girls in Chicago. For more information about Allison, visit **www.living360coaching.com**

LYNETTE LOUISE
(AKA THE BRAIN BROAD)

THROUGH THE WALL

She was a little girl of three or four. Dark curly hair, big green eyes and a protruding belly to go with her chunky legs. She was hearing the sound of chaos and knew the people around her were upset. As she grew to be eight or nine she envisioned a way to step out of the socially designed middle, and to stand on the edges where it was easier to see and her vision was farther reaching. She started grabbing people by the hand and dragging them into her version of clarity. Some came but most pulled back; as if they preferred their state of confusion which she equated to discomfort. She couldn't understand why they would prefer discomfort and pulled harder. So did they. Her frustration mounted and she grew desperate to save people. The more desperate she became the more they resisted and the farther out onto the edges she had to go for her cupful of clarity.

Some people followed, but now they were all so far away from the rest of the people that they became their own island of idiocrasy. She had wanted to save everyone not just create a community of broken pieces and social-resisters. She had wanted to overcome resistance not run it up a flagpole and claim it as a country. In her despair she let go of the need to push or pull. She gave up. The resistance against and for her was too much. She didn't know how to fix it so she quit. And it was then that she had the epiphany.

Apparently, dissolving the wall of resistance was simple. Just don't see it. And love them, completely. I know this sounds simple. But then, truth always is.

When I first entered the field of mental health I was required to certify in a goodly number of ethics and safety-in-medicine courses. Often these led from discussions of good practice into methods for preventing accusations of malpractice. Though we were taught various insurance requirements and association benefits, one of the lessons that was always included and always nothing more than a tacked on sentence at the end of the course was: "The best insurance is to have your patients like you."

This resonated with me. I have a great distaste for the trend of litigation and systematization that disintegrates the individual's needs. So my ears perked up. I chose minimal insurance and maximum kindness. What an amazing journey of discovery that has been. Let me share some of it with you.

After adopting several special needs children (many of them multiply handicapped and on the spectrum of autism) I had already learned how to dissolve emotional and social resistance. I call it "sparkle your eyes" and have been quoted as saying: "The way to make an unlovable child lovable is to love him." So I already knew that if my eye contact averse child looked to my face and he saw a sparkle in my eye, he would look again, and again, and again. I also already knew that if my sons *didn't* see that, they would look away and pull away and resist; not only my advice but my love. So I sparkled my eyes and loved them out loud enough for them to hear. Most of the time.

It was amazing. They loved me. They bonded to me. And it all happened in lightening speed. So much so that when the educators with the judgmental eyes couldn't get the same nonresistant behavior I was getting, they decided I must be doing something bad because they couldn't comprehend that I might be doing it more "correctly" than them.

This is where my understanding met resistance and I forgot to generalize what I had learned; outward and with everybody.

Then in those ethics classes I got it. I had tackled with so much teacher trouble while raising my kids because I had never sparkled my eyes for the teachers, only the children.

How silly! I was ready for a fight and I got one. Or rather, many. I had never loved the teachers. I had kept a watchful eye on them because I didn't trust them to be good enough to my children. And they had responded with resistance to the tips and tricks I was trying to share in relation to my very special children.

That ethics class opened my eyes to the value of sparkling your eyes; outward and on everyone.

The minute I understood this I felt tired. How could I possibly generate enough energy to be this loving all the time? Heck, I get irritated when the restaurant is too cold. And I am definitely not an eye sparkler when meeting the new girlfriends and boyfriends of my children and grandchildren. How exhausting to have to be happy all the time, I thought. Until I thought again.

Fortunately I am many things, and one of those things is scientist. So I researched it. Both online in various studies and in experience by just trying. As it turns out, being happy all the time works like an alternator charging a battery. The more you do the more power you have, though sometime that initial shift from *off* to *on* takes a little effort.

Now that I was loving happiness (and when I wasn't one of my daughters was able to get me there because she is a Pollyanna of sorts) I was energized and loving. I started to discover some beautiful stuff. The biggest being a dissolution of resistance by all.

This does not mean people always agreed with me or did as I asked. Far from it. It does, however, mean they heard me and made clear choices based on the information I shared and their own person goals, rather than dismiss my ideas just because they were mine.

This became especially important when working in a patient's home. I was completely exposed. An easy person to set up since many of my patients were behaviorally challenged in a big way and they often did things that were extremely inappropriate by society's standards. So if I was pinned down and slobbered on but met that with sparkling eyes, many would expect the problem to escalate. In fact, the opposite happened.

And then when the parents and/or caregivers ran in, planning to forcibly stop the situation, I sparkled my eyes at them and they too relaxed. Everyone stopped being reactive, dropped their resistance and started to learn. This was so amazing that I started bringing cameras with me to prove how powerful love can be (FIX IT IN FIVE with THE BRAIN BROAD on the Autism channel. Watch it if you don't believe meJ). I said "to prove how powerful love can be" not "how powerful sparkling eyes can be" because eyes that sparkle without warmth and love look brittle and maniacal, and then generate those feelings in place of love. To do this right, I had to actually love people.

What a gift to me.

Loving everyone.

Try it. It's freedom.

Another concrete example: On the days when a patient would call and I would see their number and think anything other than love, I would feel annoyed or put out. My energy would drop and I would want to quit working with emotionally challenged people. But then I would remember my very basic liability insurance, my very reactive patient's nature to attack and, out of self-defense, I would love them. Within seconds they would love me back and all would be right with our worlds. This was powerful. This was wall dissolving stuff, and I became extremely aware of the ways in which I was responsible for building the wall along with them. I couldn't do their work, but I could do mine.

Shortly after I entered the world of special needs parenting I began speaking to groups of parents hungry for answers and ideas. Originally I was spreading the wall of judgement that I was holding towards educators and medical professionals. Ironic because I ended up as both, educator and medical professional. People would hear me speak and get mad at someone. Some would be mad at me and some would be mad at the social constructs that handcuffed us from responding to our kiddos in a natural and effective manner. Some just got mad.

Sparkling eyes are contagious.

So are angry ones.

What world do you want to live in?

Once I started generalizing the skill of love *out toward everyone* I needed a new method for analyzing without judgement. I learned that from The Option Institute. They called it *assess-*

ing with no value judgement. I could now choose a want or a not want (like I want cooperative children or don't want an angry audience) without calling it good or bad, saintly or evil. It just was and I could choose.

Armed with the concept of assessing rather than judging, and actively loving rather than waiting to be loved, I watched my crowd of supporters grow effortlessly.

Not because I am great.

But because they are, and I see them that way.

And whenever I wake up resistant to the day ahead or find myself overwhelmed by the challenges I'm facing I stop, take a minute and ask myself: "What would a great person do with this day?"

And then I fall in love all over again.

Lynette Louise, aka **The Brain Broad**, is an award winning author, speaker, performer, host, and mental health practitioner. Lynette's publications, workshops, and presentations are crafted to entertain, enlighten, and educate. Lynette creates consistently and diversely with the intention of giving away her lifelong brain and behavior knowledge. As a result students have become confident leaders in their own success. She is the creator/host of the international docu-series series FIX IT IN FIVE with THE BRAIN BROAD, now airing on The Autism Channel. Her one woman musical comedy CRAZY TO SANE has brought mental health, abuse, and behavior awareness to venues around the world. Lynette's vast knowledge comes partially from educating with renowned experts in her field - she's doubly board certified in Neurofeedback and actively pursuing a PhD in clinical Psychology with a specialty in Psychophysiology at Saybrook University - but her understanding is credited in larger part to being the single mom of eight now grown kids; six adopted, four multiply diagnosed with cognitive challenges. Only one of her sons remains dependent and all of her children have grown beyond the limits placed on them by professionals. Lynette Louise works tirelessly to prove that limits are invented unnecessarily and with dangerous results. Inspirational and brilliant, Lynette gives her audiences the proof and the science along with the tools.

JOAN S. PECK

THE STRATEGIES FOR SUCCESS FROM A SPIRITUAL OUTLOOK

It's easy to confuse what success is because what success means for one may not be what success means for another. Does success mean more money? Just the word "money" by its self holds a power over us. We all want it and it's usually never enough for most of us – we want more. And it seems the more we have, the more we want.

Does it mean we have to work harder or spend more hours working to get more money or to become successful in whatever we are pursuing? We are taught from an early age in order to be successful in anything we have to struggle and *work hard* – that nothing comes easily. Many of us even brag about the number of hours we have worked in a day or week, throwing that number out as if it were a prize to be had.

Or can success be something simple like being happy, enjoying life? Yet, many times we misjudge others who aren't interested in grabbing the "brass ring" from the merry-go-round of big business as being lazy and less ambitious than the more showy positions, especially in large corporations.

Can we have both, money and happiness? Is that real success or not? What is the secret of success for anyone regardless of money or position?

When I began to study people who regarded themselves as successful, I was more than a little surprised to discover that it didn't matter whether that person was highly visible or living a fairly simple life because, for the most part, they all shared some common beliefs and traits. It was further fascinating to discover that the most noteworthy of those were based on their spirituality and/or their faith.

Yet, I had to get beyond what today's media portrays as success – the kind of achievement which often leads children to believe having a big house, a fancy car and all the other entrapments defines being successful. And because of the media, many of the showy "successful" people we all know, such as movie stars, sports figures, business tycoons, etc., who have the monetary means to do pretty much what they want, often end up revealing their positions by drawing attention to what they are doing. And that has not always been positive for them or a great example for others. At times, we have seen those who have a disproportionate amount of money cross the line of propriety and commit all kinds of negative behavior, leaving us to wonder if it is just because they have a large amount of money that they are allowed to escape some of the consequences of their irresponsible actions. Is that success? And there is the rub for many of us for we know that having money alone doesn't always equate with our idea of success - certainly from a more spiritual aspect.

Furthermore, we have to look at how we as a society view money for we accept and allow the idea that the more money one has, the more powerful he/she is. On the other hand, we know those with less money doesn't necessarily make them less successful, just perhaps less showy for the most part. But again, we come right back to the idea that success is perspective and we each have to reach our own understanding of what that is.

I am not a trained psychologist, behaviorist or an academic philosopher. I am simply someone who has lived long enough to understand that we as a society have gotten off the track of what I and others believe are some of the *basic tenets of living,* such as:

» Understanding and appreciating that it is a privilege to be here on earth at this time and are ready to take on what life has to offer; we look at life as something to be celebrated, not thrown away.

» Believing that each one of us deserves the best there is and that the Universe wants all of us to succeed no matter the color of skin or religious beliefs; understanding that success is not dependent on money; aware that asking the Universe for what we want empowers us to receive it.

» Being aware that we each have our own journey and allow others to have theirs; understanding that each of us is here to experience all of life and it is not our responsibility to tell others how to live theirs unless we are in positions to guide and mentor others, such as teachers, doctors, etc.

» Knowing our greatest strength for a successful life comes from doing what in our heart of hearts is the "right" thing to do; believing each of us is connected to the same source of higher power/energy (no matter what name we give it) which instills in us the most successful ways of living to the highest good of all, guiding us to know that through our intuition.

» Realizing that the only thing that matters in life is how much we love, and show love to others. Love is all there is. Nothing else counts or matters. All the rest is just fluff – good or bad.

I compiled what I learned from speaking to others, reading various books and autobiographies, listening to interviews, etc. and found that truly happy and successful people's keys to success pretty much matched the "tenets of living." Yet, if these people were asked to name these as keys to success apart from figures and profit margins, they had to stop and think about it. What came to the forefront was the realization that many of their thoughts and actions were indeed the same. Interestingly, many of these "tenets" were taught to them as children while other successful people had been forced to adapt to them from experiences that hadn't worked out for them.

Here is what I have found to be the traits of successful people who may not have listed them as keys to success but have exhibited them in the behavior and actions they demonstrate:

1. THEY LOVE THE CHALLENGE OF LIVING TODAY

Most "successful" people have a joy in living, delighted to be here on earth enjoying the human experience, and most have a good sense of humor, able to laugh at themselves, not taking everything so seriously. They celebrate each day. They believe in themselves and their own abilities and nothing is going to stop them.

In other words, successful people believe that what they do will bring the result they want. And you are not going to be able to distract them from what they want to create. They are like the "Little Engine That Could" – "I think I can, I think I can, I think

I can, I KNOW I can." If what they are trying to do or create doesn't work out, they make adjustments and steam ahead for they are determined to do it over and over again until they are successful. **They _have persistence_**, which is the number one trait behind success.

> "Success is the result of perfection, hard work, learning from failure, loyalty, and persistence."
> Colin Powell.

They _don't compare_, worry or spend their time thinking about what someone else has that they don't. They have found purpose in what they are doing and how they are living that satisfies them, not _needing_ input from others, although they are open to listening to others if it has value to them.

> "Your Highest Self only wants you to be at peace. It does not judge, compare, or demand that you defeat anyone or be better than anyone."
> Wayne Dyer

They are not afraid to ask for what they want. They are not willing to sit back and hope that what they are looking for comes their way. They do not consider themselves powerless for they know that if they want a sale or anything else, they have the power to ask for it realizing that it will simply will work their way or not. Not asking is not an option for them.

2. THEY BELIEVE THEY AND EACH ONE OF US IS MEANT TO BE SUCCESSFUL

They are optimistic and have confidence in the idea that it is their "right" and everyone else's to have wealth, not in the sense of entitlement or taking away from others but rather in the trust they have about their own purpose and capabilities.

They understand that there is more than enough money and financial abundance in the Universe for everyone, including them. They believe that the Universe wants each one of us to succeed in whatever we endeavor to do, that it is only us who gets in the way of that.

> "I actually believe that we're all meant for big things if we allow ourselves to listen to the stirring of our soul. When we let go of "perfect timing", and recognize that "too late" does not exist, it becomes easier to allow that stirring to become a rising up of awesome. I've coached 13 year olds and 70+ year olds into living their visions. If they can do it, so can you."
>
> Jordanna Eyre

Most importantly, **they *allow themselves to receive* all they want**. They don't have emotions and feelings of not being worthy enough or don't deserve it or have not earned it or believe there is not enough money in the Universe for *them*. They disassemble and throw away any blocks that hold them back from receiving success.

"By thought the thing you want is brought to you, by action you receive it."

Wallace D. Wattles

3. THEY UNDERSTAND THE IMPORTANCE OF THEIR OWN JOURNEY.

They understand themselves as part of the whole, that we are all connected to the same higher energy, no matter what we call it. Yet at the same time, they realize that it is essential to continue down their individual path without getting deterred in trying to please others to the point that they get lost in what their own purpose is. They are not selfish to do so, they simple recognize that we are here to live our lives by our choices and not anyone else's.

"It is not selfish to refill your own cup so that you can pour into others. It's not just a luxury, it is essential."

Anonymous

They **allow others their own journey in life** without taking away their choices. They are aware that one of the most difficult things to do is to allow others to live their life with their own choices, even if that is not what they would wish for them. They understand that they cannot "save" everyone and further understand that in order to have input and give their opinion, it only works when that person is open to receive it.

Truly successful people agree to disagree. They understand and work with the fact that we all can't agree on everything. They do not spend endless amounts of time trying to convince someone to think, say or do what they believe is the smart thing to do. They allow others their opinion without ridiculing them.

> "We have all been placed on this earth to discover our own path, and we will never be happy if we live someone else's idea of life."
>
> James Van Praagh

4. THEY LISTEN TO THEIR INTUITION

They are aware that our greatest strength for a successful life comes from doing what in our heart of hearts is the "right" thing to do. They are mindful of that innate knowledge within us all to know what the kindest way of dealing with people is and follow what their heart and gut tells them. They are not so willing to act on something they will regret later. They take the time to weigh decisions out so that the result is the best it can be for all.

They are very aware of that quirky urge, that funny tingle, and that little voice in their head. They let their gut "talk" in spite of so much noise, information and clutter in the world and thoughts that are clouded with distractions. They know the importance of using thoughts from the mind and memories of past experiences in addition to using clues from the body to determine the best choice at the moment. They understand their intuition shows first in feelings and then through the mind.

"Your mind will answer most questions if you learn to relax wait for the answer."

William S. Burroughs

Further, they understand how the energy of the Law of Attraction works so in **having gratitude and giving thanks to the Universe** for all they have and expect to have in the future, they will continue to receive that.

They know the importance of **giving and showing appreciation for all who report to them** in any way, whether it be a partner, colleague, employee, friend, or child. They realize by doing so, it develops the importance of mutual respect, which creates loyalty. Further, they know without a doubt that it takes more than their self to create success and are willing to acknowledge that they are dependent on others to bring it about, recognizing them as their greatest asset.

"As we express our gratitude, we must never forget that the highest appreciation is not to utter words, but to live them."

John F. Kennedy

5. THEY REALIZE THAT FOR COMPLETE SUCCESS THE ONLY THING THAT MATTERS IN LIFE IS HOW MUCH WE LOVE AND SHOW LOVE TO OTHERS.

Successful people understand that it is important for them to FLY (first love yourself) before you can fully love someone else. Yet, they are very aware that they can't fully FLY until they are willing to acknowledge the importance of our connection to each other, simply because each is part of the whole. So when we love another spiritually, we destroy any blockage that has the potential to hold *us* back from success.

They appreciate that acting in as simple a way as "do unto others as you would have them do unto you" doesn't take away their power, but adds to it by increasing good will and eliminating anger, jealousy and other negative thoughts and actions.

"There's nothing you can do that can't be done
Nothing you can sing that can't be sung
Nothing you can say but you can learn how to play the game
It's easy

Nothing you can make that can't be made
No one you can save that can't be saved
Nothing you can do but you can learn how to be in time
It's easy

All you need is love
All you need is love
All you need is love, love
Love is all you need

Love, love, love
Love, love, love
Love, love, love

Nothing you can know that isn't known

Nothing you can see that isn't shown

Nowhere you can be that isn't where you're meant to be

It's easy

All you need is love

All you need is love

All you need is love, love

Love is all you need..." The Beatles

And so it is.

Spoiler alert! What is the number one behavior holding *all* of us back from a more successful, loving life? ... LABEL-LING others and ourselves.

In spite of all the good things we do and say to live a successful life, there still is something we need to look at for we *all* continue to do and say things that we may not even be aware of doing that holds us and others back from living the highest ways. **Labelling** - nothing holds human beings back more than this. We tend to categorize people into groups with one word labels which doesn't allow the person to be more than the label we give them. It is too easy to disrespect and dismiss someone with a negative label – loser; creep; stupid; fatso; liar; ugly; cheat; jerk; housewife; dead beat dad, etc. Even when we label someone in a more positive way – teacher; handsome; beautiful; mentor; healer; doctor; poet; writer; dancer; movie star, etc., we cut away the possibility of discovering their true self which is always more than just their label. Think about it! It's something we *all* do, right? Yet, we are always more than our label or what we *do!*

We may have become aware of some of the long-term effects of labelling either from what we have experienced ourselves or what we have learned from our friends, neighbors or people we read about. It is astounding to realize how easily we are willing to label another without considering its effects. For instance, when we unwittingly give a label to children, believing it harmless to tease them, its effect can become evident later when that child becomes an adult and is in therapy because of a label given to them when they were young that they are trying to deny or eradicate. When anyone gives us a label, we begin to doubt our own thinking and belief about ourselves and begin to think that what they say *may* be true. Then when we hear it enough times, we begin to *believe* it to be so, and finally we OWN the label given to us.

We have become too comfortable inside the boxes we have created either for ourselves or given others. When that happens, it doesn't allow us the time or curiosity to figure out what makes *us* tick as an individual, whereby we can learn, appreciate, and accept our tendencies, gifts and limitations unfettered by what others may expect from us. We lose the concept that we have the power to create the life we want by the choices we make, not by the names given to us by others. And it works the same for the people we place in boxes.

How we live our lives is up to each one of us. It is as simple as that. One thing I have come to believe is the importance of recognizing the smaller or more trying successes that occur in our lives every day. Again, for each of us that is different whether it is the more ordinary yet exciting thing such as a child learning to walk or a different type of success, such as an adult learning to walk again after a bad car accident. There are so many ways to look for success for almost always there are wondrous smaller events that happen every day for each of us. We just have to be willing to become more aware of what is going on around us and begin to acknowledge any happenings as the gifts they are meant to be.

As far as I know, there is no one way or single path for lightning success; if there is, I certainly don't know it. I believe it depends on the chain of choices we make moment by moment. But what I *do* know is that when success of any kind is celebrated, life becomes sweeter, something I wish for all of us.

Joan S. Peck is an editor and author of short stories, spiritual books and a contributing author to two Life Choice books and also is a contributing writer for Recovery Today and Choices magazines.

Her latest book is ***Prime Threat – Shattering the Power of Addiction,*** a book written with her son from the other side about what addiction is and how to live without it. It is an uplifting book with him sharing some of his own lifetimes of addiction and what he is doing now to clear them.

She can be reached at:

(702) 423-4342

joanpeck39@gmail.com

www.bejeweled7.com

KATHY FRAY

PARENTING SUCCESS STRATEGIES TO GROW TEENAGERS INTO OUR FUTURE LEADERS

There fundamentally can be no role of leadership more responsible – and daunting, and intimidating, and formidable, and rewarding, and demanding – than **parenting**, especially parenting a blossoming teenage burgeoning adult.

Even as a corporate CEO with hundreds of staff, it is your own sometimes defiant, rebellious and recalcitrant teen who challenges you the most – for you can't fire them and you can't replace them. And, on top of that, you are also legally and reputation-ally (time for a new word) responsible for them. Holy shit! And they can be a little shit ... and an amazing angel, and a brilliant success, and a miserable blobbing lump, and a beautifully sensitive inspirer, and a complete friggin' nightmare, and an utterly glorious human being – sometimes all in the same week, and sometimes even all in the same day, aye. Teenagers are the breed that have baby-like hissy-fits because you're not treating them like an adult. Then you too remember being a centre-of-your own-universe teenager – it's everyone's rite of passage. But also, that's not all teenagers. Some aren't narcissistic at all. Though for many (most?) being somewhat self-absorbed is biologically what teens are supposed to be doing, because they're now truly beginning to work out *who they are* and *what they stand for.*

Amongst the most overcast days of in-the-trenches parenting a grumpy teen, we may find we need to consciously remind ourselves that all those extraordinary leaders in the world today, and throughout history, were also very likely once a hormonally-infused grouchy testy sulky snappy and sullen teen. Just like we were too! Absofrigginlutely. As the Greek philosopher Socrates complained about almost 2½ thousand years ago *"The children now love luxury. They have bad manners, contempt for authority; they show disrespect for elders and love chatter in place of exercise"*.

And from the ashes of puberty, our job as Parents, is to assist our Phoenix's to become leaders in their own right. But *what on earth* are the best strategies to do that, sometimes we wonder?

I do have to admit that hubby Mark and I have somehow managed to produce three totally awesome teenagers – but doing so, I believe, does *not* qualify me to be some 'parenting guru expert' on what the best parenting strategies are to assist your pimply whiny teenager to transform into the future leader they can be. But what does qualify for me to give advice, is all the research I did, over a four year period of reading practically every single Parenting Guidebook I could get my hands on, to research the constant themes, to then collectively summarise it all into one reference book that took another year to write titled *"OH GROW UP"*.

My strategy here, is I'm going to give you some simple specific philosophies to adopt that just might help. Embrace them all is my best advice. But I also know many of you won't bother. And that's okay too, for you need to do what is right for you and your family in your situation under your own belief systems.

NO.1 – ACCEPT WE'RE TRIADIC

Realise we're all more than just a body and mind – for they aren't the two pieces of our children we most adore. No, we adore their *Essence* ... their spirit, their chi, their soul, their *who-they-are* and their *what-they-stand-for*. We can't only focus on nutritious organic food and the best private education, as those two aspects alone don't create success. There is a third piece to the puzzle, their life-force, their spirit.

Sometimes I do wonder why as parents we can each week invest so many hours of time into a child's dance lessons or sports practice, without any real expectations the child will become a prima ballerina or pro athlete. Yet we'll invest little intentional conversations on teaching the strategies and Life Skills of how to successfully be a happy contented person. Do we as parents just cross our fingers and hope it happens by miraculous subconscious osmosis?!

Please no! Common-sense tells us it starts with us as their Leaders, showing them how we fully embrace the idea that happiness isn't having what you want; it's wanting what you have. And it starts with us in that role of Leader vocalising both how grateful we are for all our blessings, and how passionate and motivated we are to achieve our own goals and dreams.

NO.2 – USE PHYSIOLOGICAL IQ – RUBBISH IN, RUBBISH OUT

It's exceedingly well understood that the typically accepted Western childhood diet is crap – producing a generation of sedentary overfed undernourished children – a generation who, for the first time in history, are expected to live shorter lives than their parents. Society is deluding itself that sugary breakfast cereals are the best start to the day, or that chocolate nut spreads are wonderfully nutritious, or that 'muesli' bars actually contain any raw oats, or that white bread is good enough, or that fruit-juice doesn't have sugar, or that fat-free means sugar-free. Globesity is an epidemic – there are now more obese people on this planet than hungry people.

But the crazy thing is, it is us parents who pay for the groceries and stock the pantry. There is no excuse for our kids to habitually eat bad food as part of their daily routine. It's our job to teach them nutrition and provide for them whole foods (unprocessed food). It's not hard. Breakfasts of homemade muesli, or eggs on wholegrain toast. Lunches of salad sandwiches in wholemeal wraps, and fruit, and nuts. Dinners of fresh veggies, some free-range protein, and complex cards like baked potato or brown rice. It's not rocket-science. We know that body-nutrients affect mind-health, and mind-health affects emotional-wellbeing. (PS: And it's also great to give kids daily EPA-rich fish oil, which can miraculously improve dyslexia, dyspraxia, autism, ADHD, concentration problems, disruptive behaviour and depression.)

NO.3 – USE INTELLECTUAL IQ – UNDERSTAND PERSONALITY TYPES

Our children can have very different personalities from ourselves which can be perplexingly disconcerting sometimes. So I thoroughly endorse the *Personality Plus* book series, with 'compulsory' parenting reading especially being Florence Littauer's *Understanding What Makes Your Child Tick* book. Fully comprehending our children's personalities enables us to support their weaknesses and encourage their strengths. It's incredibly empowering knowledge.

Love-Language is the termed coined by author Gary Chapman that explains how we all like to receive love: Through gifts, words, acts, touch or time. I encourage you to read a copy of his parenting guide on the love languages of children – so you can make sure you're children's love-buckets are always filled to the brim.

Coz if you're a sanguine-choleric personality and you're showering your child with gifts and affirming words; but they're a phlegmatic-melancholy who's love-language is simply quality time and acts of service (like fixing the bell on their bicycle) – then you're communicating at cross-purposes and they'll always have a gnawing hunger for more love. So don't be wise-dumb, and instead get wis-dom: Know your child's innate personality and love-language.

NO.4 – USE SOULFUL IQ – TEACH THE EARTH SCHOOL RULES

Working on the philosophy that we aren't physical beings having spiritual experiences but we are actually spiritual beings having physical experiences, contained within my *OH GROW UP* book I summarise the 21 Universal Principles we need to teach our children as to how Earth School works. I encourage you to specifically and actively teach these to your children – by talking about and discussing them.

Obviously in my bias opinion the *OH GROW UP* interpretation of this universal knowledge is a wonderful explanative summary – so buy a copy, or instead google generic Universal Laws. But get some information and gain some knowledge, for these are the fundamental things we innately know as adults, which we should not assume our children don't need to be officially taught.

Such as the Law of Divine Oneness that everything is connected to everything else; and the cause-and-effect reap-what-we-sow Law of Karma that every action has a consequence; and the Law of Attraction that negative attracts negative and positive attracts positive; and perhaps most importantly of all, the Law of Dharma that finding your passion fills you with purpose.

NO.5 – FIVE PARENTING MAGICAL SECRETS TO RAISING LEADERS

Within my *OH GROW UP* book I talk of 21 Magical Parenting Secrets. Here's some that might hit the spot:

> » **Promote Wellness – not just Inhibit Illness**

If your kids do see their doctor for inhibiting illness, but don't see a naturopath for promoting wellness, then *dah?!* Or at least get actively knowledgeable yourself with over-the-counter online-orderable naturopathic herbal medicines and homeopathy. Our kids are now in their late teens, and have never yet needed a course of antibiotics for a secondary infection. Have they been unwell? Of course they have been. But we just don't use pharmaceutical drugs as our first-cab-off-the-ramp. We all need to recognise, there is way, way too much money involved in Big Pharm for corruption not to be involved, especially when the reality is that discovering simple natural inexpensive non-patentable cures to cancer and heart-disease, would likely bankrupt Big Pharm globally. So get smart. Get knowledgeable. Take charge. And learn how to help your child's body heal itself.

» Teach 'Think Big'

Show your kids how you set and achieve goals – coz we've got to walk-the-walk on this one, not just talk-the-talk. So have pictures up of the goals you're planning to achieve, teaching them that although goals-are-in-concrete, our plans-are-in-sand because that allows the God-Universe to intervene too, to make things even better than ever anticipated. Make sure they know you believe they have phenomenal potential to achieve *big* dreams. Maybe after dinner read to the family inspiring books like *Rich Dad, Poor Dad* ...and take your teens to attend TED talk conferences ...and have an array of motivational self-help books on your lounge bookcase, and a pile of inspirational biographies on your bedside table. Make sure they know that *thinking big* is the best way to achieve life goals!

» Actively Socialise

Kids need to see their parents socialising and being around lots of family or friends having a great time laughing and giggling, because a well socialised child will nearly always grow into a socially confident adult, and *social skills* is something that can only be learned by doing. So we as parents need to make it happen. Whether it's meeting up with church friends, or football friends, or school friends, it doesn't matter so long as they are good people. Bring-a-dish dinner parties, or summer bbqs, or just playing card-games with the neighbours. Again, it doesn't matter what the setting, so long as they are good people, and so long as it's not a too-rare an occurrence for your children's parents to host a social event. I encourage you: Open your home up, regularly. And another great goal is to also end up having your home as the 'local teenage hang-out pad' – all they need is a 'private space' (eg rumpus, basement, attic over the garage).

» Don't baby them – Replace fussing with worrying

Stop solving their problems!! Our job as parents is to teach our kids how to solve their own problems, and the only way that is ever going to happen is when we stop doing it for them. And the more problems our teenagers get to solve on their own, then the more experience they will have accumulated in problem-solving before becoming an 18 year old adult who is legally responsible for all their decisions. Our decisions shape our destiny, because our Life is the consequence of our decisions.

When my father left school at 14years of age in the 1940s, no-one thought he was too young to earn his keep. I managed a local superette on my own all day when I was 12-13 years of age, and regularly waitressed part-time from 14 years of age, then shifted out of home at 16-17 years of age – and no-one at the time, in the 70's and 80's thought that was unreasonable. All around the planet for thousands of years, since time immemorial, 17-18 year olds have always been respected as Young Adults. But somehow over just 1-2 generations, our Western society has utterly diminished and devalued the worth and capabilities of our young adults. On top of that helicopter-parenting has virtually become the norm. Society no longer respects 18 year olds, it fears them.

If there is ONE aspect that our own teenagers are extremely aware we have done very differently from most of their peers' parents, is in the level of independent responsibility we have given them, for which they are immensely grateful. And the undeniable result is that they are all incredibly reliable, sensible, and rational, with brilliant moral compasses and *untold* common-sense. They have likely been responsible for ten times (a hundred times, a thousand times) more decision making and judgement calls than any of their mates.

Due to the way-above-average modern levels of independent responsibility we have expected our teenagers to live up to, our normal parental fussing has been replaced with parental worrying. For example, it just it not 'common' to let your 15 year old travel from New Zealand to Nicaragua and Costa Rica for a month to do volunteer humanitarian work and several jungle treks. Hell no! But hey, she saved the $10000 needed to afford the trip, through 18 months of working at the local supermarket. Did I worry about the scorpion in her bed and the tarantula she almost stepped on and the jellyfish that stung her and the pick-pocket who grabbed her boobs? Hell yes! And yes I could have worried way, way less insisting she just stay home for the summer.

Swap your parental fussing for parental worrying, and allow your teenagers the opportunities to grow up into being a grown-up.

Our job as parents is to make ourselves redundant, and I believe that by their 18th birthday, all kids ideally need to be confident and competent to budget their money, clean their home, cook nutritious dinners, shop for food and clothing, iron a shirt, study productively, socialise enjoyably, drive responsibly, laugh gregariously, and in general be a content, kind, self reliant, passionate, and compassionate person. And if one of our children gets to 18 without having those skills mastered, then we have failed them, and shame on us. (PS: Have to admit, we're still working on our 19 year old's shirt-ironing expertise.)

In case some real specifics can help, below are the household policies we used for our age-stage expectation to help grow our children into strongly independent people.

» **The Five Age-Stage Expectations**

» By 10yrs – Responsible for their chores & pocket-money budget & lunches

Kids knowing they earn pocket money through doing their chores to a reasonable standard – without being asked. And from that pocket money they are expected to save for present buying and special occasions, and have a little play-money, and to pay for little life expenses like losing their school eraser. They are also making their own school lunches – with parents supplying a pantry and fridge full of great healthy food. It's not hard for them to do. Hundreds of thousands of 10-11 years olds all around the world are working much harder than that.

» By 12yrs – Responsible to make one dinner each week, and experiencing being home alone

Now it's time to start to find opportunities for them to be home alone for a few hours, showing that you're trusting them – but OMG they're aware the wrath of Beelzebub will be upon them if they break that trust. That is the key: Absolute black-and-white rules (which they already know well) of what is acceptable and unacceptable behaviour. Having such concrete rules gives them complete freedom to behave anyway they wish to within the confines of those expectations.

And now it's time to increase their budget too, including an ATM card of course, for them to once a week be responsible for planning a nutritious family dinner, including going to the supermarket to get the ingredients. Yes yes there will be some not so wonderful half-cooked or burned dinners, but that is how they learn.

By 12-14yrs the pocket money can potentially be increased to include them doing their own clothes shopping too – it's a great inhibitor of the whinging teen gal begging for the latest brand-name clothes – you say "Here's your budget, buy whatever you want and when it's all spent then you're broke until your next payday".

» By 14yrs – Responsible for adult household chores & local babysitting

By 14 years I believe all teens should be capable of doing adult-level chores, including vacuuming and dusting, cleaning the bathroom and toilet and oven, and are now regularly washing their own clothes.

And expected to get proactive to earn extra income, such as delivering flyers into the local neighbourhood offering babysitting and car-washing services, or helping Mum or Dad out at their work perhaps.

» By 16yrs – Independent on where they're going and a paid part-time job

From 16-18 years there is a two year 'probationary' period of complete freedom, so long as the parents are in the communication loop. The teen no longer needs to say "Is it ok if I go to the movies with my friend?" because now they can say "I'm going to the movies with my friend and will be home by dinnertime" – "Ok dear, that's great, have a wonderful time, see you later."

But if they behave irresponsibly then that freedom is not-negotiably lost for a month, with the adage drilled into them **'with freedom comes responsibility'**!

This is also the time at which you're helping them get their CV resume into the hands of as many local businesses as possible to assist them to secure their first paid after-school/weekend job, because they must start to experience developing a great work ethic before they are an adult ... and they *don't* have to LIKE their job, they just have to learn to appreciate the income.

> » By 18yrs – Respected as a young adult, own their own cheap car they've saved for, paying Board & freedom to make their own mistakes

Plop! That is the sound of you dropping the reigns. You're no longer in charge. They are officially an adult. So now treat them that way: Charge board – they *must* contribute financially. And at the same time, switch-off the parental unsolicited advice button. Instead, it is time to become their friend and confidante and mentor. Let them know you're happy to give advice on anything and everything any time they want it or need it. They only have to ask.

Deciding on parenting strategies that encourage teenagers to become our future leaders is a conundrum because of its juxtaposition: To be a disciple means to be a follower or pupil of a leader, and thus as parents our children are our disciples, because we are expected to train them to obey our rules and our code of behaviour – but to do so effectively also requires correcting dis-obedience. And you would think that such discipline surely, is the counterpart to teaching a child how to become the front-running trailblazing spearheading leader we're trying to encourage them to be.

But no, all is not as it seems Grasshopper...

Being a great parent is about being the Leader, and being a Leader is about being the manager, the organiser, the boss, and the guru, by providing guiding supervision and mentorship advice.

However, lest we forget, the word *discipline* also means a branch of knowledge studied in higher education, and I believe that is actually exactly what us parents of this modern world need to understand is our ultimate goal:

We're teaching our 'Disciples' their own Discipline (their own higher learning). We're growing Leaders.

Kathy Fray is a best-selling parenting author. Kathy is also founding creator of BabyOK Products makers of the popular and unique infant sleep-secure the Babe-Sleeper. Plus she is the founding director of SOMCANZ the global conference on Integrative Maternity Healthcare. Kathy describes herself as a wife, mother, midwife, lover of hatha yoga and general work-in-progress.

Kathy's first best-seller "OH BABY...Birth, Babies & Motherhood Uncensored" has been New Zealand's top selling childbirth and infant-parenting book since 2005 – a country respected as having the best maternity childbirth care on the planet, and she's one of the locally most respected authorities on natural labour and normal birth ... so one of the best of the best internationally you could say. And Kathy's manuscript "OH GOD – WHAT THE HELL DO I TELL THEM?! Guide for vaguely spiritual parents" was the second runner-up at NZ's prestigious Ashton Wylie mind-body-spirit book awards.

Renowned for her uniquely eclectic and soulful writing style that 'cuts through the crap' in OH GROW UP Kathy manages to walk with us, as her treasured and respected reader, along a pathway that both is, and isn't, middle-path; that is opinionated, but never judgemental; that is both revolutionary and fundamental, as she's blowing the cobwebs off antiquated ideologies, while sometimes also blowing our minds ... spiced with entertaining realism.

OH GROW UP includes comprehensive explanations of each age stage of childhood development; the good, the bad and the ugly of pharmaceutical medications; effective natural health remedies and healing therapies; nutrition as you've probably never seen it explained before; enlightenment about fully grasping our children's innate individual personalities. Kathy describes OH GROW UP as being about 'parenting with spirit: strength, guts and soul'. The result is a truly remarkable fusion of ordinary old-school middle-of-the-road methodologies, with extraordinary old-age new-age philosophies.